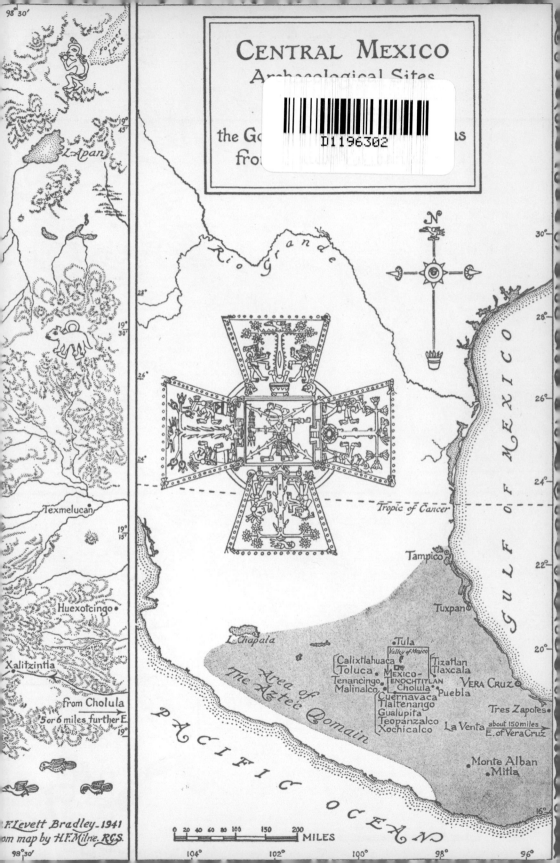

12 50

THE AMERICAN MUSEUM OF NATURAL HISTORY
Science Series

Aztecs Of Mexico

 *One of the strangest feelings left to us by prehistory is the sensation of omen. It will always exist. It is like an eternal proof of the non sequitur of the universe. The first man must have seen omens everywhere, he must have shuddered at each step.* GIORGIO DE CHIRICO

Aztecs Of Mexico

ORIGIN, RISE AND FALL OF THE

AZTEC NATION

By George C. Vaillant

DIRECTOR, UNIVERSITY MUSEUM, UNIVER-
SITY OF PENNSYLVANIA; HONORARY CURA-
TOR, MEXICAN ARCHAEOLOGY, AMERICAN
MUSEUM OF NATURAL HISTORY; HONORARY
PROFESSOR, NATIONAL MUSEUM OF AN-
THROPOLOGY, MEXICO

GARDEN CITY, N.Y.   1950
Doubleday & Company, Inc.

PRINTED AT THE *American Book–Stratford Press, Inc.*, N. Y., U. S. A.

To
My Wife

ACKNOWLEDGMENT OF SOURCES OF PLATES, PHOTOGRAPHS AND ORIGINALS

THE WRITER acknowledges his deep obligation to the American Museum of Natural History for allowing him to use the blocks illustrating articles in the Museum magazine, *Natural History,* and other publication series of this institution. In some cases plates in other publications were copied, following general scientific procedure. The list below designates the source of the illustrations taken from such published material and later used in the magazine or guide-leaflet series. Where the photograph was made directly from a Museum original for the journal the term Natural History is used. Unless otherwise designated the originals are all in the Middle American collection of the American Museum. The writer, therefore, wishes to express his thanks to those scholars whose illustrations are copied here.

PLATE
1. *The Scientific Monthly.*
2. *Natural History.*
3. *Natural History,* except for top right, from C. Seler, *Auf Alten Wegen,* p. 129; original in Berlin Museum.
4. *Natural History.* Top: photograph by Lilo Hess. Middle: model in Peabody Museum, Cambridge, Mass. Bottom: original photograph by Sylvanus G. Morley.
5. *Natural History.*
6. Top, *left:* after Maudslay, *Biologia Centrali Americana,* 1889–1902; *right: Natural History;* original in Museo Nacional, Mexico. Bottom: after Totten, *Maya Architecture,* 1926; after Catherwood, *Views,* 1844.
7. Top: after Gordon and Mason, *Maya Pottery,* 1925–28; original in British Museum. Bottom: after Morris, Charlot and Morris, *Temple of the Warriors,* 1931; original fresco in Temple of the Warriors, Chichen Itza.
8. Top: Wide World Photograph. Middle: *Natural History;* original in Musée de l'Homme, Paris. Bottom: after Batres, *Monte Alban,* 1902.

PLATE

9. Top, *left: Natural History; right:* photograph by Miguel Covarrubias; original in Oaxaca Museum. Bottom: *Natural History.*

10. *Natural History.*

11. Top, *left: Natural History;* original in Oaxaca Museum; *right:* after Joyce, *Maya and Mexican Art,* 1927; original Codex in British Museum. Bottom: after Charnay and Viollet-le-Duc, *Cités et Ruines Américaines,* 1862–63.

12. Top: after Morris, Charlot and Morris, *Chichen Itza,* 1931. Middle: *Natural History;* original in Merida Museum. Bottom: *Natural History;* photograph by Department of Historical Monuments, Mexico.

13. *Scientific Monthly.*

14. Top: *Scientific Monthly.* Bottom: *Natural History.*

15. Top: Archaeological Papers, American Museum of Natural History. Bottom: *Natural History.*

16. *Natural History.*

17. *Natural History.*

18. Top: *Natural History.* Bottom: *Natural History;* photograph by La Rochester, Mexico.

19. *Natural History.*

20. *Natural History.*

21. *Scientific Monthly.*

22. Top: after Gamio, *Teotihuacan,* 1922. Bottom: *Natural History;* photograph by Fairchild Aerial Surveys de Mexico, S. A.

23. After Lehmann, *Aus den Pyramidenstädten,* 1933.

24. Top: *Natural History.* Bottom: after Gamio, *Teotihuacan,* 1922.

25. *Scientific Monthly.*

26. Top: *Natural History.* Middle: *Scientific Monthly,* photograph by La Rochester, Mexico. Bottom: *Scientific Monthly.*

27. Top: after Lumholtz, *Unknown Mexico,* 1902. Middle and Bottom: *Natural History.*

28. Top: *Natural History.* Bottom: *Natural History,* photograph by La Rochester, Mexico.

29. *Scientific Monthly.*

30. *Natural History.*

31. *Natural History.*

32. Top: *Natural History.* Bottom three rows: *Scientific Monthly.*

33. After Keith Henderson, in Prescott, *Conquest of Mexico,* 1922.

34–35. After Codex Florentino, 1905.

36. After Keith Henderson, in Prescott, *Conquest of Mexico,* 1922.

37. Top: *Natural History;* drawing by Ignacio Marquina. Bottom: *Natural History;* photograph by Ewing Galloway.

Foreword

THIS BOOK *is a history of the Indians of the Valley of Mexico and the civilizations which they wrought. It was a hard book to write. It will be a hard book to read. There are two reasons for this unfortunate circumstance. First, the Indians did not have the same goals in life which we have, so that their pattern of life is different from our own and difficult to understand. Second, Indian history has to be reconstructed from what we can find, so that much of the material, like techniques of making household implements, does not fall within the scope of our usual historical reading. The first four chapters deal with such reconstruction, and the reader is warned in advance that the going will be very difficult. These pages may be skipped if he is not particularly interested in such a historical background.*

The remaining chapters are based on contemporary observations made by the conquering Spaniards and by the Aztecs themselves. They deal with people who were seen alive, their culture functioning. We can form an impression of what the Aztecs were like, and this makes easier reading, since we can envisage people in terms of what they did, not in terms of the objects which they made. Even so, this will not be a crystal-clear process, for their customs, habits and motives differed from ours. However, I hope that I shall be able to show that it was a perfectly good way of life and the result of considerable experience. Our Western civilization, on the social side, is nothing to boast of today, so we need not be scornful of the Aztecs.

I want here to express my thanks to some of the many people who helped me write this book: to the authorities of the American Museum of Natural History for providing me with the sinews of research and the time to exercise them, to the authorities of the Mexican government for their consistent courtesy and co-operation in making my work possible, to my colleagues in my own and other lands, who by their friendship, counsel and collaboration make one proud to be an Americanist. To my wife I owe especial thanks for her unfailing aid and comfort during the long hours spent in the field and laboratory and in the preparation of this book.

To Colonel Theodore Roosevelt, Mr A. P. Tedesco and Mrs Mary Slavin of Doubleday, Doran I am grateful for stimulation and counsel. To Dr Edward Weyer I am under deep obligation for permission to incorporate illustrations and articles from Natural History. *I wish to thank Miss D. Levett Bradley for her excellent end sheet maps of Aztec Mexico and, last, but by no means least, Miss Frances Jay for her unflagging patience and judgment in preparing this manuscript and smoothing the path of the reader who traverses the ill-marked trail of this aspect of Indian history.*

To Mr Clarence L. Hay I am deeply indebted for collaboration in field and laboratory as well as for supporting much of my research and to Mr Willard Carr for underwriting our last field season, which brought this book into being.

Contents

Tables

HALFTONE PLATES

CHAPTER I
Plates 1–12

CHAPTER II
Plates 13–20

TEXT ILLUSTRATIONS

Aztecs Of Mexico

CHAPTER I

THE HISTORICAL AND CULTURAL
BACKGROUND OF AZTEC CIVILIZATION

*A somewhat speculative summary of the social and
economic factors which directed the rise of Indian
civilization*

THE HISTORY of the Americas records the colonization and settlement of a great continent. We take a just pride in our European ancestors, who, from the Vikings down to the most recent political exiles, set forth to find a new life in the changing conditions of a new land. Our histories and traditions describe the evolution of these colonies into the present group of American republics, and it is a remarkable episode in the story of mankind. Yet the European settlement of the Americas, for all its modern political significance, is just a late phase of the history of man on the American continent. The Asiatic colonization of the New World, which preceded the European infiltration by many centuries, has its own proud place in the annals of Continental America.

This immigration from Asia produced the American Indian. Without his preliminary development of the resources of the continent it is dubious whether the European occupation would have succeeded as it did. The great Indian civilizations of the Aztecs and the Incas challenged the European

imagination and opened a rich life for their military conquerors. The humble farming skill of the tribesmen of North
America's eastern seaboard sustained religious exiles until
they could live off the land and create their own type of
commonwealth. The Indian and his culture were soon
plowed under, but they enriched a soil which otherwise
would never have produced the lavish harvest of Pan-American civilization.

The most violent clash between the Indians and the Europeans took place in the Valley of Mexico during the early
summer of 1520, when Cortes and his Spaniards achieved the
Conquest of Mexico and overthrew the Aztec civilization,
the most advanced Indian culture at that time. Cortes' success was the loadstone which drew to the Americas the iron
might of Europe. Stone could not withstand steel, and the
days of the Indian were numbered. The history of the Aztecs
and their forebears is a synopsis of the rise of Indian civilization and its doom.

The Aztecs were a populous group of independent Indian
tribes who occupied a restricted section of central Mexico.
Their history and social customs are better known than their
neighbors' because their conquest had such a far-reaching
significance for the European world. Spanish observers of
military, priestly and civil status wrote careful accounts of
the Aztec life and history, and Indian authors a generation
later augmented these records, drawing on the tribal lore
still only thinly veneered by Christianity. A few pictographic
records, either prepared before the Conquest or copied
afterward, are precious additions to the Aztec annals. However, our chief data on Indian history come from archaeology, that branch of research which recovers social his-

tory through the study of the surviving remains of human handiwork in ages past.

Most of the American Indian tribes had not developed writing, so that archaeology is the one available medium for reconstructing their past; and the Aztec records reveal only a few centuries in the life of a single tribe. To sketch the broad background of Aztec culture before we turn our attention to the people themselves, we should realize that the earth must be our archive, the shovel our reading glass, and that nature, eternally destroying to create anew, has scattered our materials over mountain, plain and forest, from Greenland to Tierra del Fuego. Aztec history, like that of the American republics, begins with the discovery of this continent. (See Plate 1.)

Long before the Aztecs existed the ice sheets began to retreat northward, as the last glacial era was ending. Those animals accustomed to cool climates gradually moved north, and small nomadic bands of hunters followed the game on which their lives depended. Some of these groups moved up through Siberia and reached the shores of the Bering Strait. With so much water held in suspension by the ice sheet, the sea level was probably lower than now, so that the islands were larger and the extent of water between them less. In winter the sea was doubtless choked with ice, and crossing over this ice, hunters and hunted could reach Alaska. Thus man discovered America and made his first settlements there.[1] *

Other hunters may have constructed rafts and boats and passed from island to island until their ceaseless search for game led them to the mainland. The process must have been

*See Notes, beginning on p. 283.

slow and the migrating units small. We can reconstruct conditions from what we know of modern hunting tribes, who,
as social fossils, still pursue a precarious existence in the old,
old way. The primitive hunting group moved on foot and
had no effective beasts of burden. Therefore they carried
little in the way of food or equipment. Their progress was
no faster than that of the oldest man or woman, or youngest
walking child. Food had to be secured even on the march,
and hunting was a slow and arduous process. Such conditions
necessarily kept the group units small, for a large cluster of
people, when on the march, besides requiring food in quantity, must also scare away the very game on which its nourishment depends.[2]

This nomadic hunting life had its effect on language and
physical type. The tendency for hunting groups to split into
smaller units whenever their numbers threatened the balance
between consumption and available food supply, encouraged
the establishment of isolated bands. This loss of contact with
other groups intensified mannerisms of speech and thought,
so that profound dialectic differences resulted after several
generations. Inbreeding also followed, and strains of physical
type became established. Such conditions, already existent in
the Asiatic life and continued under American conditions,
probably account both for the linguistic diversity among the
Indian tribes and also for their great physical variation within
a more or less homogeneous frame of dark eyes, straight or
wavy black hair and a yellowish skin color.[3]

When this infiltration took place, or how long it continued,
has yet to be expressed in exact dates. No examples of Old
World palaeolithic industry have been uncovered in the
Americas, but excavations on the campus of the University

of Alaska have turned up tools like those found in neolithic stations on the Gobi Desert. Other stone implements, defined by archaeologists as Folsom culture, occur in association with the remains of extinct bison at sites in Colorado and New Mexico. Far to the south, in a cave on the southern tip of the Argentine, the dung of an extinct sloth is mixed with the tools and refuse of men who hunted and ate an extinct type of American horse. Sloth dung also seals in the remains of Nevada hunters. These human vestiges may not have the great antiquity of geologic man in Europe, nor may the fact of extinct species have the same implication of age that obtains elsewhere, but man may well have come to America between ten and twenty thousand years ago.[4]

Hunting techniques have thus been established as an early form of Indian life in America. Some of the first hunters fished with net and line and gathered shellfish as their chief nourishment. Deep accumulations of discarded shells are found along the coasts of the Atlantic and Pacific and along some of the great inland rivers of North America. In one such heap in Tennessee the earliest layer disclosed bone implements, and no stone tools appeared until very much later. How old these heaps are we cannot guess, and we have no way of dating them by geology or palaeontology. Yet man, from his earliest beginnings, must have used these rich and relatively stable sources of food.[5]

Another primitive livelihood is disclosed along the shores of dried-up lakes in California and Texas. Mortars and grinding stones found here indicate that the early people ground nuts and seeds into flour, while a lack of well-made stone points suggests that they found the gathering of vegetable foods a more reliable way to fill their larders than the hunting of game. These desert cultures are highly important since they provide early evidence of an economy which led eventually to the development of agriculture.[6]

These three early ways of life—hunting, fishing and gathering—were often combined in whole or in part. There is no hunting group in the Americas which does not take advantage of vegetable products to some extent, and in North America the properties of four hundred species were known and utilized. Some tribes found their hunting economy so satisfactory that they never abandoned it. Other peoples, like the Eskimos, were so situated geographically that they had to hunt or starve. The Plains tribes, when they acquired the domesticated horse from the Spanish colonies, turned from a successful if drab farming life to a highly dramatic existence, living off the wandering buffalo herds and exalting masculine virtues in war and the chase. Fishing groups, like the tribes of the Northwest Coast, were able to live in sedentary villages and create an elaborate social and material culture on the rich abundance yielded by forest, stream and ocean. In California one of the densest populations in the Americas maintained itself by gathering wild nuts and fruits, supplementing this diet with shellfish and game. Yet in spite of these successful primitive techniques the Indian would have never attained really high cultures without the domestication of plants.[7]

In the New World there were two centers of intense agricultural development, Middle America and the Andean region, which likewise represent the peaks of Indian social and material culture. There is considerable discussion among botanists as to which area first had domesticated plants, but the problem is not yet resolved. Perhaps the answer to this question may have a botanical rather than a social significance, since there are several other areas where plants not cultivated in Mexico and Peru are agricultural staples. The presence, early in the history of America, of peoples who lived largely by gathering must have led almost inevitably to the independent development of several different types of agriculture, based on the food plants common to particular regions.[8]

The great staple of Brazil, for example, was manioc or cassava. Before the introduction of corn in eastern North America, sunflowers, the giant ragweed and other plants of prairie and savanna were cultivated for their seeds. The highlands of Peru yielded the white potato, but at the time of the Conquest the great basic American foods, corn and beans, were diffused over most of agricultural America. Whether they were first domesticated in Peru or Middle America is a point still arguable: each may have had its own separate point of primary cultivation. However, the great principle to bear in mind is that no plant cultivated by the American Indians was known to Asia, Europe or Africa prior to the white settlement of America. The introduction of these plants more than doubled the available food supply of the older continents.

The development of agriculture accomplished, in America as elsewhere, the liberation of man from the constant search for food. A permanent food supply which could be enlarged by bringing fresh land under cultivation allowed the tribal population to grow. The precarious equilibrium maintained by nature between population and food supply became more stable, and man had leisure to invent techniques and to develop rules for societal behavior. It became possible to support aggregations of people large enough for the individual to specialize according to his skill and for the community to carry out public projects like irrigation systems and temples.

The successful growth of agriculture was not paralleled in the raising of animals. True, the dog, which may well have come in with the immigrants from Asia, was almost universally domesticated. In the north it was a beast of burden; in Mexico, an article of diet. The Mexican and Pueblo tribes tamed the turkey. The Peruvians ate guinea pigs and raised llamas and alpacas for wool and transport; bees were kept for honey in Middle America and northwest Brazil; some southern Mexican tribes raised cochineal for dye. But the native horse, which might have proved as useful here as in the Old World, became extinct early in America; the cow and sheep were unknown, and the caribou and bison, which, if domesticated, might have taken their place, had their chief range in regions occupied by primitive groups who were content merely to hunt them.[9]

This lack of suitable domestic animals prevented man's migration on an extensive scale, comparable to that of the great hordes from Asia which beat against the walls of Rome. At first the nomadic groups in the Americas were too small to threaten seriously the sedentary groups, and the question of population pressure, so often an indirect cause for war in the Old World, was virtually nonexistent in Indian America. War techniques in consequence were little developed in the Indian cultures, and the killing and rapine which took place during the white colonization did not have its origin in the usual Indian political attitudes.

The invention of agriculture accentuated rather than

changed the basic structure of Indian social organization. Those groups which gradually shifted their economic reliance from hunting to farming were in thinly populated country. As their population increased they could enlarge their fields without infringing on the rights of previous inhabitants. A growing population scared away game, forcing neighboring hunting groups to withdraw to regions where wild life was more plentiful. If the available arable land became insufficient for the community a number of people drifted away to found a new settlement.

According to the environment, be it forested or semiarid and consequently open, there tend to be two types of settlement. In dry open country the minerals which plants need remain near the surface, so that fields can be farmed over and over again. The people, therefore, can maintain a permanent village. Forest country, on the other hand, presents a serious problem to Stone Age people. To clear ground for planting, trees must be girdled and, after they die, burned. The soil, therefore, rapidly becomes exhausted and incapable of supporting crops. The Indians met this situation in two main ways: by moving the entire village, or by allowing each family group sufficient land so that crop rotation would permit exhausted fields to recover by lying fallow. This last method tended to decentralize the population except in very small communities.[10]

The social implications of these two methods of life are highly important for reconstructing the genesis of American Indian culture. The food plants used by the higher civilizations in the Americas seem largely derived from highland, open-country species, emanating from the kind of region permitting the maintenance of a permanent village. In a community where the village street was a forum, technical school and social center, interests were pooled and techniques improved by emulation and inherited experience. The opportunity to store accumulated equipment, as opposed to the bare essential minimum of portable implements used by nomads, led to specialization in tools and techniques. The decorative arts became fixed according to style, since custom channels shapes and forms into directions approved by communal practice. Enterprises involving the man power of the whole village could be undertaken with a resultant benefit to the whole community. The long stretches of relative leisure when crops did not need care afforded time for technical experiment and intellectual speculation.

The complete series of steps by which an early farming group converted itself into a high civilization has not been recovered in any one area. However, North America, which preserved so many tribes at various stages in the development of Indian civilization, yields, in the case of the history of Anasazi or northern Pueblo culture, an example of such an evolutionary process.[11]

At the bottom of the scale are found the remains of people (called the Basket Makers by the archaeologists) who lived by hunting, gathering and the cultivation of corn. They occupied shallow dry caves in small units of twenty or thirty individuals. They were skillful weavers of fibers of apocynum, fashioning baskets, bags and sandals. They had no pottery but constructed rude images of sun-dried clay and modeled trays and lined baskets with this material. They did not use the bow but propelled long darts with the throwing board or *atl-atl*. Their equipment in the way of nets, tools of stone, bone and wood, was relatively elaborate. In their later phases they learned how to make a hard, flinty pottery in simple forms, decorated with designs derived from their weaving.

About the year 700 A.D. a new people drifted into the Southwest and changed the direction of the local economy. New varieties of corn enriched the larder, and the cultivation of beans supplied the protein content in a diet impoverished by lack of game. Cotton tended to supplant apocynum for weaving clothing, while the bow superseded the *atl-atl* for hunting. The underground house gave place to clusters of joined rectangular rooms, although the older form was retained for a men's clubhouse and ceremonial chamber. Pottery improved greatly in shape and design. There is every evidence of a considerable increase in population.

By the eleventh century the number of settlements decreased, but the towns became much larger. The Anasazi constructed great communal apartment houses of two, three and even four stories not only in the open, but also in shallow caves high in the canyon wall. Their arts and crafts changed in style but not in character, and the manner of life developed then has lasted to the present day, despite the infiltration of nomadic groups like the Apaches and Navajos and the intrusion of white conquerors from Spain and the United States.

In Middle America and the Andean region the earliest *discovered* cultures begin where the Pueblo left off. Our investigations have not yet brought to light the early hunting and sedentary aspects of human history in this area. The cultural level which the Pueblo attained in the eleventh century is represented in strata assignable to the centuries immediately preceding and succeeding the birth of Christ. This base discloses people living in permanent villages, supporting themselves by the cultivation of corn, beans and other vegetables. They raised cotton and wove it for clothing. They made pottery for the storage and service of food. They developed techniques for the manufacture of tools of stone, bone and wood, as well as ornaments for themselves and designs for their utensils. They achieved a tribal government and evolved a religion which centered around the natural forces that control the growth of plants.[12]

The term "Middle Culture" best expresses this level of development, which is midway between the meager resources of a hunting group and the splendor of a ceremonial civilization. Dr Spinden and Mr Means defined this stage by the broad term "archaic," and the writer coined the clumsy phrase "Early Culture" to describe this phase in Central Mexico. Neither term allows for the naming of older or more primitive cultures which will eventually be discovered. Consequently the phrase "Middle Culture" appraises more justly than the other terms a cultural situation and emphasizes less strongly the element of historical position.

In Middle America and the Andes man and his works progressed and prospered from a Middle Culture base, but in somewhat different directions. The Andean peoples, to generalize broadly, concentrated on the material technique of supporting life; the Middle American on spiritual or, more accurately, supernatural methods. In the Andes, especially in the coastal valleys of Peru, enormous cities were built and vast irrigation systems watered the fields. Weaving was developed to a point unequaled by man in the whole course of human history, and pottery in excellence of construction and richness of design had no peer in the Americas.

This civilization culminated in the Inca Empire, the original benevolent, monolithic state, unique in American annals as the only governmental system which combined territorial expansion with the amalgamation of conquered peoples into a social whole.[13]

The Middle Americans, on the contrary, lived in independent tribal or civic groups and created a religious art and architecture without rival in the Americas.[14] The ceremonial aspect of life dominated the civil structure, and the remains of temples, not cities, gauge the splendor of the past. The cause or causes for this difference are shrouded in the past, but the more primitive North American scene suggests that here again agricultural conditions played a part.[15]

The Indians of the arid Southwest, as we have seen, built permanent towns but did not devise an imposing ceremonial architecture. In the southeastern United States the more sophisticated tribes reared great earthen platforms to support their temples and the houses of their chiefs, and to serve as centers at which the community membership might congregate at specified times. The demands of a forest agriculture did not permit the occupancy of permanent towns like those of the Pueblo country, since the southeastern tribes had to move their villages, whenever the soil of their farm clearings was exhausted. A good part of the year saw the able-bodied men and women virtually abandon the villages to hunt and gather wild food. But they all united for tribal rites at the ceremonial centers and thus strengthened the bonds of social solidarity, loosened and frayed by the conditions of their ecology. The ceremonial center occurs late in the history of the Southeast and bears the earmarks of a trait imported from Mexico. Yet it answered a very definite need for maintaining social unity in the growing population of a forest area.

Therefore it seems reasonable to suppose that some such ideas germinated centuries before in the lowland forests of Middle America, since the elaboration of this social and ceremonial requirement became a dominant theme in Middle American civilization. There is nothing strange in this practice which characterizes the earlier culture patterns in the development of western Europe and the colonial United States. The great cathedrals of the Middle Ages loomed massively out of a countryside wherein miserable villages, set in tiny clearings, made a violent contrast between the poverty of man's individual material existence and the rich glory of his corporate spiritual life. In New England communities still survive where the church, the store and the town hall are the social center for people scattered in isolated farms over the forested hills. The master artists who covered the miles of sculptured temple walls in Cambodia lived in flimsy towns now totally consumed by the jungle. Both the act and the fact of ceremonial building coalesce into a tangible expression the relationships of man to society and of society to the universe; so it is not surprising that different tribes have independently adopted this practice which, in the modern United States, we follow in structures like libraries, hospitals, colleges and governmental buildings, used primarily for the public benefit.

This assumption carries further weight when we examine the broad spread of Middle American cultural history. No evidence of truly primitive communities has been discovered as yet. The earliest materials represent a mid-point between the rude life of hunters and the complex society in developed American Indian civilization. From Salvador to

Zacatecas, from the high mountain valleys to the forested coast, we find evidence of tribal cultures which had reached a competent plane of technical development and, implicitly, social adjustment as well. The surviving remains consist of ably made implements of pottery, stone and bone. Handmade clay figures show that the religions in vogue required simulacra of the gods as a part of worship. The flat grinding stones and mullers, still used in Mexico and called *metates** and *manos*, prove that the people relied on corn as their principal food. The regional differences in form and decoration of the figures, pottery and other utensils indicate that several different tribes remained at this Middle Culture stage for several centuries, to judge from the deep layers of refuse in the Valley of Mexico.[16]

Between the Middle Cultures and the elaborate ceremonial civilizations which succeeded them there are transitions in the design and form of implements, a sure sign that the authors of the various Middle Cultures were the creators of the later civilization. Those transitions appear to be gradual and not abrupt, so that the impression is strengthened of cultural development *in situ*. The existing evidence gives no valid reason for assuming any source for the high civilization of Middle America except the inventiveness of the local population.[17]

Monuments of these highly developed tribes are found between a southeastern limit in western Honduras and Salvador, and a northwestern boundary in the state of Zacatecas in Mexico. On the basis of their art styles and the reports of the Spaniards we can identify a number of distinctive tribal cultures. In the lowlands of Guatemala the Mayas had their

*Me-ta'-tays.

imposing ceremonial centers, which in the mountain regions were much less elaborate. In the state of Oaxaca* in Mexico the Zapotecs were the authors of a rich civilization. The coastal region of Vera Cruz yields evidence of several high civilizations which archaeological research is just beginning to distinguish. Most notable among these are the works attributed to the Olmecs and the Totonacs. On the northern border the Toltecs and the Aztecs created the great civilizations of Central Mexico. North and west of them tribal cultures of lesser development represented in some cases persistences and survivals from the Middle Culture plane, in others distorted reflections of the more elaborate civilizations.[18]

Just as in fifteenth and sixteenth century western Europe, where distinctive national and regional art styles were developed under the aegis of the Roman Church, so in Middle America there was sharp stylistic differentiation in the arts and crafts of tribes whose broad culture pattern was the same. This civilization was grafted to a Middle Culture base and comprised such elements of advanced culture as a polytheism based on nature worship, the representation of various divinities through drawing and sculpture, the erection of temples on platforms to honor these gods, a system of writing for religious and tribal records, a calendar and an astronomy designed primarily for ritualistic purposes. The Middle Americans probably did not develop these practices simultaneously but evolved and elaborated first one, then another, trait.

Other tribal units gradually absorbed and adapted these customs to suit their local needs. To maintain a civilization

*Wah-ha'h-cah.

along these lines a tribe had to be numerous, stable and successfully adjusted economically. Men had to be freed to a very considerable extent from the bare struggle for existence to perform and direct the elaborate ritual, to build the ceremonial structures and to develop the arts and crafts which gave the religion its outward expression.

The Mayas of Guatemala, Yucatan, southeastern Mexico and western Honduras attained the greatest eminence in the elaboration of this cult. Their temples and priestly dwellings were built of masonry and roofed by means of the corbel or false arch. The sculpture in stone and plaster adorning these buildings has the elaborate sophistication of a matured art. Their carefully pondered delineation of their gods and goddesses reflects theological maturity. Their writing is set forth in conventionalized hieroglyphs, of which only the calendric texts can be deciphered. It is this calendar which particularly excites the admiration of our Western civilization, for it is based on a highly evolved mathematical and astronomical system.[19] (See Plates 4–7.)

The Maya calendar should be a great aid in reconstructing history, but opinions differ as to how it should be correlated with Christian dates. There are several calculations designed to reconcile the Maya with the Christian calendar, but each correlation involves a difference of some two hundred and sixty years in the expression of Maya dates in Christian terms. This lack of agreement has led to quite divergent interpretations of Maya history, although the main trends are well established.[20]

The complexity and elaboration of the Maya civilization, barely touched on here, have challenged the imagination of explorers and students. Extravagant theories have been woven by seers and visionaries as to the origin of the Mayas in lost continents like Atlantis or Mu. Soberer judges see them as American in origin and credit them with the invention and spread of Middle American culture. However, in view of the unanswered correlation question it would seem more just to consider the Mayas as carrying to a higher degree, without implication of greater antiquity, a civilization shared by their neighbors.[21]

The excavation and study of remains in Middle American sites disclose a symmetrical cultural development which began at Middle Culture plane and passed through a long period of highly stylized local development, only to be cut short by a sudden decline and the intrusion of cult practices from Central Mexico (Table I). In the Maya area even the Middle Culture plane is not uniform at the several sites where it is represented. Pottery and figurines differ so strongly in style and ware as to suggest their manufacture by unrelated tribes.

These Middle Culture forms gradually became more sophisticated as the people began to build temples, erect stone time markers and develop a mature religious art. The differences in style observable at the Middle Culture plane became strongly accentuated in this civilized period. Yet pottery vessels made at one site have been found as trade objects in another, so that in the broad sense we know that the local cultures were contemporary. A vast amount of building and, in places, deep refuse beds suggest that a long span of time elapsed during this period. Whenever this civilized epoch crystallized, be it the years preceding the Christian Era, the early centuries afterward or the fifth century A.D., according to the correlation one adopts for the Maya calendar, we do know from traditional sources that about the twelfth century

A.D. tribes of Mexican stock moved into the Maya country, where they founded various local dynasties. This movement is reflected in the archaeological remains which show influences from the Mixteca*-Puebla culture complex and reveal a degeneration of the local tribal civilization.[22]

The Maya region, prior to the twelfth-century infiltration from Mexico, contained peoples speaking different dialects and having distinctive regional styles in their material culture. Their religion and calendar, however, were essentially the same throughout the area. On the mainland of Mexico we find that the regional populations had not only distinctive arts but also different theological conceptions. Yet these Mexican civilizations, like that of the Maya, had their roots in the Middle cultures and succumbed at the end to Mixteca-Puebla influences.

The recent discoveries in southern Vera Cruz and Tabasco suggest a tantalizing explanation for the origin of Middle American civilization. At the sites of Tres Zapotes and La Venta great ceremonial centers occur, producing huge stone heads and religious and calendric formulas inscribed on stone doorjambs and stelae. Little clay figures made by hand follow the aesthetic tenets of Middle Culture art, but some types reflect the more matured modeling of the stone sculpture. The religious art portrays strange beings whose faces are either swollen and infantile or else grotesquely reproduce the visages of tigerlike monsters. This art has been called Olmec, after a gifted and civilized people whom the traditions say lived in the region but whose handiwork has never been securely identified.[23] (See Plates 3–4.)

The sculpture has relationships with other tribal arts that

*Mish-te′ca.

suggest great antiquity. The tigerlike mask has close analogies with the plaster decorations on the oldest temple at the Maya site of Uaxactun,* a building which exhibits none of the characteristic features of Maya art. Masks and infantile faces were also present in the earliest occupation of Monte Alban, the great ceremonial site of the Zapotecs of Oaxaca.† The "baby face" was repeated on figurines from Upper Middle Culture sites in the Valley of Mexico, and an associated type of figurine also marked the close of the Lower Middle Period in that area. (See Plates 3, 8.)

The associations between "Olmec" art and early culture levels in the Maya area, Oaxaca and the Valley of Mexico, would suggest that the first steps toward ceremonial civilization were taken in southern Vera Cruz and Tabasco, except for one very perplexing feature: the writing and calendar system were those used by the Mayas, but the dates expressed seem to be earlier than those they inscribed on their own monuments. Further excavations undoubtedly will resolve this problem, which is like the old one of which came first, the hen or the egg.

The majority of scholars consider that "Olmec" art was later than early Maya, and that its creators understood so little of the complexity of the Maya calendar that they made errors, giving a fictitious impression of antiquity. Others claim that the early sculpture is a decisive argument for the antiquity of "Olmec" art and that the inscriptions are contemporaneous. Furthermore, they argue that the position of the Olmecs in the midst of Maya, Zapotec and other tribes with different art styles and calendar systems indicates a center from which such elements were diffused. However, later research is bound to answer this question.

*Wash-ac-to'on.   †Wah-ha'h-cab.

The excavation of Tres Zapotes discloses that after the first period the inhabitants developed a well-defined local style which had connections with the so-called Totonac cultures northward up the Vera Cruz coast. This period seems to have been a long one, to judge from the amount of mound building and the quantity of pottery and figurines dug up. In the final epoch Mexican influence seeped in, testifying to the spread of the Nahua-speaking peoples of the Central Plateau. Since the work at Tres Zapotes is still in progress we cannot yet sum up the final conclusions as to the historical and cultural affiliations of the occupants of this site. Nonetheless, the pattern of development followed the same lines we have noted before. (See Plate 10.)

On the uplands of Oaxaca, southwest of the Olmec country, another local civilization flourished, that of the Zapotecs. Their chief ceremonial site, Monte Alban, has been extensively excavated. It covers a small mountain, leveled and terraced into a gigantic natural platform which supports lesser artificial structures such as temples and ball courts. The five periods of occupation disclose the same sort of culture history that we have sketched previously, but Zapotec art styles and writing were quite different from those of their eastern neighbors.[24]

Monte Alban, in its earliest period, was the home of a people who made pottery and figurines of Middle Culture quality. They were advanced enough to rear platforms for their temples and they carved in relief human figures reminiscent of "Olmec" art to adorn their buildings. Hieroglyphs accompanied some of them, suggesting further connection with Vera Cruz; and two "Olmec" divinities, the infantile god and the tiger god, were represented in ceremonial vases of the period. But a later phase showed a gradual shift away from "Olmec" influence. Stones were inscribed in a distinctive writing, and calendric calculations were set forth, not in the elaborate long count of the Mayas, but in an abbreviated system which fixed a date in terms of a fifty-two-year cycle. The art, also, reveals a vague suggestion of Maya influence, and occasional vessel forms recall shapes found early in Maya history. (See Plates 8–9.)

The third and fourth stages of Monte Alban were of long duration. The Zapotecs grew less susceptible to foreign influence and developed a strongly regional theology and art. At the close of this era they appeared to be in contact with northern peoples, like the Toltecs of Central Mexico, and their culture underwent a transformation in its fifth and final period. A new people, the Mixtec, came into the Valley of Oaxaca and brought with them a new art, new gods and a new type of calendar and writing.

This later religious civilization was also spread into the Maya country by members of a totally different linguistic stock, the Nahua, and it reached its zenith among the Aztecs of Central Mexico. Research has not progressed to the point where we can identify the formulators of this civilization. Its place of origin seems definitely to center in the lands of the Mixtecs in northern Oaxaca and in the territory of Nahua tribes in Puebla. Thus to call the civilization Mixteca-Puebla and to identify its latest carriers under their tribal name, when this is known, seem the best ways to reconcile cultural with political history. In much the same way we use the term Western civilization to cover those culture elements shared by the nations of Europe and the Americas. (See Plates 7, 11, 12.)

In Central Mexico, at the northwestern frontier of the zone of high civilization, we find the same sort of sequence which we have set forth for the Mayas, the Olmecs and the Zapotecs. First, there was a long Middle Culture occupation; second, a shift in culture whereby another group, basically Middle Culture, took on the beginnings of a civilized status as shown by the presence of mounds and the sculptural definition of one or two gods. Out of a branch of this Upper Middle Culture a third phase developed, a majestic ceremonial civilization called Teotihuacan* or classical Toltec, which was surpassed by its southern contemporaries only through their superior development of sculpture and the religious calendar. A fourth interval in the history of the Valley of Mexico was known as the Chichimec† Period and comprised a phase of decline when the Teotihuacan Toltecs disintegrated and migrant tribes vied with each other for supremacy. Finally a fifth phase saw the introduction of the ceremonial civilization, developed by the Mixteca-Puebla peoples, which culminated in the domination of the Aztecs.[25]

The Aztecs and their forebears grew up on the outer borders of an intensely civilized area in which the cultural history of its various peoples seems to have been very similar. Out of a long period of exploration and experimentation, the processes of which we have to reconstruct from our knowledge of the archaeology and ethnology of surviving cultures in North America, some of the tribes developed the sedentary life based on agriculture, typical of the Middle Cultures. This economy persisted for many centuries and in some places was never modified. However, somewhere in Guatemala or southern Mexico the conception of a cere-

*Tay-o-tee-wah-ca′n.   †Che′e-chee-mec.

monial center for religious practices changed the older pattern of life. Conditions in forested country, as we have noted, would seem to offer the most urgent reasons for such a practice, but it spread over the Highland area as well.

In the train of this ceremonial architecture followed closely the ritualistic definition of the gods and, elaborated in various degrees, a calendric system closely tied in with their worship. The development of these practices followed tribal lines, creating regional art styles and special religious modifications. There seems to be a correlation between the evolution of these tribal styles and the spreading out of an increasing population. Yet these populations at first do not seem to have had close enough contact to modify specifically the patterns and styles of each other's cultures. Eventually this protracted phase of independent civilization ended with a spread of ideas and peoples, derived from Central Mexico, which continued for the last four centuries before the Spanish Conquest.

Estimates of time are hard to make in the absence of specific dates. Yet to allow eight centuries for the duration of the independent civilizations does not seem excessive, and to assume a similar length of time for the Middle Culture phases appears to be well within the bounds of probability. However, several thousand years could have elapsed between the first immigrations to America and the establishment of sedentary agricultural settlements like those of the Middle Cultures.

Rhythms of development are obviously not the same in all areas. The conditions of the natural environment had a profound effect on the progress of the American Indians, and the causes which affect the rise and decline of the birth rate likewise played a part in their history. The forces leading to invention and to the development of techniques, the status of the various tribal societies, and many other important factors must have operated in this historical evolution, but it is next to impossible to reconstruct them from the mute evidence of archaeological remains.

Since the history of the Aztecs and their forebears is better known than that of any other American Indian population, it is worth while to see how closely we can reconstruct the social, economic and environmental forces which affected them. Indian and Spanish sources illuminate the Aztec period, and dim traditions shed a faint light on the decline and fall of the Toltecs of Teotihuacan. Only for the Middle Culture peoples do we have to rely solely on material remains; nevertheless, in the Valley of Mexico the deep refuse heaps accumulated through the centuries present a record more detailed and capable of interpretation than elsewhere in Middle America. Therefore, the history of the Aztecs and their forebears presents in small compass the major trends which governed the rise of Middle American civilization.

TABLE I

PRINCIPAL CULTURE SEQUENCES IN MIDDLE, NORTH, AND SOUTH AMERICA

Approximate Dates	NORTH AMERICA		Central Mexico	MIDDLE AMERICA					SOUTH AMERICA		Approximate Dates
	U.S. Southeast	U.S. Southwest		Cholula	Oaxaca	Vera Cruz	Highland Maya	Lowland Maya	Peru North Coast	Peru South Highland	
1600		Pueblo V									1600
1500	Temple Mound II		Aztec 4	Cholula 5	Monte Alban 5		Chipal 3		Late Chimu plus Inca		1500
1400	Temple Mound I	Pueblo IV	Aztec 3			Cempoala		Chichen Itza 3	Inca Conquest Late Chimu	Inca	1400
1300	Burial Mound II		Aztec 2	Cholula 4							1300
1200	Burial Mound I	Pueblo III	Aztec 1				Chipal 2	Chichen Itza 2		Inca Conquest	1200
1100			Mazapan	Cholula 3		Cerro Montoso			Black-White-Red		1100
1000	Early Stages	Pueblo II	Teotihuacan 5		Monte Alban 4		Chipal 1	San José 3-5		Decadent Tiahuanaco	1000
900			Teotihuacan 4			Ranchito de las Animas	Chamá 4	Uaxactun 3	Tiahuanaco		900
800		Pueblo I	Teotihuacan 3			Tres Zapotes 3	Chamá 3	Holmul 5	Gallinazo-Chavin II	Chiripa	800

Mixteca-Puebla Period (spanning the Middle America columns, upper portion)

Late Independent Civilizations (spanning the lower portion below 1100)

Chronological correlation chart

Date	Southwest	Valley of Mexico	Cholula	Monte Albán	Tres Zapotes / La Venta	Kaminaljuyú	Maya Lowland	Peru Coast	Peru Highland	Date
700										700
600	Basket Maker III	Teotihuacan 2	Cholula 2	Monte Alban 3		Kaminaljuyú		Early Chimu B	Pukara / Classic Tiahuanaco	600
500						Chamá 2	San José 2 / Holmul 2-4 / Uaxactun 2			500
400	Basket Maker II	{ Teotihuacan 1 / Cuicuilco / Ticoman / Gualupita 2		Monte Alban 2	Tres Zapotes 2	Chamá 1	Holmul 1	Early Chimu A		400
					MIDDLE CULTURES					
300	Basket Maker I(?)	Gualupita 1	Cholula 1	Monte Alban 1	Tres Zapotes 1 / La Venta		Uaxactun 1b	Chavin I	Early Tiahuanaco	300
200		{ Copilco-Zacatenco / Early Zacatenco / Early El Arbolillo I				Miraflores	Uaxactun 1a			200
100										100
0					**EARLY CULTURES**					0
100										100
200										200
1000	Desert Cultures(?)									1000
2000										2000
5000	Cochise								Argentine Caves	5000
10000	Folsom									10000
20000										20000

FULL INDEPENDENT CIVILIZATIONS

CHAPTER II

THE MIDDLE CULTURES IN THE
VALLEY OF MEXICO

*An attempt to interpret the history and society of the
earliest peoples found in Central Mexico through their
archaeological remains*

THE FIRST PEOPLES of whom we have a record in the Valley of Mexico lived on the Middle Culture plane in the centuries immediately preceding and following the birth of Christ. They occupied permanent villages, subsisted chiefly on the products of their fields, made adequate implements of stone, bone and clay, and fashioned little idols of terra cotta. Their level of development was about midway between a relatively primitive hunting or farming society and the more elaborate social and technical systems of the ceremonial civilizations. In the Valley of Mexico there were two occupations of this type, which we may distinguish as Lower and Upper. The people of the Upper Middle Cultures introduced the ceremonial mound or platform and made occasional images of gods, defined according to the laws of their ritual, while the Lower Middle population followed a simpler religious presentation.[1] (See Plate 13.)

The Valley of Mexico was a superb place to live at that time. Seven thousand feet above sea level high mountain chains walled in a fertile valley in which lay a great salt lake,

Texcoco,* fed at the south by two sweet water lagoons, Xochimilco† and Chalco; at the northwest by two more, Xaltocan‡ and Zumpango, and at the northeast by a sluggish stream, the Acolman River, which drained the fertile Valley of Teotihuacan.§ The lakes were shallow and their marshy shores, thick with reeds, attracted a teeming abundance of wild fowl. On the wooded mountain slopes deer abounded. During the rainy season thick alluvial deposits, ideal for primitive agriculture, were washed down along the lake shore.

As village sites, the Middle Culture peoples selected points along the lake where they could take the greatest advantage of the natural resources of lake and forest, and cultivate most easily their crops of corn, cotton and other plants. Once located in a suitable spot, they stayed there for a long, long time, enough for twenty-five feet of refuse to accumulate at the site of El Arbolillo‖ and fifteen at Zacatenco.¶

Their homes were impermanent affairs which left no remnants of foundations, floors or fire pits. Little fragments of burned clay, impressed with stick marks, suggest that the dwellings were of wattle, daubed with mud and covered by a thatched roof, like the homes of modern Indian communities in this very Valley. The inhabitants were not troubled by ideals of sanitation or civic neatness and threw their refuse on their own doorsteps. Broken pottery, animal bones, all the nameless trash that man rejects, found their way to the dump heap, but its most conspicuous element was corn shocks which, in the absence of domestic animals, had no

*Tes-co'-co.
†Sho-chee-me'el-co.
‡Hal-to'-can.
§Tay-o-tee-wah-ca'n.
‖El Arb-o-le'e-yo.
¶Zacate'nco.

possible use. This vegetable matter, disintegrating into earth, caused the middens to accumulate rapidly and, indirectly, has aided archaeological research, for an object dropped into this mess was as lost as the proverbial needle in a haystack. Even the dead found their way into the middens, not, however, because of their survivors' lack of respect, but because graves were dug more easily with wooden tools in the soft, churned earth of the refuse heaps than in undisturbed soil.

Mexican myths and annals give no clue to the identity of these men or the language they spoke. The study of their skeletal remains reveals a people of medium height, composed of several physical strains; but not enough material has been amassed to trace these affiliations precisely. The middens, however, filthy and flyblown as they may have been, are real historical documents. Laid down gradually through the years, the successive layers disclose the different types and styles of the people's tools and utensils.[2]

Archaeological research refers to these Lower Middle remains in the Valley of Mexico as the Copilco-Zacatenco culture, named from the sites where the material was first studied. The stylistic sequences also receive their names from the places where they were first determined. Specimens of both the Lower and Upper Middle phases were referred to under various names until 1917, when the first real excavation defining the Lower Middle material was made under the lava quarry of Copilco. In the winter of 1928–29 excavations at Zacatenco showed that the Copilco remains were a late stage in the history of the Lower Middle occupation of the Valley. Two years later the excavation of El Arbolillo produced deep beds of Early Zacatenco material, enabling us to detect three stages of which the earliest, El Arbolillo I, preceded Early Zacatenco.[3] (See Plate 1.)

Thus archaeology works with two sets of factors, peoples in the past and their material remains; the terms used in distinguishing the one do not always apply justly to the other. A style of pottery may be very useful and important in defining the presence of a people at a given time, but it is a mere adjunct to the reconstruction of their history. The making of the style is not an important historical fact in itself. The technical literature of archaeological research must concern itself with the methods of reconstructing Indian history, but such findings appall the general reader, who quite reasonably wants to know the history itself.

This digression, it is hoped, will explain Table II, on which is summarized the material evidence for the history of Lower Middle Culture peoples of the Valley of Mexico, the creators of the Copilco-Zacatenco culture. Their life history seems to have been a peaceful one, without external indications of war or revolution. They made numerous tools of stone, the forms of which were so satisfactory to them that there was little change through several centuries. For many purposes they used obsidian or volcanic glass. Hard but fragile, it could be chipped into projectile points or scrapers and flaked off into long narrow blades. Discarded fragments could be used without retouching, since the edges of a freshly broken piece are as sharp as a razor blade. Projectile points, which required careful shaping, show changes through the years, caused by technical improvements. For example, the stoneworkers of the later periods found that by notching the butt of an arrowhead it could be more firmly lashed to its wooden shaft. (See Plate 16, middle.)

Metates and *manos*, the grinding stones and mullers used to grind corn kernels into flour, were made of lava rock and, being efficiently developed for the purpose, were not changed through the centuries. Axes and celts were rare, and the examples recovered were made of serpentine, porphyry and jade, rocks not found in the Valley of Mexico. An occasional beautifully worked jade ornament, like an earplug or pendant, indicated trade and the existence of more advanced cultures south of the Valley limits.

The tribesmen found deerhorn and bone very useful for fashioning various kinds of tools, such as flakers for working obsidian and awls for perforating hide or aiding in weaving basketry, and they sometimes notched a deer shoulder blade to beat out a rhythm by rasping a stick along the serrations. A few crude shell ornaments made from Pacific coast species testify to trade to the south and west. Wood and basketry have all disintegrated so that we cannot tell whether the people used the bow or the *atl-atl*, or what their techniques of weaving were. However, we know that they did weave and possibly beat out bark cloth, for some of their little clay images are represented as wearing turbans. Furthermore, a tiny fragment of cloth, miraculously preserved, was woven from cotton thread in one direction and apocynum fibers in the other.[4]

These people were practical potters but were not troubled unduly by an aesthetic urge. Ninety per cent of their vessels were solidly constructed storage and cooking jars, ranging in color from a light tan to the shade of a bay horse. At first they made black bowls with three little feet and incised a rude geometric design into which they rubbed red paint. Later they grooved a pattern before applying a slip or wash,

a practice which led ultimately to handsome channeled designs. In their later days they gave this practice up, changed
the vessel shape and, after the bowl was fired, took a piece of
obsidian and etched a running pattern that had the same relation to the previous stiff geometric design that script has
to block lettering. (See Plates 16, top; 17, second and third
rows.)

Painted decoration was not very popular. At one village,
Zacatenco, in the early period, there was a fashion of painting white geometric designs on red clay. Later on this style
shifted to spreading white slip on vessels and adding a simple
solid design in red. There was some further experimentation in trying out different types of slip, but the most conspicuous change was the shape of the bowls which, in the
later period, differed markedly from the earlier forms.

This impression of smug competence, uninspired by
artistic yearnings, is borne out by the little baked-clay images
which the people made in abundance. They were usually
female and may have represented a mother goddess, symbolizing growth and fertility, a conception common among
the religious ideas of mankind. The figures were not valued
in themselves, as they are almost always found broken and
discarded in the refuse heaps. Distinctive styles seem to have
developed in different regions. Among the vastly more
numerous locally made figurines there are a few which are
the standard types elsewhere, so that if the little idols were
not traded they must have been brought in by pilgrims.
When we consider how carefully, even if naïvely, the figures
were made and how clay idols were manufactured in later
periods to represent specific gods, we must conclude that
they had religious significance even at this early date.

The early sculptor did not work in stone or wood, but clay. His figures were small, seldom over six inches high. His method was to model the head and torso first and then add details, like arms and legs, nose, eyes and ears, by pinching on little pieces of clay. Later the figurine was fired, and often after firing the face and body were painted with ornamental designs. The sculptor strove for a naturalistic effect rather than following a rigid convention. Yet standardized ways of doing things produced styles that vary according to tribe and to changes in fashion or in technical development and degeneration. (See Plate 14, top.)

In our modern world we are accustomed to sophisticated and self-conscious art forms. Seen objectively, these Early Middle Culture figurines are dumpy and gross. Short, fat bodies, blobby noses, protuberant eyes and stubby arms and legs are not attributes of a graceful form, according to our way of thinking. Yet handling one of these figurines and tracing each step in its formation, one is conscious of an intense seriousness and comprehends a whole world of thought dammed by the want of technical facility in expression. An intuitive person sometimes sees a populous world of shining fantasy behind the meager scribbling of a child. Behind these figurines must have existed an austere realization of the complex rhythms of birth, growth and death in nature, epitomized in the miracle of woman and her bearing of children. (See Plate 14, bottom.)

The process of experimentation kept on throughout the early part of the Lower Middle Period. A careful observer can see how certain manners of presentation dominated the sculptor's interest from time to time. The work of one cluster of settlements differed from that of another, and figurines seem to have been exchanged between communities. Perhaps the most attractive type developed in this era had its center in Puebla and Morelos, but was so liked by the people of the northern Valley of Mexico that a small but constant quantity has been found at almost every village. These figurines, in contrast to the matronly bearing of the local images, have something of a girlish grace. They are too distinctive and differ too sharply from the northern-Valley forms to have been copies made by the local artisans. (See Plate 15.)

However, as time went on, the importation of another new style (Type A) stimulated local adaptations. This sculpture reproduced in relatively accurate proportions the rounded contours of the Central American face. The artist, by sinking his wads of clay into slots, was able to reproduce the curves of the nose and lips more accurately in relation to the face planes. This new style had no discovered prototypes in the Valley of Mexico and seems to have been evolved originally by Tres Zapotes sculptors during the early "Olmec" occupation. Its introduction to the Valley also brought distinctive changes in the form and decoration of certain types of pottery bowls and had a pronounced effect on the local tradition of clay modeling. The painstaking methods of the early work were neglected for the slap-dash fashioning of flat gingerbread forms, coarsely conventionalized. One contemporary style was so crude that it may have been made as an intentional grotesque. Another quaint concept evolved at the time was a two-headed being which must have represented some god or mythological personage. (See Plate 17, top, bottom.)

Thus to judge from the material remains, the Lower Middle Culture people existed for centuries, developing their own techniques without being affected very much by outside peoples. Then they suddenly showed signs of being strongly influenced by external groups from whom they borrowed an art style and new types of pottery. The social significance of this typological change is hard to interpret. (See Plate 17.)

The history of art is also the history of artists who, in a primitive community, are not a specialized class but the people themselves. When an art is created for religious purposes the development of the content of the religion and the requirements of ritual are as important as the evolution of the artistic technique. These little figurines, judged by the standards of the great arts of the world, are feeble and fumbling examples of the social process which, in our own culture, we designate as aesthetic. Even as the dissection of a frog leads to the understanding of the biology of more advanced organisms, so we can see how the plastic art of this Lower Middle Culture passed from a period of convention to one of experiment, and then settled back to convention again. Contact with a foreign source of inspiration brought in a new manner of presentation which may have withered interest in the older technique. Such rhythms appear over and over again in art history.

The religious significance of the figurines is less intelligible. A common concept in the religion of farming peoples is that of a female principle or generative force, tied in with growth and productivity. A goddess frequently symbolizes that belief, since man often invests the processes of nature with his own attributes and motives. The little clay figures of Zacatenco and El Arbolillo always represent women, some of whom carry children in their arms, but no two wear precisely the same costume. A few exceptional examples have two heads.

Such evidence is little to build on, but it is all we have. We do not know what lay behind the sculpture in the way of theology, philosophy and ritual. The modern Pueblo Indians of our own Southwest have few ceremonial objects which could survive destruction and decay, yet such implements by no means reflect the full complexity of religion and ritual which these people possess. We should not, therefore, leap to the assumption that the Lower Middle Culture people were lacking in religious development because of the crudeness of their surviving ceremonial equipment.

The only other index to the religious practices of this period is the treatment of the dead. They were buried, but seldom according to a set plan. Some were contracted, others extended; usually a single person was buried at a time. Yet group burials occurred, and the differences in the age and sex of the occupants of a single grave suggest a family interment. The skeletons exhumed show no marks of death by war or sacrifice. Disease has left no trace, but over a quarter of the dead were children, and few individuals reached old age. Offerings like pots, tools, weapons and ornaments often accompanied burials, but prosperity in life may have had something to do with the practice. At El Arbolillo one half the dead, irrespective of age and sex, had offerings, but at Zacatenco, less than five miles away, only one out of eighteen were so honored. The mourners covered a few of the corpses with red paint made from hematite; they left with one man his ornament of turquoise mosaic and endowed a tiny baby with two jade ear ornaments and two pottery bowls, an unprecedented gift, suggesting exceptional parental grief or wealth. Some of the dead they dumped into shallow pits, while they stretched others out in formal tombs, lined and covered with stone slabs and floored with clean beach sand.[5]

The government of these Lower Middle Culture people is not told in this earthy record. The economics are only faintly outlined: hunting, farming and a little trade to the south. Status in society was apparently recognized, since the burials differed in richness of equipment, and most people grant honor to the dead in the same proportion as prestige to the living. The tenor of life was peaceful in the main, but nature seems to have intervened with occasional violence. At Zacatenco the lake level suddenly rose just at the dawn of the late period. Whether the changes in art styles were brought in by refugees, driven from their homes by the rising waters, or were due to modes and fashions from farther afield, is still a moot question. Some communities, inhabited at the end of this period, were abandoned as local floods swept over them, sealing the remains under several feet of silt.[6]

Yet abruptly the Lower Middle Culture people disappeared, and their stylistic traditions did not linger on into later periods. Immigrants took their place who were the makers of the Upper Middle cultures of Cuicuilco-Ticoman* (named for Cuicuilco, the great mound erected to honor their gods, and Ticoman, their most carefully studied village site) (Table III).

The Upper Middle Culture throve in the Valley of Mexico, Morelos, Puebla, Michoacan and in Vera Cruz. It was already in existence during the later phases of the Lower Middle Culture, in Morelos, south of the Valley of Mexico.

*Kwee-kwe'el-co-Tee-co-ma'n.

Whereas the Copilco-Zacatenco styles ceased abruptly, the Upper Middle techniques persisted into the later Teotihuacan civilization and the high cultures of western Mexico. The Upper Middle art, in contrast to the unity of the Lower, had strong local variations. Yet the Upper Middle Cultures were the scaffolding used to erect the ceremonial civilization of the Teotihuacan Toltecs, and as such take an important place in Mexican history.[7] (See Plate 13.)

A meager listing of objects found in the earth constitutes the historical record of the Upper Middle Cultures, but by contrasting these pots and tools with those of the preceding era social forces may be seen at work. At Ticoman, the most carefully studied village site, the population terraced their rocky peninsula to make level places for houses which were too perishable to leave traces for later archaeological reconstruction. In the refuse beds deer bones are less in evidence than in the adjacent sites of the preceding period, indicating that game was gradually being hunted off. The Ticomanos made a greater variety of stone tools, both in shape and in purpose, and they found out that the flakes of obsidian could be more easily worked than the more solid fragments used in Lower Middle times. Yet as techniques became more complex the capabilities of the individuals differed. We found two graves of leatherworkers who were buried with the tools of their trade; one carefully fashioned his implements, while the other contented himself with chips and flakes, as if he cared more about finishing the job than taking pride in sheer workmanship. (See Plate 16, bottom.)

The potters showed this same interest in improving the manner of living. They made a much higher proportion of carefully fashioned vessels for the service of food than did their Lower Middle predecessors. They were attracted more by shape and finish than by painted designs. Not content with little tripods to hold the vessels steady, they modeled the legs with care and often filled them with pellets to make them rattle pleasingly. At first they had trouble painting designs because the burnishing process caused the red paint to run. They tried to correct this after firing by outlining the blurred pattern with an obsidian blade. Later they found that painting a heavy white outline gave a pleasing trichome effect, which at the end of the era they abandoned for simple polishing. (See Plates 19–20, bottom.)

They also experimented with a new process, negative painting, the same technique as batik. A vessel was coated with wax or gum, which was then scraped away to make a pattern. The pot was next covered with paint, and when fired the gum burned away, leaving only the scraped portion colored. This method of decoration may have had its origin in Central and South America, where the practice is more common, and the technique may well have passed from tribe to tribe until, at this early date, it reached the Valley of Mexico in an imperfect form. Archaeology does not reveal the use of an analogous method for textiles, but, in the early days of Indian Peru, garments were beautifully treated in batik.[8]

Trade was much more extensive than in Lower Middle times. Shell was more abundant and more carefully worked, but the varieties were those of the Vera Cruz coast, in contrast to the west-coast origin of the Lower Middle shells. Ornaments and axes of jade, porphyry and serpentine also pointed to an eastern origin, but fragments of pottery seemed to disclose a wide radius of commercial activity.

The figurine cult was still very important, and the imaginative person can read into these little votive objects the art history of a forgotten people. Before the Upper Middle Culture spread out into the Valley of Mexico there was a little settlement in the present ward of Gualupita in Cuernavaca.* The inhabitants made clay idols, stiff and clumsy like the Lower Middle figurines of the Valley but distinct from them in style. Sporadic examples traded from one region to another show that early Gualupita was contemporary with the Lower Middle Cultures of the Valley. These Gualupita forms, obviously representative of a much more widely distributed art, later crystallized into a happy little style wherein the conventionalized treatment of the face was balanced by the variety of the headdress and of the posture. This type was being made by the Upper Middle people when they filtered into the Valley of Mexico.[9] (See Plates 19, 20, top.)

The wave of technical experiment that affected the other artisans also stimulated the sculptors, and they began to elaborate these shapes, making grotesques as well as naturalistic human beings, in which they tried to depict different positions and even actions. They polished the surfaces to enhance the form by the luster of its finish. To our modern eye the results are not particularly impressive, but they marked a step in the technical development of the art. Finally out of this chaos in miniature two styles developed that must have been satisfactory to the tribal sculptors since they were in vogue to the exclusion of all others. In one the figures were coated with a polished white paint, sometimes touched up in red. They were shown seated or standing, arranging their hair, covering their eyes, holding a bowl and performing

*Kwayr-na-va'-ca.

various different acts. In the other there was a return to applying pieces of clay in meticulous detail, emphasizing ornaments and hairdress, as well as the limbs and features of the individuals. While most of the figurines were female, a few were obviously male, a suggestion, even though tenuous, that the theology was becoming more complex.

Supporting this theory, we find two carefully individualized beings portrayed with more or less skill. One is a figure with a contorted mouth and the general lineaments of a baby. In the Valley of Mexico this personage was crudely conventionalized, but at Gualupita a sculptor made superb and large-sized representations that stand far above the general artistic norm. They seem truly to reflect in clay the strange infantile beings, hewed out of gigantic boulders or graven on stone slabs, that dominated the religious art of the Olmecs in Vera Cruz.[10] (See Plate 20, top.)

The other being, portrayed both in clay and stone, is an old man who sits with bowed head, supporting on his head and shoulders a bowl for burning incense. This god was also important in the Teotihuacan civilization and in Aztec times, when he was appropriately called Huehueteotl,* the Old God, and sometimes Xiuhtecuhtli,† Lord of Fire. Such a divinity is peculiarly fitting for a volcanic region, and his presentation as an old man suggests the manifest antiquity of mountains. His continuous worship for many centuries would seem to make him the oldest god ritualistically shown in Middle America, even though the mother goddess of corn and growth may represent an earlier concept.[11] (See Plate 18, top left.)

Yet the full impact of Middle American religion on those

*Way-way-ta′y-otl.   †Shee-oo-te-co′otli.

Central Mexican villagers is symbolized by the great adobe mound of Cuicuilco. On the skirts of the volcanic range of Ajusco,* at the southwest of the valley, tribesmen built a massive oval mound, approximately 369 feet in diameter and 60 feet high, to the top of which led a wide ramp. They faced the sides with river boulders to guard against the erosion of seasonal rains and, perhaps, to add to the effect of rugged majesty. They reared no stately temple on the summit but instead constructed an altar, open alike to the sky and to the eyes of the congregation. With its lack of the stiff rectangles of formalized direction the mound seems, to a modern, almost a spontaneous evocation of the mass religious spirit. The altar is a direct contrast: here sloping rectilinear walls and a pair of steps flanked by low balustrades presage the developed architecture of a later day. The sides are faced with smoothed adobe to approach as nearly as possible the plasterwork of religious architecture fully developed elsewhere. The whole beautifully symbolizes the introduction of a cherished ritual, as exemplified by the altar, to the mass need of a large population, represented by the mighty mound.[11] (See Plate 18, bottom.)

The people of Cuicuilco added twice to their temple, each time replacing the altar by setting another above it. Once they added a new facing to the structure, utilizing jagged blocks of lava instead of the river boulders. They allowed refuse to pile up around the base, covering up a narrow passage of stones set on edge, which answered some forgotten purpose of the early builders. In time they paid little attention to their creation, and the rains weakened the stone veneer and let the sides slump down. Then a volcano, Xitli,†

*A-hoo's-co.   †Shee'-tly.

erupted, and molten lava poured down along the slopes and flowed over the countryside, creating the volcanic desert of the modern Pedregal. Cooling, it left many feet of solid stone, sealing in the lower third of the platform. The flow was stopped by the lake after it had also covered up several abandoned sites of earlier date, like Copilco. However, the molten flood affected directly only a small part of the Valley of Mexico.

The desert of the Pedregal is a wasteland. The lava quarried from the congealed stream is now the principal building-ing stone of Central Mexico and the ballast for its tracks and its motor roads. In exploiting the quarries the early discovery of Copilco was made. Then the artificial mound projecting through the Pedregal challenged the imagination of Dr Gamio, who requested Dr Byron Cummings to undertake the excavation of Cuicuilco. Finding traces of man underneath this impenetrable sheet of rock suggested a culture of immeasurable antiquity. When did the volcano erupt? On the answer to that question hinges the date of these Middle Cultures, first traces of man in Central Mexico.

The vast and precise learning of geology was brought into play, and the geologists concurred that the flow was recent and gave it the trivial age of two to ten thousand years, nothing in terms of the millenniums and multimillenniums in which they usually measure time. But two thousand to ten thousand years are enormous units by which to count the history of man. The oldest legendary history of Mexico reached back only to 500–700 A.D. for the founding of Teotihuacan. What happened between that date and the cataclysm of the Pedregal? That was a problem for archaeology to answer, if it could.[12]

PLATE 1

EXCAVATIONS IN CENTRAL MEXICO

Top: *Left:* Deep pit at El Arbolillo, Federal District, Mexico. The earliest discovered figurine types (Plate 14) were found at the bottom of this trench. *Right:* Clearing out a canal in the Nonoalco district of Mexico City, which was filled with pots from the cyclical destruction of 1507. Middle: Excavation at Nonoalco. Bottom: *Left:* Peeling layers of refuse at Zacatenco, D.F. This work led to the formulation of the Middle Culture sequence described in Chapter II. *Right:* Dissecting a palace at Chiconauhtla, State of Mexico; for plan see Plate 43.

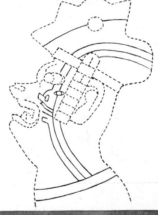

PLATE 3

SCULPTURES IN THE "OLMEC" STYLE

TOP: *Left:* Clay figure from Middle Culture site at Gualupita, Morelos. *Right:* Jade bead from Chiapas in similar style; note face marking. MIDDLE: Outline of jade tiger (below) with facial marking like that of the bead. BOTTOM: *Left:* Jade tiger, Necaxa, Puebla, a superb example, in miniature, of the jade cutter's art. *Right:* Stone mask representing the same tigerlike god, see Plate 4.

PLATE 4

SCULPTURES IN "OLMEC"
AND EARLY MAYA STYLE
TOP: Porphyry mask from T
basco; note the simplification of th
details of the tiger gods on Plate
MIDDLE: Model of Temple E VII
sub Uaxactun, Peten, Guatemal
Later structures seal in the earli
monument of rubble covered b
plaster. The second tier of mask
closely resembles the sculpture
the top of the page. BOTTOM
Temple E VII-sub after excavatio
The stela, or stone time marker,
left bears the earliest date found
Uaxactun.

PLATE 5

MAYA ARCHITECTURE AND SCULPTURE

Top: Model of Temple II, Tikal, Peten, Guatemala. The human figures at the top give an idea of the scale of this monument. The temple is almost completely decorative in function, the massive construction reducing the room size to mere slots. Middle: God, Copan, Honduras. These figures show the complete mastery which the Maya sculptors held over carving in the round. Bottom: Grotesque head from Copan, Honduras.

PLATE 6

MAYA ARCHITECTURE AND SCULPTURE, LATE PERIOD

Top: *Left:* Stela, twenty-five feet high, from Quirigua, Guatemala. These stone time markers bore calendric calculations. *Right:* Figure in low relief, Jonuta, Tabasco. This is a superb example of Maya art. Contrast the dignity of the kneeling man with the vivid realism of the parrot. Bottom: House of the Dwarf, Uxmal, Yucatan. Late Maya temple architecture increased the size of the rooms and lavished decorative detail on the façades.

PLATE 7

MAYA PAINTING

TOP: Detail from a vase, Alta Verapaz, Guatemala. A high dignitary receives an offering. Notice the sure outlines of the figures, recalling the masterly draftsmanship of the priest on the opposite page. The inscription, being textual and not calendric, is undecipherable. BOTTOM: Detail from a Mexican period wall painting at Chichen Itza. Warriors are raiding a town and taking prisoners, suggesting the troubled days of the Mexican expansion.

PLATE 8

ZAPOTEC SCULPTURE AND ARCHI-TECTURE, OAXACA, MEXICO

Top: The ruins of Monte Alban, near Oaxac, Oaxaca. This was the great Zapotec ceremoni center, where a whole hill was terraced to mak space for temples and tombs. Middle: Jade bea Oaxaca. The head is bearded, as is the case with number of other sculptures and paintings fror southeastern Mexico and Guatemala. Bottom Relief from the earliest period at Monte Alba. This earliest art has certain resemblances to th "Olmec" style. Glyphs accompanying some o the figures show that a form of writing wa known.

ZAPOTEC SCULPTURE IN CLAY

TOP: *Left:* Mortuary urn depicting a rain god. Ritual demanded a formal and conventional treatment in defining this god. *Right:* This figure in the Oaxaca Museum shows how Zapotec sculptors could break through the bonds of convention to produce fine realistic art. BOTTOM: This tiger god recalls the "Olmec" divinity of Plates 2 and 3. It is a splendid example of the Zapotecan style, combining the freedom and the conventionalization manifested in the sculptures above.

PLATE 10

"TOTONAC" SCULPTURE, VERA CRUZ

Impressive art forms have been found in this state and have been inaccurately grouped under this single term. TOP: *Left:* Palmate stone, of undetermined use, representing a dead wild turkey. *Right:* Back of a slate mirror which probably had a reflecting surface of iron pyrites. Note the masterly sense of design. BOTTOM: Model of Temple of Tajin, Papantla. The niches held small idols, and the temple proper was at the top. This building is an impressive example of the versatility of the Middle American architect.

PLATE 11

MIXTECA-PUEBLA ART

This culture became dominant after the eleventh century and had a wide influence on the established regional styles shown on the preceding plates. TOP: *Left:* Gold ear ornament representing a falling eagle, symbolic of the setting sun. *Right:* Page from the Codex Nuttall depicting warriors attacking a town in a lake. The band at top left represents the heavens, and the other symbols the name and number of the characters' birthdays. BOTTOM: A temple or palace at Mitla, the largest roofed room in Middle America. Observe how each block of the façade is carved to combine into a mosaic pattern.

PLATE 12

MIXTECA-PUEBLA INFLUENCE
IN YUCATAN

At the turn of the twelfth century
Mexican tribes conquered Yucatan
and built a ceremonial center at the
former Maya city of Chichen Itza.
TOP: Reconstruction of the Temple
of the Warriors by Kenneth Conant.
MIDDLE: Head of the Mexican Rain
God Tlaloc. BOTTOM: The Castillo, a
majestic temple blending Maya and
Mexican elements, the central struc-
ture of the Mexican city of Chichen
Itza.

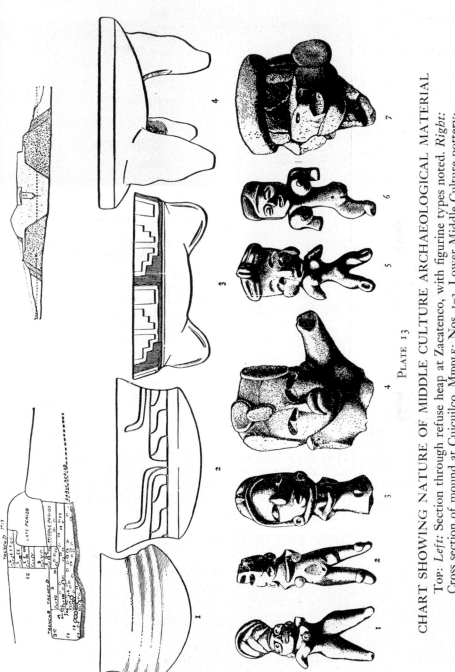

CHART SHOWING NATURE OF MIDDLE CULTURE ARCHAEOLOGICAL MATERIAL

TOP: *Left:* Section through refuse heap at Zacatenco, with figurine types noted. *Right:* Cross section of mound at Cuicuilco. MIDDLE: Nos. 1–2, Lower Middle Culture pottery; Nos. 3–4, Upper Middle Culture pottery. BOTTOM: Nos. 1–4, Lower Middle Culture figurines, C 3, C 1–2, B–C, A; Nos. 5–6, Upper Middle Culture figurines, E, H 2; No. 7. Teotihuacan I figurine, E 4.

PLATE 14

LOWER MIDDLE CULTURE FIGURINES

Top: Figurines (Type C 3) from earliest level. The features are made of applied bits of clay. Although the general appearance is crude, the technique shows long experimentation. Bottom: These figurines (Types C 1 and C 1–2) develop from those above. They seem to show a more slovenly procedure, but there is more variety in form than in the earlier style of female figures above.

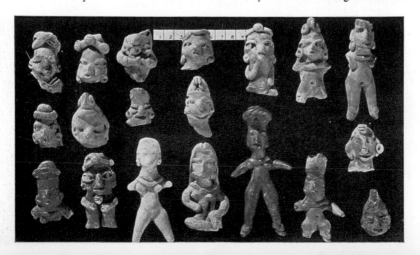

PLATE 15

LOWER MIDDLE CULTURE FIGURINES

Top: The head (D1) in this much enlarged reproduction represents a style in which the craftsmen exercised more care and skill. The source of the type seems to have been outside of the Valley of Mexico in Morelos. Bottom: A group of similar heads from Central Mexico, showing the variations within a single style. The scale is in centimeters.

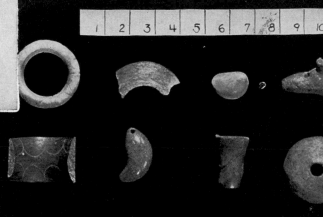

PLATE 16

MIDDLE CULTURE POTTERY AND IMPLEMENTS

Top: Pottery from the early phase of the Lower Middle Culture Period, *L.* to *R.*, trade piece, red and orange on white; bowls, white on red; bowl, black ware. MIDDLE: Obsidian tools; *top row,* Upper Middle Culture; *middle and bottom rows,* Lower Middle Cultures. BOTTOM: *Left:* Equipment of an Upper Middle Culture leatherworker, awls, grainers, scrapers and rodent teeth for cutting and scraping. *Right:* Lower Middle Period ornaments, earplugs, beads and whistle. Note the jade ornaments, second in both rows.

First the materials from Copilco and Cuicuilco, the two buried sites, were compared and found to be different. Then these styles were discovered in other parts of the Valley in open sites, unaffected by the local eruptions which formed the Pedregal. Next several seasons of work in these open sites disclosed that not only was Copilco older than Cuicuilco but that Copilco-Zacatenco culture was represented by rubbish heaps twice as deep as those at Cuicuilco-Ticoman. There is no way to measure the rate of accumulation of such heaps. However, on the basis of a deposit at Pecos,* New Mexico, the beginning and ending dates of which are more or less known, it does not seem unreasonable to compute six or seven centuries' duration for the Lower Middle Culture of Copilco-Zacatenco and three hundred years or so for the life span of the Upper Middle Culture of Cuicuilco-Ticoman.[18] (See Plate 13.)

The next step was to fit Cuicuilco-Ticoman to the later phases of Indian history in Mexico. Cuicuilco and Ticoman material is stylistically akin to pottery and figurines found at mound sites in Puebla and Morelos, suggesting that the massive shrine of Cuicuilco in the Valley was an outpost. The baby-face divinity leads back to the highly ceremonialized "Olmec" culture in Vera Cruz, and the Fire God occurs not only at Ticoman and Cuicuilco and the Upper Middle Culture site of Jalapazco,† in Puebla, but also very frequently at Teotihuacan.

Actual examples of Teotihuacan culture have appeared in Gualupita and Ticoman. Yet much more significant was the discovery at Teotihuacan that its earliest phase was closely affiliated to pottery and figurines commonly occurring at

*Pa'y-cos.   †Hah-lah-pa'hz-co.

Cuicuilco, Ticoman and Gualupita. Thus the beginning of the Teotihuacan civilization was a part of the same cultural manifestation that we have characterized as the Upper Middle Cultures. The lava flow of the Pedregal must be dated in terms of the continuous history of the Valley of Mexico tribes. Cuicuilco was abandoned before the flow took place and, to judge from the destruction, an appreciable time before. Six or seven hundred A.D. then is none too late a date for the eruption.[14] (See Plate 21.)

Therefore, we must conclude that one or two centuries prior to the dawn of the Christian Era sedentary farmers were maintaining themselves in the Valley of Mexico. Their culture was sufficient for their needs, and very little in the way of outside influence affected them. Toward the end influences in art or, more precisely, religious representation began to modify their culture. Finally, in the third or fourth centuries after Christ, they seem to have withdrawn from the Valley, giving way before the pressure of a new people.

These new people may well have come from the regions east and south of the Valley of Mexico, now embraced in the states of Morelos and Puebla, and seem to have been in a ferment of technical and religious experiment. They showed greater interest than their predecessors in modeling and technique and exercised something of an artistic independence between villages. Their most impressive contribution was the introduction of religious architecture and the beginnings of defined ritualistic art. Their contacts in trade and in intellectual inspiration were with the peoples of the east coast, but they worked out their styles in their own way. Some groups built clusters of mounds; others seem not to have taken up this type of architecture. They abandoned Cuicuilco, where they built their largest platform, possibly owing to warnings of the cataclysm that later took place when the Pedregal was formed. Another site, fifty miles away across the lake, eventually evolved into the great ceremonial center of Teotihuacan, the first and mightiest of the temple cities of Central Mexico.

With the foundation of this new capital the frontier of Middle American civilization shifted from the south and east of the Valley of Mexico to the territory north and west of it. The Valley was no longer the haunt of tribes taking their first steps toward ritualized civilization, but the proud domain of the Toltecs, traditional founders of civilization in Central Mexico, who had their capital at Teotihuacan.

TABLE II

SUMMARY OF HISTORY OF LOWER MIDDLE CULTURES

EARLY PHASE: Permanent villages, gradual evolution and changes in pottery and figurine types. Long occupation, stages of which are better defined at some sites than others.

Early El Arbolillo I: Figurines, C_3a, C_3b, C_{1-2}, C_2, pottery incised black with red paint.

Intermediate El Arbolillo I, Early Zacatenco: Figurines, C_{1-2}, C_2, pottery incised black, thick black, white, white on red, vague olla necks; laurel-leaf points.

Late El Arbolillo I, Early Zacatenco: Figurines, C_1a, C_1b, C_3c, C_3d, D_1, early F; pottery as in intermediate period.

LATE PHASE: Permanent villages, sharp shift in figurine and pottery styles, introduction of new figurine style, type A; evidence of local floods at beginning and end of Late Phase, which seems shorter than Early Phase.

Transitional El Arbolillo I, Transitional Zacatenco: Figurines, B–C, B–F.

Copilco, Middle Zacatenco, El Arbolillo II: Figurines, A, B, F, C_5; pottery thin black with etched design, red on white, red on yellow, trade wares; stone points with tangs.

TABLE III

SUMMARY OF HISTORY OF UPPER MIDDLE CULTURES

EARLY PHASE: Permanent villages in Puebla and Morelos; pottery and figurines in distinctive styles; trade connections suggest contemporaneity with Late Phase of Middle Cultures of Valley of Mexico.

Gualupita I, Cholula I: Figurines, D1, D2, D3, K, O; pottery, simple silhouette bowls and bottles in brown and red ware.

LATE PHASE: Permanent villages, introduction of platforms and altars; evolution from Early Phase in Morelos and Puebla; replacement of Lower Middle Cultures in the Valley of Mexico without transition; distinctive figurines and pottery which go through gradual evolution; ritualized presentations; some sites better defined than others; first settlement of Teotihuacan; lava flow of Pedregal after abandonment of Cuicuilco.

Early Ticoman-Cuicuilco I: Figurines, E1, E2, E3, I3; red-on-yellow incised pottery; disk earplugs.

Intermediate Ticoman, Cuicuilco II: Figurines G1, G2, I1, I2, E4, J, M, N; red-on-yellow pottery with white outline; incised earplugs.

Late Ticoman, Cuicuilco III, Late Zacatenco, Gualupita II, Teotihuacan I: Other sites in Puebla and Morelos; figurines, H1–5; in Gualupita, C9 and hollow figures; fire gods at Cuicuilco and Ticoman; pottery polished and elaborate tripod supports; carved earplugs hollowed in center.

CHAPTER III

TEOTIHUACAN AND THE CLASSICAL TOLTECS

A description of a civilization, the monuments of which are the wonder of Mexico, and an attempt to reconstruct the history of its creators from the meager and distorted sources available

THE TOLTECS or Master Builders were the first people mentioned in the annals of the Valley of Mexico. Their customs and achievements are so wrapped in the mystery which myth draws over the raw facts of history, and so confusing and illogical are the references to them, that a leading Mexicanist once challenged their very existence.[1] The facts of the case seem to be that, in the late migration period between the tenth and fourteenth centuries, marauding tribes applied the term Toltec to whatever settled population they met and later assumed that name themselves as a badge of advertisement of being civilized. In our own culture history we have frequent cases of the names of stately European capitals being similarly applied in wistful hope to the tiny hamlets of the first settlers of North America. (See Plate 21.)

One set of annals refers to an imposing civilization whose creators we may call Toltecs of Teotihuacan from their majestic capital.[2] Other histories recount the lineage of chiefs of different tribes, which we may distinguish as Dynastic

Toltecs.[3] If the history of Europe were recounted in fragmentary records without consecutive dates we should have a similar difficulty in distinguishing between the Roman Empire of Caesar and Augustus and, say, the Holy Roman Empire, which one writer has defined as neither holy nor Roman nor an empire.

The Teotihuacan Toltecs have been described as great architects, carpenters and mechanics. They were skilled likewise in agriculture, cultivating corn, cotton, beans, chili peppers and all the other domesticated plants known to Mexico. From cotton they spun thread to be woven into cloth which ranged from the fineness of linen to the thickness of velvet. The men wore robes and breechclouts, supplemented in cold weather by sleeveless jackets, and were shod with sandals of henequen, the fiber of a variety of maguey. Women dressed in *huipiles*,* sleeveless blouses, and *enaguas*, skirts made by wrapping a long strip of cotton around the waist and legs, a costume which still persists in the Indian villages of modern Mexico. Warriors wore armor made of quilted cotton and used spears and wooden clubs set with blades of obsidian. The club wielders carried shields, and Ixtlilxochitl† says that some soldiers had copper helmets, although no trace of this metal has been officially reported from Teotihuacan-Toltec sites. Priests were distinguished by a more elaborate costume composed of a headdress and a long black tunic which touched the ground.[4] (See Plate 24, bottom.)

The "kings" wore robes like the priests and adorned themselves with necklaces and earrings. They wore socks as well as sandals, a great elegance for sandal-wearing people. They distinguished themselves as much by conduct as by dress,

*wee-pe'el-ess.   †Eesh-tleell-sho'-cheetl.

rising early and eating only at daybreak and at nightfall. They spoke little but to the point. A "king" had one "queen," and neither could remarry upon the death of the other, although commoners might take a second or even a third wife. A "queen" could inherit the realm from her husband, and her legitimate sons succeeded her, a statement suggesting that the austerity of the marital ideal did not interfere with the royal pleasure.

The Toltecs built their palaces and houses of stone and mortar and used the *temascal* or steam bath, which still persists among the modern Indians. They held a market every twenty days, or each month in terms of the Middle American year. These markets were located in Tula, Teotihuacan, Tulancingo, Cuernavaca, Cholula, Tultitlan and several other towns where remains of Teotihuacan occupation still may be seen. There is additional evidence that the Toltecs counted their years and used the sacred almanac of 260 days, according to the pattern followed by their successors.[5]

The religion of this bygone era is difficult to interpret, for both the sixteenth-century Christian mentality and the late Aztec theology distort for us its true structure. Ixtlilxochitl reported a supreme being, Tloque Nahuaque,* who surpassed all other gods. However, to a Sun God and his wife, the Moon Goddess, tradition persistently dedicates the two largest structures at the sacred city of Teotihuacan. Tlaloc,† a Rain God, was mentioned as highly important, and a Frog Goddess was also honored by a sumptuous temple. Quetzalcoatl,‡ Feathered Serpent, was worshiped as the bringer of civilization, but the same name was used as a title for the chief priests. There were persistent myths referring

*Tlo'-kay Na-wa'h-kay.   †Tla'h-loc.   ‡Ka'yt-zal-co-atl.

to the conflict between an old worship and a new, symbolized by a struggle between Quetzalcoatl and the war and sky gods of the later Aztec religion.[6]

Apparently a basic nature worship was transformed into an elaborate polytheism. Later history tells of the struggles between the votaries of one god as opposed to those of another. The elevation of a god to the role of tribal protector led to the domination of his worshipers in the community and was as important to the ancient Mexican as the domination of an economic or political system is to our modern populations. There was then, as now, the same masking of desire for power with conviction of rectitude. Probably, too, there was the same confusion of motives in the individual.

The history of the Teotihuacan Toltecs is as tenuous as their sociology and religion. The two chief sources, Ixtlilxochitl and the *Annals of Cuauhtitlan*,* refer to different localities, one at Teotihuacan, the other at the west of the lake near Azcapotzalco.† [7] The eastern history, written by Ixtlilxochitl, began very properly with the creation of the world and the four or five Suns, or eras, through which life has survived. The first era, the Water Sun, was when the supreme god, Tloque Nahuaque, created the world; and after 1716 years floods and lightning destroyed it. The second era, the Sun of the Earth, saw the world populated by giants, the Quinametzin,‡ who almost disappeared when earthquakes obliterated the earth. The Wind Sun came third, and Olmecs and Xicalancas,§ human tribes, lived on earth.

*Kwow-ti-tla'n.   ‡Keen-a-me't-zeen.
†Az-ca-pot-z'al-co.   §Shee-cah-la'ncas.

They destroyed the surviving giants, founded Cholula and migrated as far as Tabasco. A marvelous personage, called Quetzalcoatl by some, Huemac* by others, appeared in this era and brought civilization and ethics. When the people did not benefit from his teachings he returned to the east, prophesying the destruction of the world by high winds and the conversion of mankind into monkeys, all of which came to pass. The fourth age, the present, is called the Sun of Fire, and will end in a general conflagration.

These four eras are mythological, with a small amount of historical information incorporated (Table IV). The Aztec versions, which had five Suns, were more purely theological. Yet these mythical floods and fires may recapitulate calamities, such as inundations and volcanic eruptions, which, according to evidence found at Middle Culture sites, beset man in Mexico.

Toltec history, when it breaks through the background of myth, describes a people wandering through Mexico. Under the guidance of an astrologer priest, Huemac, they founded the city of Tollan and elected a king whose reign was fixed at fifty-two years. This was the length of an Aztec year cycle, a major time unit having the same function as our century. The list of the nine rulers is given on Table V, but tribal events were seldom recorded until the end of the period. Huemac died at the age of three hundred in the reign of the second ruler, after compiling a book of history and prophecy. This observation may be a backhanded explanation of the introduction of established ritualistic practices, including a calendar and architecture. The sixth ruler, Mitl, broke the order of length of rule, enlarged his kingdom and

*Wa′y-mac.

built the splendid Temple of the Frog and many other sumptuous structures. Mitl's association with extraordinary building operations had a possible basis in fact, as we shall see in describing the Temple of Quetzalcoatl.

Significant events for the reigns of the last rulers are recorded. The eighth had a dominion extending over Toluca, Cuernavaca, Yolotepec, Cholula and Jalisco. The old gods were still worshiped, but the cult of two new ones, Tezcatlipoca,* the great Sky God, and Huitzilopochtli,† the War God, were introduced. During the reign of this king a lady, Xochitl,‡ popularized an intoxicating drink named pulque,§ made from the fermented juice of the maguey, which is today the standard tipple of Highland Mexico.

Topiltzin, the ninth king, who introduced the ball court, had a reign fraught with disaster. In his time the domain of the Toltecs disintegrated because of local revolts, invasions and the bitter toll exacted by famine and pestilence. Teotihuacan was abandoned. When they could, the people emigrated south to Tabasco and Guatemala. Those who remained were absorbed into the new tribes, and their lineage was assumed as a mark of honor by the ruling houses of the succeeding Chichimec or Dynastic Toltec period. Such is the story of the eastern Toltecs as set forth by Ixtlilxochitl.

The dignity and awe in which tradition holds the Toltecs affect the modern visitor to Teotihuacan. Here in the valley which bears its name, a vast area, three and a half miles long and nearly two miles wide, was given over to clusters of imposing buildings. The whole zone was paved with a plaster floor, not once but many times. This was no residential city

*Tez-cat-li-po'-ca.　　‡Sho'-chitl.
†Weet-zeel-o-po'tch-tly.　　§po'ol-kay.

but a great ceremonial center given over to temples and houses for the people engaged in religious activity. There is little trace of the humble refuse of communal life. Teoti-huacan is an impressive monument to the toll which men exact from themselves for their salvation.[8] (See Plate 22, top.)

The architects built their city in several successive precincts, extending southward from the mighty Pyramid of the Moon. This was not a true pyramid but was truncated at the top to give space for a temple, and the ascending planes were skillfully broken to provide terraces. A broad stair led up the south side from a wide rectangular court. Additional buildings flanked this plaza, and several hundred yards to the east and west two smaller precincts added to the symmetry of the plan.

Two rows of buildings of impressive size lead south from the Moon Plaza. Excavation of one revealed lovely frescoes, the content of which suggest a temple of Agriculture. Another group of small mounds lies off to the east, and directly south is a second large unexcavated group of temples, which, from the emplacements found in the vicinity, is called the Group of the Columns.

The Pyramid of the Sun dwarfs all the other buildings in Teotihuacan. This great truncated pyramid, almost seven hundred feet at the base, rises in four terraces to a height of over two hundred feet. The slopes were varied by their builders to create an impression of greater mass. The exterior was faced with stone and covered with plaster, but the pyramid proper was built of adobe bricks, made from the refuse beds of an earlier era. The fragments of pottery, figurines and tools, imbedded in the interior, were transitional between the developed culture of Teotihuacan and the Upper Middle Culture group. (See Plate 22, bottom.)

The Pyramid of the Sun is surrounded by a wide platform, constructed of square cells, walled by adobe and filled with refuse and rubble. Outside the enclosure are situated the houses for the priests. Smaller mounds still unexplored extend southward, until another great enclosure is reached, in this case surrounded by masonry dwellings. Rooms with pilastered porches open on inner patios. There are no two-story buildings, but by means of platforms some apartments are raised higher than others.

A river makes a natural terminus at the south, but across it lies a magnificent platform, the walls of which are faced with carved stone blocks; but the crowning temple has disappeared. The feathered serpent is the dominant decorative motive, and great heads carved in rugged simplicity project from the balustrade and from the façades. These were originally painted, and some still glare at the onlookers through eyes of burnished obsidian. Along the façade the serpent heads alternate with those of a strange being, who may be Tlaloc, the Rain God. On the wall behind them the undulating bodies of the snakes are carved in low relief, and sea shells, all Caribbean varieties, are used to fill the spaces left by the curves of the bodies. The effect is massive and awesome. Though lacking the sinuous grace of Maya relief, the decorative scheme, nonetheless, is that of an achieved art. There was no fumbling in this work of many craftsmen, laboring through the years, cutting stone with stone. This building, called by modern investigators the Temple of

Quetzalcoatl, Feathered Serpent, the God of Learning, is splendid enough to qualify as the edifice for which Mitl was renowned. The ancient name, Temple of the Frog, may have arisen from the symbolic association of frogs with Tlaloc, the God of Rain. (See Plate 23.)

Once the city was completed in all its mighty scope, a transformation took place. From the Pyramid of the Moon, at the north, to the Temple of Quetzalcoatl, every single building was rebuilt. Rooms were filled in and façades covered up to form platforms for new temples. Not even the gigantic hulks of the Pyramids of the Sun and Moon escaped the addition of new stairs and façades. The Temple of Quetzalcoatl, as was fitting, received the most extreme alteration. The original shrine became the core of a high platform which dominated a huge enclosure, surrounded by a broad rampart. This wall supported four lesser platforms on each of three sides and, on the eastern wall behind the main structure, three such temple foundations.

The later building is less massive than the earlier. There is less use of hewed stone, and rubble is extensively employed. Although the reconstruction extended eventually to rebuilding the whole sacred area, no violent shift in the styles of pottery or figurines suggests conquest by new tribes. The new architecture has all the earmarks of a religious reformation which destroyed the symbolism of one cult to uplift a new. Moreover, in one sector of the city, the filling between the late and the early pavements produced much burned material such as charcoal, adobe, pottery, and the like, as if the debris from incendiary fires had been utilized for foundation material. The events recounted in the annals seem to reflect this architectural change, and possibly the new religion of Huitzilopochtli and Tezcatlipoca replaced the old cult of Quetzalcoatl and Tlaloc. Certainly the levies of man power, time and materials sufficient to achieve the rebuilding of Teotihuacan would have been enough to bring about serious popular disorders.

People continue to live, though their religion change and their kingdoms perish. Their basic techniques for maintaining life persist likewise. Therefore, tools and pottery give a more continuous guide to tribal history than the annals of chiefs or the soaring bulk of religious architecture. The material culture of Teotihuacan is an important index to the history of the early Toltecs. The contrast between articles for household use and for ritual became sharper as the Teotihuacan culture reached its full development. The rhythms of change in different types of activity do not always synchronize, and in the Teotihuacan culture we distinguish two building periods, three ceramic phases and five successive styles in clay figurines.

The beginnings of Teotihuacan culture are revealed by the contents of the adobes in the Pyramid of the Sun. The pottery fragments and figurines show an amalgamation of four culture strains, one deriving from the Upper Middle Culture, another containing the germs of the later Teotihuacan periods, a third tying in with the tribes of western Mexico and a fourth of unknown provenience. The little clay figures are handmade and closely affiliated with Upper Middle Culture types. The early Teotihuacanos developed a new kind of idol made of crudely incised stone. A combination of three-colored pottery, like that of Ticoman, with a lost-color process, resulted in a four-color polychrome which was highly characteristic. Clay earplugs were as common at Teotihuacan as at the Middle Culture sites. While the early Teotihuacanos did not make, style for style and piece for piece, implements identical to those of their contemporaries at Ticoman or Cuicuilco or Gualupita, their material culture comprised specific elements drawn from each particular site. The early Teotihuacanos took part in the same Upper Middle Culture migration.[9] (See Plate 21.)

When the Teotihuacanos began their first big building operations their handiwork had become more conventionalized and more stylistically unified. Polychrome pottery gave way to simple lustrous wares of black and brown or vases and large jars painted in red on yellow. A flourishing trade sprang up in the importation of a thin orange ware that attains at times almost an eggshell delicacy. For use in their religious rites the Teotihuacanos constructed cylindrical wares of black or brown which they carved in ritualistic patterns, utilizing such techniques as simple incision, champlevé and, very rarely, intaglio.[10]

Their stone and bone tools were not capable of much elaboration. However, since abundant deposits of obsidian were close at hand, the Teotihuacanos used this material lavishly, flaking blades to a scalpel-like narrowness and chipping tools of every variety. They made little animals of this hard and brittle substance and ground it to mirror-like smoothness to make eyes for their great stone idols. In addition they used lava, not only pecking out great blocks for facing their buildings but also carving designs and creating a sculpture. The great step taken by the Teotihuacan Toltecs was to formalize their religious art. Clay figurines which carried the main trend of artistic development in the Middle Cultures, became conventionalized into simple little figures of men and women whose faces were reduced to their bare anatomical essentials. Women were shown dressed in *huipiles* and *enaguas*, men in the *maxtli** or breechclout. The sculptors painted the faces and the costumes of both male and female figures. The growth of ritualistic definition may also be seen in representations of the Old God, of a god in a human skin, later known as Xipe† (Our Lord the Flayed One), and in composite figures, having attributes of men and animals among which the jaguar predominated.[11]

Their mastery of stone sculpture was most evident at the Temple of Quetzalcoatl, where able presentation was subordinated to the decorative demands of architectural ornament. To make incense burners the sculptors embodied the idea of the Old God seated under his bowl. Other artists traded for jade and porphyry and wrought these hard substances into beautiful masks and figures, which stand out as masterpieces of Middle American sculpture. Much of the work in stone has disappeared, smashed by the Spanish priests or broken into building stones, but two colossal examples still survive. One is the ten-foot statue of the so-called Goddess of the Waters, now in the National Museum. Jade ornaments, *huipil, enagua*, sandals, every detail is set forth, not as graceful accents to a suave naturalism but as the ornament to an architectural creation. This goddess is a monument, a sort of monolithic building, that symbolizes the implacable force of nature. The other statue was never finished. It lies still anchored to its matrix of living rock in a ravine near Texcoco.§ Larger by far than the Goddess of the Waters, battered by the elements, the deity of Coatlinchan‡ cannot fail to impress the modern visitor. Its concept is

*ma'hsh-tly.   †She'e-pay.   ‡Co-at-lin-cha'n.   §Tess'-co-co.

grandiose, but the engineering skill was lacking to cut the sculpture free of its base. Prometheus in his chains may symbolize the tragedy of European thought, but to me this goddess, still an integral part of the land that made her, represents the paralysis of Indian civilization. (See Plate 24, top right.)

Painting and drawing found an outlet in the requirements of ritual.[12] The frescoes of the Temple of Agriculture show an appreciation of decorative design combined with a sense of natural values. One fresco which has now disappeared but which fortunately was copied at the time of discovery depicts a ceremony before two divinities like the Goddess of the Waters and confirms Ixtlilxochitl's description of the Toltec costume. Carved vases present in full ritualistic detail the attributes of tiger gods and other divinities, and little definitive symbols indicate that some sort of writing was in priestly use. Unfortunately no sacred books have survived. (See Plates 24, bottom; 58, top.)

A ceremonial center like Teotihuacan must have exemplified the best work of which a culture was capable. The civil centers have been little explored. In the neighborhood of Teotihuacan, some few miles from the sacred city, great communal dwellings were built, embracing fifty and sixty rooms set about patios connected by passageways. The rooms were made of adobe and rubblework covered with plaster, and supported a life of comfort and security. There was also an altar prominently placed, for religious duty was not confined to the ceremonial zone.[13]

Another huge settlement lay across the lake at Azcapotzalco. Here the land is tremendously fertile, so that the old buildings have been razed to level the fields for present-day agriculture. Modern excavations to get the clay used in brick and tile have yielded a rich stream of objects, and a few days' digging produces hundreds of specimens. Thus we may judge of the abundance of life in Toltec times from the quantity of human possessions.

At Azcapotzalco and at Xolalpan,* near Teotihuacan, hundreds of skeletons were buried under the floors of the houses. Adults were usually seated, and the quantity of pottery vessels accompanying them suggests the richness of the economy. At Azcapotzalco sometimes the people had great feasts, and after partaking they cast their dishes into pits prepared for the purpose. Since clay idols were thrown in likewise, we may be sure that these festivals were religious in character. Once we found a great red-and-yellow bowl in such a deposit. It contained the remnants of the *pièce de résistance*, the upper legs and hips of a human being, the most succulent portions for festive consumption. There is also other evidence of human sacrifice. At the Temple of Quetzalcoatl individuals were buried under the corners as foundation deposits. At both Teotihuacan and Azcapotzalco shallow dishes, cut from the top of skulls, testify to other rituals involving sacrifice and death.

The Toltec dominion had its widest extent in the first architectural and second ceramic period. Confirming the statement of the annals, remains are found in the Valley of Toluca, in Morelos, and most abundantly in Puebla. At Cholula the Toltecs constructed a whole temple site of enormous extent, which later peoples covered with the single great pyramid so renowned for its size. This Toltec site has produced no carving, but one temple had a fresco decora-

*Sho-la'l-pan.

tion portraying the Butterfly God, a mythological being, important to Teotihuacan religion.[14]

The third phase of Teotihuacan consisted of a tremendous reconstruction of the city, followed by a decline in the arts. The architectural activity evoked no corresponding elaboration in stonework or ceramic techniques, save in one respect, the clay figurines. The idols of this period represent some of the finest modeling ever achieved in Mexico. The faces were so carefully constructed that some students have considered them portraits. At first handmade, later they were copied in molds and retouched to bring them to a detailed perfection. Finally, like the other arts and crafts, the portrait style degenerated, to be replaced by moldmade heads of coarser workmanship. At this time, the fourth figurine period, Teotihuacan ceased to function as a sacred capital.

Ixtlilxochitl has related that religious conflict, revolt and crop failure contributed to the downfall of Teotihuacan. To some extent we can corroborate this statement from archaeological interpretations. The architectural change has the appearance of having been made simultaneously, in contrast to the gradual development of the original city. Teotihuacan was built over hastily with the maximum use of original construction. The abrupt change in figurine styles suggests that a new god was honored by this new presentation. The drain on human resources, implicit in such large-scale construction, would lead readily to revolt under the strain.

Crop failure could have resulted from deforestation and the consequent drying up of streams. At Teotihuacan lime cement covered all the buildings and formed the entire paving. The modern Maya Indians burn ten times as much wood as the quantity of limestone to be reduced, and they have the advantage of steel axes.[15] It is not too fanciful, therefore, to assume that the Toltec masons, lacking metal of any kind, found it easier to use hearths of charcoal, obtained by burning over the forest, than to try to obtain the requisite fuel by chopping out their logs with stone axes. If this interpretation is correct, the hills must have been widely denuded of timber, with a consequent drying up of streams and erosion of fields. Furthermore, the barren aspect of the hills of Teotihuacan today must be due to something more than the requirements for fuel and timber of the post-Conquest population. The Toltecs and their successors, Chichimecs, Acolhuas and Aztecs, undoubtedly contributed their fair share to this wastage of the forests.

Tradition ascribes the abandonment of Teotihuacan to the tenth and eleventh centuries, whatever the basic causes. However, Teotihuacanos still occupied the outlying villages, and across the lakes the enormous city of Azcapotzalco continued to flourish. Teotihuacan, however, was a city of ghosts. In Chichimec times the makers of the Mazapan* culture occasionally crept onto the ruins to bury their dead, but they never disturbed the silence by building houses in the zone. A persistent tradition describes the great Aztec ruler Montezuma as visiting Teotihuacan to make sacrifices, but no evidence exists in the shape of ceremonial equipment left behind.[16] The three or four Aztec potsherds found among the hundreds of thousands of Teotihuacan fragments certainly cannot be testimony to the pomp and ceremony of Aztec worship.

Azcapotzalco was an enormous city, where dwelt a large

*Ma-za'h-pan.

TABLE IV

SEQUENCE OF TRIBES IN THE VALLEY OF MEXICO ACCORDING TO VARIOUS AUTHORITIES

	Phillips[a]	Ixtlilxochitl I[b]	Ixtlilxochitl II[c]	Veytia[d]	Duran[e]	Muñoz Camargo[f]	Clavigero[g]	Sahagun[h]	de Jonghe[i]	Mapa Tlotzin[j]	Mapa, Quinatzin[k]	Codex Xolotl[l]	Motolinia[m]	Garcia Icazbalceta[n]
Maceguales (created by Gods)	1	–	–	–	–	–	–	–	–	–	–	–	–	–
Quinames (Giants)	2	1	1	1	1	–	–	–	–	–	–	–	–	–
Tarasco	–	–	–	–	–	1	–	–	–	–	–	–	–	–
Olmeca-Xicalanga	–	2	2	3	–	2	–	–	–	–	–	–	–	–
Zacateca	–	–	–	–	–	2	–	–	–	–	–	–	–	–
Toltec	4	3	3	4	–	–	1	1	–	–	–	–	–	–
Nomad Chichimec	3	4	4	2	–	–	2	–	1	1	1	1	1	1
Chichimec	–	–	–	5	2	3	–	2	–	–	–	–	–	–
Teo-Chichimec	–	–	–	–	–	4	–	2	–	–	–	–	–	–
Otomi	–	–	5	6	–	–	2	2	–	–	–	–	–	–
Acolhua I Tlailtoque	–	5	–	–	–	–	–	–	–	–	–	–	–	–
Chimalpanecs	–	5	–	–	–	–	–	–	–	–	2	2	–	–
Chalco-Toltec	–	–	–	–	–	–	–	–	–	–	–	2	–	–
Acolhua II Texcoco	–	6	5	6	–	3	3	–	(4)	3	–	–	2	2
Culhua { 7 Tribes	–	–	–	–	3	–	–	3	3	–	–	–	–	–
Culhua { Tepanec	–	6	5	6	–	–	–	–	–	–	–	3	–	–
Culhua { Culhua	5	–	–	–	–	–	–	–	–	–	–	3	–	–
Culhua { Aztec	–	6	6	7	4	–	–	–	–	–	3	3	3	3
Culhua { Huitznahua	–	6	–	–	–	–	–	–	–	–	–	3	–	–

[a]Phillips, Codex Ramirez, 1883, 618–19, 622–24.
[b]Ixtlilxochitl, Relaciones, 1891, 17–21, 75–103.
[c]Ixtlilxochitl, Historia Chichimeca, 1892, 21–45, 61–65, 69–71.
[d]Veytia, Historia Antigua, 1836, Vol. 1, 139–156; Vol. 2, 3–10, 39–46, 87–101.
[e]Duran, Historia de las Indias, I, 1867, 10–14.
[f]Muñoz Camargo, Historia, 1892, 5–116.
[g]Clavigero, History, 1787, 93–136.
[h]Sahagun, Historia General, 1938, Vol. 4, Book II, 106, 116–17, 138–47.
[i]de Jonghe, ed., Histoire de Mechique, 1903, 8–20.
[j]Aubin, Peinture Didactique, 1885, 58–74.
[k]Aubin, Peinture Didactique, 1885, 75–85.
[l]Radin, Sources, 1920, 41–45.
[m]Motolinia, Historia, 1914, 3–5.
[n]Origen in Garcia Icazbalceta, 1886–92, Vol. 3, Origen de los Mexicanos, 283–92.

TABLE V

SUMMARY OF TOLTEC HISTORY

TEOTIHUACAN I

Manufacture of materials inside adobes of Temples of Sun and Moon.

Eastern Lineage		*Western Lineage*
Chalchiuhtlanetzin	510–62	
Ixtlilcuechahauac	562–614	
Huetzin	614–66	

TEOTIHUACAN II

Construction of first-period buildings at Teotihuacan, culminating in the Temple of Quetzalcoatl under Mitl; establishment of center at Azcapotzalco (El Corral I); wide distribution of culture to Cholula, Morelos.

Eastern Lineage		*Western Lineage*	
Totepeuh	666–718		
Nacoxoc	718–70	Huetzin	869–(?)
Mitl-Tlacomihua	770–829	Totepeuh (?)	(?)–887

TEOTIHUACAN III–IV

Construction of second-period buildings; introduction of mold; complex ritual in figurines; trade with Mayas; introduction of new religion; abandonment of Teotihuacan; incursion of Chichimecs.

Eastern Lineage		*Western Lineage*	
Queen Xihuiquenitzin	829–33		
Iztaccaltzin	833–85	Ihuitimal	887–923
Topiltzin	885–959	Topiltzin	923–47

TEOTIHUACAN V

Shift of Toltec center to Azcapotzalco, possibly under Topiltzin; great ritualistic development of figurines; influence from Oaxaca; new religion and destruction by Culhuas.

Eastern Lineage	*Western Lineage*	
	Topiltzin	923–47
	Matlacxochitl	947–83
	Nauhyotzin I	983–97
	Matlaccoatzin	997–1025
	Tlilcoatzin	1025–46
	Huemac	1047–1122

population. The decline of Teotihuacan and the gradual abandonment of the eastern towns must have added substantially to its numbers. Its people did not follow the architectural practices of earlier times and have left no great monuments. It originally seems to have been founded at the time of the first great building period at Teotihuacan, because the same handmade figurines and pottery styles exist at both sites. However, the religious reformation at Teotihuacan suggested by the rebuilding of the city and the making of the "portrait" type of figurines left no trace at Azcapotzalco. No true "portrait" heads occur among the thousands of figurines found in the western district.

A fully developed moldmade figurine cult replaced the older handmade techniques, but this practice was absent from Teotihuacan. Just as Byzantium for centuries carried on the tradition of Rome after the barbarians had sacked the parent city, so, in smaller scale, Azcapotzalco maintained the older tradition of Teotihuacan. Yet the figurine cult was carried to an extreme development. The introduction of the mold led to mass production of images by skilled workmen. Thus the details of dress and ornament, which defined the gods represented, could be rigidly fixed. Each household could be equipped in miniature with the outward elements of a ritual previously confined to special centers. Elaborate incense burners studded with molded decorations reproduced the main temple altars with their ritualistic ornament. The origin of this practice may well have been in Oaxaca among the Zapotecs, who not only made elaborate incense burners of this type, but since fragments of Oaxaca wares are found in Toltec sites, also shipped pottery to be traded to these northern people.[17]

This archaeological situation clears up a discrepancy in the annals that has made modern scholars tear their beards. The *Annals of Cuauhtitlan* recorded a list of Toltec rulers that only partially in name and not at all in date corresponds to Ixtlilxochitl's list of the rulers of Teotihuacan (Table V). It would seem highly probable that the lineage of Cuauhtitlan referred to the chiefs of this western settlement which endured after the parent site had been abandoned. The Azcapotzalco region was protected by the lakes from invaders on the east. There was no such tax on the population as at Teotihuacan, where the people had to carry out a religious reformation in architectural terms. Therefore, the pressures from within and without, which caused Teotihuacan to crumble, were not manifested in the west until over a century later.

Civil war, religious strife and the yielding of the Quetzalcoatl cult to that of Tezcatlipoca contributed to the downfall of the western Toltecs at the close of the twelfth century. A large cluster of baby burials at El Corral, Azcapotzalco, suggests that starvation with a resultant stepping up of infant mortality may have played its part as well. Yet the conquerors of the western Valley were the first to take the name of the conquered and aggrandize their lineage by the assumption of great age. Toltec arts and crafts disappeared, and their styles had no continuation in the work of the later people. But the name continued, and so did that old, old cult of making images, though the idols were now in honor of a religion with a new personnel of gods.

The Toltec era, the classical period of the builders of Teotihuacan, saw the full emergence of a Middle American

civilization. The culture was unified and seems to have been
diffused by an increasing population. In the emphasis on ritual
and the direction of technical skill toward the requirements
of worship this frontier civilization recapitulated the culture
history of Middle America.

CHAPTER IV

THE CHICHIMEC PERIOD AND THE DYNASTIC TOLTECS

In which are set forth the complex events, political, social and cultural, which led up to the formation of Aztec civilization

THE CLASSICAL ERA of the Teotihuacan Toltecs was an age of cultural unity. The people of Central Mexico made the same things, lived the same way and worshiped the same gods for centuries. Dissolution set in as famine, religious disagreements and the incursions of strange peoples corroded the structure of Teotihuacan civilization.

The succeeding era in Mexican history, 1100–1300, was a chaotic one which eventually resulted in that mixture of cultural unity and political independence which we know as the Aztec civilization. A tempting analogy is to compare the Chichimec Period to the European colonization of North America, where groups of many conditions and sorts struggled to populate the land and eventually incorporated the sum total of their experience into the North American republic. (See Plate 25.)

Religions and social systems and peoples competed for domination of the Valley. Several of the powerful tribes at the time of the Conquest had their origin in this era of confusion, and from their tribal annals we may extract a fairly clear picture of what went on. As each tribe recorded its own affairs with relatively little attention to those of its neighbors, cross references are rare. History, in our modern sense of utilizing past trends to chart the present and the future, did not exist in the intellectual structure of ancient Mexico, and the traditions of the successive tribal immigrations are in confusing disagreement (Table IV).

The histories of five towns summarize this period: Culhuacan,* Texcoco, Azcapotzalco, Cholula,† and Tenochtitlan‡ (Table VI). According to the *Annals of Cuauhtitlan*,§ a long, confused record referring to Culhuacan, Tenochtitlan and the politically insignificant Cuauhtitlan, the Culhuas conquered the Toltecs and lived for a time at their ancient capital Tula. The location of this Toltec capital is not clearly stated, but it was on the west side of the lake and may have been either the late Toltec site of Azcapotzalco or the modern Tula, which has some late Toltec remains but presents more evidence of a heavy Mazapan occupation.[1]

The Culhuas later withdrew southward to Culhuacan, where they established a lineage of chiefs, the length of whose reigns they carefully recorded in their annals. In the middle of the thirteenth century a new dynasty came in which the historians called "Chichimec"; it replaced the older line which they called "Toltec." References were made to struggles with other tribes, chiefly at the northern end of the lakes, but there was trouble with the southern towns as well (Table VI).

At the end of the fourteenth century civil war broke out and people deserted Culhuacan, which became weak and a

*Cool-wah-ca'n.   ‡Te-no'tch-ti-tlan.
†Cho-lo'o-la.   §Kwow-ti-tla'n.

shadow of its former self. The rise of a new power, the Tepanec, who had as allies the vigorous but ill-established Tenochcas,* contributed to its downfall. Yet before Culhuacan succumbed completely to vassalage under the new order, members of its reigning house had twice been sought to found the lineage of Tenochtitlan.

On the documentary evidences Culhuacan was an extremely important city-state. The consecutive reigns of its chiefs stretched from the time of the fall of the western Toltec Empire to that of the rise of the important Aztec state of Tenochtitlan. Culhuacan was considered a center of civilization and for three centuries was a major power in the Valley of Mexico. Yet a visit to the modern town discloses no lofty remains, for the ancient city is razed completely. Only the temple on the Hill of the Star, which rises behind the town and dominates the lakes, is a memorial to its past splendor. For here took place, even after the Culhuas had lost their power, the New Fire Ceremony which ushered in each new cycle of fifty-two years and epitomized the spirit of Aztec religion.

Texcoco on the eastern shore of the lakes of Mexico was the most civilized town in the Valley of Mexico at the time of the Conquest. Ixtlilxochitl, a descendant of the ruling house, had access to the annals of his people and left a full history, distorted though it was by his wish to make his lineage rival the noble lines of Castile; but he had a strong historical sense, doubtless absorbed from the Spanish priests who educated him. His ancestors were a nomadic group which lived mainly by hunting and eventually, under a chief named Xolotl,† occupied the territory around Teotihuacan.

*Te-no'tch-cas.   †Sho'-lottle.

They pushed west to Tenayuca* and in the process learned agriculture and assumed a sedentary life. While there they met other tribes of varying degrees of culture and assumed the practice of choosing a chief from a special lineage instead of electing him directly from the clan leaders.[2]

About 1300 two brothers were in line for succession to the chieftainship and one Tlotzin, who was not selected, moved back to Texcoco and headed his own line. When he died and his son Quinatzin† took the throne two tribes moved into his territory from the Mixteca area in northern Oaxaca and southern Puebla. They brought with them the worship of the god Tezcatlipoca, the art of writing and many other useful skills. So completely did these people transform life at Texcoco that the picture manuscripts portrayed the local population clad in skins and the immigrants in woven clothing to emphasize the contrast between their own culture and the superior talents of the newcomers. Quinatzin, who was an extraordinarily competent ruler, extended his dominions greatly by conquering many adjacent communities. The idea of absorbing conquered towns into the victorious state, so obvious to a modern member of western civilization, had not yet occurred to the Mexicans. Instead, defeated towns retained their local autonomy; but they paid a yearly tribute and their chiefs had to make a state visit to acknowledge their fealty to the conqueror. Quinatzin had some seventy towns as fiefs, and his dominion projected down to the shore of Vera Cruz. His successor, Techotlala, succeeded in unifying the Valley dialects into one language, Aztec.

Texcoco and Culhuacan never came into direct conflict, for they were situated at opposite ends of the Lake of Mexico.

*Te-nah-yo'o-ca.   †Kee-nat-se'en.

There is evidence, too, that the Valley was not completely settled, for in the mid-thirteenth century the Tenochca were able to thread their way south to Chapultepec* without coming into serious conflict with the settled populations.[3]

However, in the mid-fourteenth century there was serious conflict. A tribe called the Tepanec, which lived at Azcapotzalco, outgrew its boundaries. Led by an able and vicious chief, Tezozomoc,† it began to extend its territories. Culhuacan felt the pressure first, and internal discord developed, as it must when a nation cannot feed itself and has no room to expand. Some of the Culhuas moved up to Texcoco along the eastern shore and added their long-practiced skills to those of the Texcocan community. The Tepanec, blocked to the south by dense populations and to the west by high mountain walls, turned north and east to raid and occupy Texcocan lands. Otomi‡ tribes, whose territory lay on the islands and the eastern shore of Lake Xaltocan, were pinched between the opposing forces who would brook no neutrality. They moved north, and the two great powers, Tepanecs and Texcocans, came into direct contact and war ensued. Tezozomoc won a signal victory, broke Texcoco and alienated her vassals. He quickly dominated the rest of the Valley towns, almost obliterating the empty shell of Culhuacan's former dominance. His son Maxtla§ succeeded this vigorous and ruthless conqueror in 1427. Having the northern Valley at his feet, he oppressed the conquered and interfered in the affairs of former allies like Tenochtitlan. Yet he was to enjoy his conquests only a bare two years.[4]

Indian governmental practice extracted tribute from conquered tribes, but had not developed a technique for forcing

*Cha-po'ol-tepec.   †Te-zo'z-o-moc.   ‡Ot-o-me'e.   §Ma'sh-tla.

payment without declaring a new war and making a fresh campaign. Consequently a bond of sympathy forged from mutually shared ill-fortune grew up between otherwise somewhat hostile communities. Tenochtitlan and Tlacopan,* towns at the backdoor of Tepanec territory, made a pact with Texcoco across the lake; and the allies, rising suddenly, overthrew the new power. Maxtla was slain, his city burned and, contrary to the practice of the time, his people incorporated into the allied tribes. Land was apportioned to warriors who had performed notable feats of valor. So completely did the allies break the Tepanecs, that all that remains of their history is the memory of Tezozomoc and Maxtla and some petty local chieftains who succeeded them.

The Texcocans regained their prestige after this war, but the Tenochcas, who had begun as mere vassals, grew so rapidly in strength that at the coming of the Spaniards they had managed to eclipse their former lords, as we shall see in the following chapter.

These events disclose a picture of expanding populations and ensuing intertribal conflict. This cultural history shows a diffuse background of tribal arts and practices gradually welded into a closely similar whole, Aztec civilization. The process was achieved before Tenochtitlan attained eminence, so at the cost of academic tediousness the term Aztec has been reserved for the civilization, Tenochca for the people who so conspicuously made it known.

The civilization of Teotihuacan disappeared before the infiltration of intruding tribes. The nomadic groups referred to in the chronicles have left no identifiable remains. Hunters reduced to the bare necessities which they can carry on their

*Tla-co′-pan.

backs do not leave much trace of their presence. Other immigrants came from established communities and, after founding their settlements, resumed building houses and making pottery, thus reverting to their normal life as sedentary Mexican villagers. There were two well-defined cultures of this type which are called Mazapan and Coyotlatelco,* after the sites where their remains were first discovered. What temples and towns the makers of these cultures constructed have disappeared during architectural revamping in the Aztec period, so that we have to rely on pottery and other imperishable equipment to find out their tribal connections and their significance for the history of man in Mexico.[5]

The Mazapan culture was definitely later than Teotihuacan, for its graves penetrated through Teotihuacan floors and its refuse overlay deposits of Teotihuacan discard. These remains were strongly concentrated at the northwest of the Valley of Mexico but extended to the west as well. While in general they seem to have been associated with villages, refuse heaps did occur at the ceremonial site of Tula. In the modern town of that name stone sculptures in a distinctive style, neither Teotihuacan nor Aztec, may, by the process of elimination, be assigned to these people. The lavish equipment of their burials suggests that the Mazapan folk were prosperous and well to do. At Chiconauhtla,† a frontier town subject to Texcoco, the population, originally Mazapan in cultural affiliation, shifted to Aztec styles with no transition. (See Plate 25.)

The pottery of these people falls into three main types sufficiently distinctive to suggest that three independent groups were united. One ware comprises deep hemispherical

*Coy-o-tlah-te'll-co.   †Chee-co-no'w-tla.

bowls with decorations made in wavy parallel lines as if by a comb. Allied are other bowls with vaguely outlined maroon designs. A second ware is used for heavy bowls with tripod support and floors scored for use in grinding pepper. A third consists of bowls with flat floors and slipped in distinctive colors of white or orange. Such vessels were traded to Puebla, to the slopes of the volcanoes and to other areas bordering on the Valley.

In return the Mazapan peoples received pottery from distant sources. From Puebla and Vera Cruz they acquired a popular fine orange ware that was commonly traded to Chichen Itza* in Yucatan, to Guatemala, and even as far south as Salvador. They had also the distinctive pseudo-vitreous ware called plumbate, which had a wide orbit of commercial distribution, centering in Salvador and Guatemala but reaching south to Panama and east to Vera Cruz, west to Tepic and north to Tula. This ware is never found in classical Maya centers but appears in the later sites. In the Valley of Mexico it never reached the Teotihuacan Toltec, and its distribution ceased in Aztec times. Wares decorated in plaster cloisonné were also esteemed by the Mazapeños, and a few examples appear far from their chief source of manufacture in northern Jalisco.[6] (See Plates 26, top; 27.)

The Mazapan people made or acquired by trade beautiful spindle whorls with lustrous slips and stamped designs. Their obsidian work was excellent, and the scalpels flaked off by pressure were the finest in Mexico. Figurines were moldmade but poorly fashioned, a mother god and a warrior god presaging the Tonantzin† and Tezcatlipoca of the Aztec period. They worshiped also the flayed god Xipe, who wears a

*Chi-che'n Eet-za'.   †To-nan-tse'en.

human skin, and in his honor they broke through the lowly limitations of their clay sculpture to make two life-size representations of him, monumental examples of the potter's art. A smaller figure, carrying in his hand a little vase of Zapotec type, was prepared with closer detail. Thus archaeological evidence confirms the traditional origin of Xipe worship in Oaxaca, territory of the Zapotecs and Mixtecs. (See Plate 28.)

This Mazapan culture was cosmopolitan and was in touch with the products of all of civilized Middle America. Its basic wares indicate a western origin. The suggestion of fused tribal elements in the pottery hints at the tribal amalgamations mentioned in Ixtlilxochitl's accounts of the history of the Chichimecs of Texcoco. Thus archaeological evidence corroborates the native histories, assigning this period to the twelfth and thirteenth centuries when Mexican influence spread south to the territories of the Zapotecs and Mayas.

The Coyotlatelco culture is confined chiefly to the western shores of the Lake of Mexico. Excavators have not had the luck to find clearly demarked sites. It may well be old in origin, for fragments of simple vessels have been found at Tenayuca, underlying fully developed Coyotlatelco ware; and similar fragments occur in Mazapan territory prior to that occupation. A collection in the American Museum of Natural History from somewhere near Tula suggests a cross-fertilization of this early ware with decadent Teotihuacan elements, resulting in a potential prototype of the full Coyotlatelco style. The developed ware comprises bowls with well-executed patterns in red, which reveal mastery of design.[7]

The chronological position is a little uncertain. Beds of unmixed Coyotlatelco debris occur at Azcapotzalco and on the

Hill of the Star, behind Culhuacan. Dr Tozzer, who named the ware, found it mixed with late Teotihuacan material at the type site, but my wife and I excavated a Teotihuacan site of the same period without finding a single sherd among the 200,000 fragments we examined. At one or two places west of Tenayuca, Coyotlatelco sherds have appeared with Mazapan material. Mr Noguera found the extreme limit in lateness at Tenayuca where Coyotlatelco and Aztec II fragments were mixed. The geographical and chronological associations of this ware suggest that the makers were Culhuas or Tepanecs.

Culhuacan, so important in the annals as the seat of a famous line of chiefs, shows today little sign of its past greatness. Yet excavations undertaken twenty-five years ago prove that its historical importance was not overestimated, for it seems to have been the base from which Aztec culture spread over the Valley. Pottery, so dismal to read about, so important in reflecting tribal patterns, tells the story of this process.[8]

Aztec pottery is found everywhere in the Valley of Mexico, and, due to the Aztec custom of destroying household goods at the end of each fifty-two-year cycle, it can be identified in terms of relatively exact periods: IV, 1507–19 (the date of the Spanish Conquest, which prevented the cyclical celebration of 1559); IIIb, 1455–1507; IIIa, 1403–55; II early and late, perhaps a century prior to 1403, and I. Periods III and IV are represented everywhere. Period II is common on the mainland but less so in Tenochtitlan, which was politically insignificant until after 1400. To date, Period I is represented in quantity only at Culhuacan. The standard ware of Periods II–IV goes through a consecutive evolution but has a close generic resemblance throughout, while Period I pottery is much closer to the fine orange wares of Puebla which were traded widely throughout southeastern Mexico. There is also a trade connection between Aztec I and Mazapan.[9] (See Plates 25, 29.)

In the history of Culhuacan digested on pp. 72–73 the fact was noted that there was first a Toltec dynasty, which was succeeded by a Chichimec or foreign regime. It may not be stretching the manipulations of the historian too far if we suggest that the Culhuas changed their culture with their dynasty. Coyotlatelco ceramics, which have vague affiliations with Teotihuacan pottery, may represent the material culture of the Toltec dynasty, while the Aztec I pottery, completely alien to the preceding styles, seems to embody the material presence of the new regime.

Seeming confirmation of this situation comes from the site of Tenayuca, where great Mexican archaeologists like the late José Reygadas Vertiz, Ignacio Marquina, Alfonso Caso, Eduardo Noguera and others have carried out a superb dissection of one of the temples. It was completely rebuilt five, or possibly six, times. The renovation answered the ceremonial requirement of rebuilding and refurnishing at the beginning of each fifty-two-year cycle in compensation for the destruction at the close of the previously elapsed period. As the site was occupied during the Conquest, the reconstructions probably followed the cyclical ceremonies of 1507, 1455, 1403, 1351 and 1299, with the first building erected some time earlier. The fourth, fifth and sixth constructions (1403, 1455, 1507) are purely Aztec; the third temple built (1351) is a transition between the Aztec style and the simpler, more archaic methods employed in the two earliest

structures (1299 and the original temple). The three completely developed Aztec temples correspond closely to the
distribution of Aztec III and IV pottery, between 1403 and
1519. The transitional temple and the second building suggest that cyclical renovations were adopted everywhere
along with the Aztec II pottery of the fourteenth century.
The original platform of this Tenayuca temple could have
been constructed almost any time in the thirteenth century,
since the building of a shrine did not entail the celebration of
the beginning of a fifty-two-year cycle.[10] (See Plates 25;
26, bottom; 29.)

The Aztec civilization was brought into the valley at Culhuacan, where it gradually supplanted the defined local
cultures. Where, then, was its true source? The most probable answer is Cholula, in the state of Puebla, where still
exists the largest structure in the world in terms of cubic
content. The devoted group of Mexican archaeologists,
whose co-ordinated efforts have organized the rich background of their Indian past, have been analyzing this monument by excavation and archival research for many years.
The results are important. (See Plate 26, top, middle.)

Originally Cholula was occupied by an Upper Middle
Culture tribe which later fell under the domination of Teotihuacan-Toltec civilization. At this time the inhabitants built
a large ceremonial precinct, a maze of temples, platforms
and stairs, constructed of rubble covered with plaster. Eventually newcomers, possibly with the aid of the resident
population, performed the stupendous task of converting
the Toltec precinct into a single great platform, traditionally
in honor of the god Quetzalcoatl. This mammoth construction entailed filling in every building and courtyard with

adobe bricks. On its top they erected altars and quarters for the ceremonial personnel. In one of the altars, Altar de los Craneos, they buried two people and made a mortuary offering of pottery vessels, some of which resemble Aztec I in many respects, while others show affiliation with Mazapan types.[11]

Later on the Cholulans gave up these forms for ornate creations in polychrome, in which pure design and ritualistic decoration were elaborated to an extraordinary degree. The skill of workmanship, the proliferation of ritual and the quantity of production from Puebla and the south, surpass the work of the Valley tribes even though the content is the same. Therefore, it seems reasonable to assume that in Puebla lay the source and inspiration of Aztec civilization.

The few annals preserved relate chiefly to this period, and their pages are filled with the history of Teo-Chichimec and Toltec-Chichimec lineages. Breaking off from their parent communities, groups wandered away to found homes in new territory. Occasionally they settled in unoccupied lands, but they usually imposed themselves as a ruling class on some already established tribe. Often the conquerors called themselves by the proud name of Toltec, usurping the title of the chief civilization they destroyed. Thus arose the confusion of the early annalists, who, without the countercheck of archaeology, were hard put to distinguish references to the classical Toltec of Teotihuacan from tales of the warlike interlopers who assumed the name of the vanquished civilization.[12]

Most of these wandering groups spoke Nahuatl, the native tongue of the Aztecs, and of many other peoples in western Mexico. Some, like the conquerors of Oaxaca, spoke the unrelated Mixtec tongue. Yet whatever their language, these invaders joined in spreading over southern Mexico, Guatemala, Salvador, even Nicaragua, such kindred cultural elements as chiefly lineage, formal war, distinctive gods and characteristic ceremonial practices, which we classify as Mixteca-Puebla culture. Other tribes moved north, leaving a strong imprint on the cultures of Sinaloa in the northwest, and elements of this religion affected tribal communities as far distant as the southeastern United States.[18] (See Plates 11–12.)

This movement of people, in contrast to that of their civilized predecessors, was not the process of settling unexploited territory. Overpopulation seems the most logical cause, since it forces nations to risk the hazards of war rather than submit to the pangs of slow starvation. The vanquished, whose people had expanded into unpopulated territory during the previous epoch, had had no need to develop military techniques and so fell easily under Chichimec domination. However, in view of the intimate relation between government and religion in ancient Mexican society, such conquest meant the worship of new gods as well as the acceptance of new chiefs. It is likely that some tribes adopted the new religion previous to actual physical contact so that they could the better resist invasion. Yet the factor of conquest strongly influenced the spread of Mixteca-Puebla culture by tribesmen of Nahuatl and Mixtec speech.

War has its advantages when made on the unwarlike. The thin coating of Western civilization which Europe laid over the globe has its minor counterpart in the late Mexican influence spread over Middle America by these restless tribesmen. The winner's gods must be good gods, so cults of

Mexican origin spread through the length and breadth of Middle America. Just so the Christian religion had a ready acceptance in Indian America when the missionaries were backed by such redoubtable exponents of our gentle faith as Cortes, Pizarro and their coadjutors.

TABLE VI

SUMMARY OF CHICHIMEC AND DYNASTIC TOLTEC HISTORY

950–1100, EARLY CHICHIMEC PERIOD

Eastern Phase: Contact with Toltecs at Tula (Teotihuacan) under Xolotl; Tenayuca I pottery; rude culture.

Western Phase: Teotihuacan V and western Toltec Empire at Tula (Azcapotzalco).

1100–1247, MIDDLE CHICHIMEC PERIOD

Eastern Phase: Tenayuca occupation by immigrants; replacement of Toltecs at Tula (Tula); tribal government; foundation of Texcocan Chichimec lineage in 1232; development of fiefs; introduction of Mazapan culture.

Western Phase: Destruction of Toltecs at Tula (Azcapotzalco); movement to Culhuacan; foundation of Culhuacan "Toltec" lineage in 1114; adoption of Coyotlatelco ceramics; first Aztec cycle counted, 1143–95; second Aztec cycle counted, 1195–1247.

RULERS

Culhuacan	Cuauhtitlan	Cuitlahuac	Texcoco	Tenochtitlan
Nauhyotl (d. 1124 after 60 years)			Xolotl 1115–1232	
Cuauhtexpetlatzin 1124–81	Teiztlacohuatzin 1160–1226			
Huetzin 1181–1202				
Nonoalcatl 1202–1223				
Achitometl 1223–37	Quinatzin 1226–99			
Cuauhtonal 1237–51				

1247–99, LATE CHICHIMEC-AZTEC I PERIOD

Eastern Phase: Establishment of Texcoco as Chichimec capital under Quinatzin in 1298; persistence of Mazapan culture in east; penetration of Coyotlatelco and temple cult to Tenayuca(?).

Western Phase: Foundation of new dynasty at Culhuacan in 1251; introduction of Aztec I pottery at Culhuacan, with Pueblan origins; construction of Building I at Tenayuca(?); Cholula rebuilt (Altar de los Craneos); Cholula III pottery; Tenochcas at Chapultepec; third Aztec cycle counted, 1247–99.

Culhuacan	Cuauhtitlan	Cuitlahuac	Texcoco	Tenochtitlan
New Lineage			Lineage Begins	
Mazatzin 1251–74			Nopaltzin 1232–63	
Quetzaltzin 1274–87		Coatomatzin 1282–88	Tlotzin 1263–98	Huitzilhuitl 1235–98
Chalchiuhtlatonac 1287–1304				

CHAPTER V

THE AZTEC PERIOD

*In which is recorded the history of the Tenochcas and
the political background of Aztec civilization*

THE CHICHIMEC PERIOD witnessed invasion of the Valley
of Mexico by various tribes and the gradual domination of
these tribes by a culture and manner of life that seems to
have emanated from Puebla and northern Oaxaca. The basic
political unit consisted of a tribe resident in a town supporting itself from its own land with the supplement, if
possible, of supplies derived from the tribute payments of
vassals. At the head of the state was a chief of lineage who
also performed ecclesiastical functions. Craftsmanship was
highly skilled, and trade flourished to furnish raw materials
for the artisans. This productivity, however, was directed
toward religion and ritual rather than the creation of personal wealth. Religion was an elaborate polytheism based on
nature worship, with some god or gods singled out for
special adoration, but the working of the *tonalpohualli*,* or
sacred almanac, brought the full force of divine powers to
aid man in his life on earth. (See Plate 29.)

The history of the Tenochcas, the Mexico City Aztecs,
shows how a tribal body lived and acquired the position of an
important state. According to their own records, the Tenoch-

*to-nal-po-wa'hl-li.

cas started their wanderings in 1168 A.D., though this date is arbitrary and possibly represents the date of the invention of the calendar system in vogue in Central Mexico.[1] At first they lived on an island in a lake in western Mexico and crossed in boats to the shore. In a hillside cave they found an idol of Huitzilopochtli (Hummingbird Wizard), which had the useful ability to speak and give them good advice. The accounts differ, and some have the Tenochcas starting off on their travels with several other tribes from a group of caves in which they originated. The names of the tribes are seldom the same in any two annals, but they always refer to important tribal entities at the time the particular history was inscribed (Table VII). These beginnings may be considered as formalized origin myths without historical significance.[2] (See Plate 62, middle left.)

The Tenochcas carried their new god's image with them on their journey. At each stopping place they set him up to be worshiped, and in return he advised them. Their method of procedure was to stay a year or more at a given place, while pioneers searched the land for another site and planted a crop there to harvest when the whole tribe arrived. The list of stopping places is highly dubious, and the different traditions disagree. Not until the tribes reached the lakes of Mexico are the localities mentioned easily identifiable or in common accord.

The Tenochcas entered the lakes from the northwest, via Tula and Zumpango, so there may be a basis for believing their original home was in Michoacan.* They seem to have made every effort to avoid fighting by keeping away from settled lands. At one place they split up; at another they sac-

---

*Mich-o-a-ca'n.

rificed three individuals, according to the prescribed ritual of opening up the stomach and tearing out the heart; and at a third place they learned how to make pulque.

Their records make little reference to the tribes already in the Valley, and their own entrance was relatively unnoticed by the others. However, the hieroglyph of Tezozomoc in one manuscript suggests the obvious conclusion that they had to have Tepanec permission to pass through Azcapotzalco and settle at Chapultepec, where the beautiful park now is. Here they remained happily for nearly a generation. Their neighbors seem to have been small but growing communities, so that conflict was inevitable. The Tenochcas began the strife because their young men went up the lake to Tenayuca to raid and steal wives, a common North American Indian method of gaining prestige. Their more powerful neighbors became irritated and made up a punitive expedition in which Tepanecs, Culhuas and Xochimilcas took part. The result was horrid: the Tenochca chief Huitzilhuitl* and most of the tribe had to go to Culhuacan territory to dwell in serfdom, while the rest escaped to the lake where some low-lying islands offered refuge. The main body stayed in Tizapan,† near the present San Angel, where they were under the eye of Coxcox,‡ the chief of Culhuacan. The Tenochcas detested the waste which was barren in all except poisonous snakes and insects. Huitzilopochtli they still enshrined, but his worth had sunk so low that the Culhuas came to mock him at his shrine and toss nameless filth into the temple.³

Finally, however, the tide turned. Coxcox became involved in a war with Xochimilco and called upon his vassals to aid him. When the Tenochcas reached the field of battle

---

*Wee-tze′el-weetl.   †Tee-za-pa′n.   ‡Cosh-cosh.

they rushed to the attack and took no less than thirty prisoners, from each of whom they detached an ear with their obsidian knives before sending him to the rear. After the battle Coxcox made a speech praising the valor of his forces in taking so many prisoners but denigrating the Tenochcas who came back empty handed. The vassals waited until their lord had finished speaking and then inquired of him why each captive was short an ear. The attention of the Culhuas being riveted to this extraordinary circumstance, the Tenochcas opened their pouches and displayed the missing ears, proving beyond cavil the measure of their prowess. Clearly the war-sacrifice cult had reached the Valley by this time, for the emphasis set on the taking of prisoners indicates that this was one of the chief purposes of war. Furthermore, a drawing shows the later sacrifice of the prisoners, a cult practice the accomplishment of which was to make the Aztecs dreaded by other tribes throughout the length and breadth of Mexico.

So great had the prestige of the Tenochcas become that they went to their lord, Coxcox, and asked for his daughter as a wife for their chief so that they might found a dynasty. Coxcox granted their request, and the Tenochcas were so overcome with gratitude that they sacrificed the luckless girl and draped her skin on a priest to impersonate a nature goddess, Toci. Then with somewhat less than tact they invited the father to the ceremony. He, expecting a marriage celebration, was utterly horrified and summoned his warriors, to exterminate the Tenochcas who forthwith fled to the lake, rejoining their brethren already there.

There were two communities on the islands at the middle of the fourteenth century: Tenochtitlan, which seems to have become an entity in 1325, and Tlaltelolco,* which was founded about the same time. They both were havens for malcontents from the mainland, and about the middle of the century each was large enough to petition the mainland tribes for a chief to found a dynasty. Tlaltelolco received a leader from the Tepanecs, and the Tenochcas again induced Culhuacan to provide them with a chief, Acamapichtli.† The accounts vary as to whether or not he arrived as a lad accompanied by his mother. The *Annals of Cuauhtitlan* mention that at this time the Tenochcas were erecting houses of stone, an indication that a community had to reach a definite stage of development before enjoying the prestige of an important lineage.⁴

In the time of Acamapichtli the Tenochcas were tributaries and allies of the Tepanec and fought successfully against Tenayuca and Culhuacan. Yet their field of operations was minute, and a morning's automobile ride will enable the curious to see the whole scene of Tenochcan history. Huitzilhuitl II succeeded Acamapichtli at his death and prudently ensured the future of the nascent state by marrying the daughter of Tezozomoc. He was chief during the final struggle between the two great lake powers, the Tepanecs and the Texcocans, a war which ended in the death of the Texcocan chief, Ixtlilxochitl, and the dispersal of his fiefs.

Chimalpopoca‡ succeeded his half brother Huitzilhuitl, and his reign was fraught with disaster. Tezozomoc died, and his son Maxtla succeeded him at the cost of murdering a brother. Maxtla was frankly out for power and kept the city-

*Tlal-tel-o'l-co.   ‡Chee-mal-po-po'-ca.
†Ah-cam-a-pe'ech-tli.

TABLE VII

MIGRANT TRIBES, ACCORDING TO VARIOUS AUTHORITIES, COMPARED TO CERAMIC GROUPS IN CENTRAL MEXICO

	Histoire Mexicaine[a]	Codex of 1590[b]	Codex of 1576[c]	Cubas–vd. Muñoz Camargo[d]	Historia de los Mexicanos[e]	Codice Ramírez[f]	Codex Boturini[g]	Durán[h]	Sahagún[i]	Codex Telleriano–Remensis[j]	Codex Vaticanus A[k]	Clavigero[l]	Motolinia[m]	Muñoz Camargo[n]	de Mendieta[o]	Suggested Correlation of Pottery Styles with Tribal Groups
Aztec	x	x	(x)*	–	x	x	(x)	(x)*	(x)*	–	–	(x)*	x	–	x	Regulation Aztec of Tenochtitlan[p]
Xochimilca	x	x	x	x	x	x	(x)*	(x)*	(x)*	–	–	x	–	(x)*	–	(?)
Tepaneca	x	x	–	x	x	x	x	x	x	–	–	x	–	(x)*	–	Tenayuca II (?)[q]
Acolhua	–	x	–	–	[x]†	x	x	x	x	–	–	x	(x)*	(x)*	–	Mazapan[r]
Culhua	–	x	x	x	x	x	–	–	x	–	–	–	x	(x)*	–	Culhuacan (like Aztec)[s]
Cuitlahuaca	x	x[t]	x	x	–	–	x[u]	x	–	–	–	x	–	–	–	(?)
Chalca	x	–	–	x	x	x	x	–	x	–	–	–	x	(x)*	–	Some styles resemble Cholula wares[w]
Tlahuica	–	–	–	–	–	x	x	x	–	–	–	x	–	–	–	Gualupita III[v]
Tlaxcalteca	–	–	–	–	[x]†	x	–	x	x	–	–	x	(x)*	–	–	Some styles resemble Cholula wares[w]
Cholulteca	–	x[x]	–	x	–	–	–	x	x	–	–	x	–	–	–	Cholula wares[y]
Huexotzinca	x	x	x	x	[x]†	x	x	–	x	–	–	–	–	–	–	(?)
Matlatzinca	x	–	x	x	–	x	x	–	–	–	–	–	–	–	–	Matlatzinca[z]
Malinalca	x	–	x	–	–	x	x	–	x	–	–	–	–	x	–	(?)
Quauhquechollan-Xelhua	–	–	–	–	–	–	–	–	–	–	–	x	–	–	–	(?)

																		Monte Alban 5[aa]	
Chichimeca	x	–	x	x	–	x	–	–	–	–	–	x	x	–	(x)*	–	–		(?)
Nonoalca	–	–	–	–	–	–	–	–	–	–	–	x	x	–	–	–	–		(?)
Michoaca	–	–	x	–	–	–	–	–	–	–	–	x	x	–	(x)*	–	–		(?)
Couixca	–	–	–	–	–	–	–	–	–	–	–	x	x	–	–	–	–		(?)
Totonaca	–	–	–	–	–	–	–	–	–	–	–	x	x	–	–	–	–		(?)
Cuexteca	–	–	–	–	–	–	–	–	–	–	–	x	x	–	–	–	–		(?)
Xicalanga-Olmeca	–	–	–	–	–	–	–	–	–	–	–	x	x	–	(x)*	x	–		(?)
Mixteca	–	–	–	–	–	–	–	–	–	–	–	–	–	–	x	–	x	x	
Otomi	–	–	–	–	–	–	–	–	–	–	–	–	–	–	x	–	x		(?)

*Implied but not specifically listed.

†"These people, say the Mexicans, and no more sallied forth, although those of Tezcoco and Tlaxcala and Huexotzinca boast . . . that they too . . . are also of that land." Phillips, Codex Ramirez, 1883, p. 625.

[a] Histoire Mexicaine in Boban, Documents, 1891, Pl. 60.
[b] Codex of 1590 in Boban, Documents, 1891, Pl. 24; Muñoz Camargo, Historia, 1892, p. 8, footnote.
[c] Codex of 1576 in Aubin, Histoire, 1893, p. 4, both of text and translation.
[d] Muñoz Camargo, Historia, 1892, p. 7. A footnote by Chavero gives a list taken from Cuadro Historico-Jeroglifico de la Peregrinacion de las Tribus Aztecas Que Poblaron el Valle de Mexico, No. 2, published in the Atlas Geografico of Antonio Garcia Cubas, Mexico, 1858, usually called the Codex Boturini.
[e] Phillips, Codex Ramirez, 1883, pp. 624–25. Forty tribes.
[f] Historia de los Mexicanos in Biblioteca Mexicana, 1878, p. 18.
[g] Radin, Sources, 1920, p. 33, Pl. I taken from Kingsborough, Vol. 1.
[h] Duran, Historia de las Indias, I, 1867, p. 10.
[i] Sahagun, Historia General, 1938, Vol. 3, Book 11.
[j] Codex Telleriano-Remensis, 1899, p. 34, Pl. 25.
[k] Codex Vaticanus A, 1900, Pl. 67.

[l] Clavigero, History, 1787.
[m] Motolinia, Historia, 1914, pp. 7–10.
[n] Muñoz Camargo, Historia, 1892, pp. 5–68. The list of tribes given under this authority has been extracted at random points from the text. Muñoz Camargo does not specify the list of migrants.
[o] de Mendieta, Historia, 1870, p. 145.
[p] Noguera, Caracteristicas de Ceramica, 1930, Pl. 32.
[q] Noguera, in Tenayuca, 1935.
[r] Vaillant, Correlation, 1938.
[s] Boas, Album, 1911–12, Pls. 1–36; Brenner, Influence of Technique, 1931.
[t] Chavero, in Muñoz Camargo, Historia, 1892, p. 7, misreads this sign Cholula.
[u] Radin, Sources, 1920, misreads this sign Cholula.
[v] Vaillant and Vaillant, Gualupita, 1935, Figs. 19, 27.
[w] Noguera, Caracteristicas de Ceramica, 1930, Pl. 31.
[x] Peñafiel, Nomenclatura Geografica, 1897, gives this sign as Cholula.
[y] Noguera, Caracteristicas de Ceramica, 1930, Pl. 31; 1937 b.
[z] Noguera, Caracteristicas de Ceramica, 1930, Pl. 6.
[aa] Caso, Monte Alban, 1938.

TABLE VIII

SUMMARY OF AZTEC HISTORY BEFORE THE RISE OF TENOCHTITLAN

1299–1351, EARLY AZTEC II PERIOD

Eastern Phase: Introduction of picture writing and other arts at Texcoco by people from the Mixteca; adoption of Aztec IIa pottery.

Western or Culhua Phase: Cyclical reconstruction at Tenayuca, Building II; adoption of Aztec IIa pottery, retention of Coyotlatelco (?) pottery; revolt of Tenochcas at Chapultepec, settlement of Tenochtitlan; fourth Aztec cycle counted, 1299–1351.

Culhuacan	Cuauhtitlan	Cuitlahuac	Texcoco	Tenochtitlan
Cuauhtlix 1304–11	Tezcaltecutli 1299–1338	Miahuatonaltzin 1290–1300		
Yohuallatonac 1311–21		Axayaltzin 1300–08		Tenoch (?)
Tziuhtecatzin 1321–34	Vactli 1339–49	Atzatzamaltzin 1308–24	Quinatzin 1298–1357	
Xihuitlemoc 1334–52		Totepeuhtecutli 1324–43		*Lineage Begins*
		Epcoatzin 1343–54		Queen Ilancueitl 1349–83

1351–1403, LATE AZTEC II PERIOD

Eastern Phase: Unification of language by Techotlala; political and cultural dominance of Texcoco; Aztec IIb pottery and homogeneity of culture; Cholula IV pottery; cyclical dumps at Chiconauhtla.

Western Phase: Decadence of Culhuacan; rise of Tepanecs at Azcapotzalco; cyclical reconstruction of Tenayuca, Building IV, Aztec transition; captive Tenochcas escape to build in stone and adopt lineage pattern with Acamapichtli; fifth Aztec cycle counted, 1351–1403.

Culhuacan	*Cuauhtitlan*	*Cuitlahuac*	*Texcoco*	*Tenochtitlan*
Coxcox 1352–76	Queen Ehualyenitzin 1368–72	Quetzalmichin 1354–65		
				Acamapichtli 1375–95
Acamapichtli 1376–88	Tematzacocuitzin 1373–78	Mamatzin 1369–89	Techotlala 1357–1409	
Achitometl 1388–1400	Tlacateotzin 1379–89	Pichatzin 1389–92		Huitzilhuitl II 1395–1414

TABLE IX

SUMMARY OF AZTEC HISTORY AFTER THE RISE OF TENOCHTITLAN

1403–55, EARLY AZTEC III PERIOD

Eastern Phase: Political elimination of Texcoco in first half of period with later recovery; prosperity and cultural advance under Nezahualcoyotl; expansion of palace at Chiconauhtla; Aztec IIIa pottery; Cholula V pottery; cyclical dumps at Chiconauhtla and Los Melones, Texcoco.

Western Phase: Political extinction of Culhuacan; rise and fall of Tepanecs; rise of Tenochtitlan with organization of Triple Alliance; growth of conquest and war-captive pattern; cyclical reconstruction at Tenayuca, Building IV; cyclical dump in Zocalo, Mexico City; broad diffusion of Aztec IIIa pottery; sixth Aztec cycle counted, 1403–55.

Culhuacan	*Cuauhtitlan*	*Cuitlahuac*	*Texcoco*	*Tenochtitlan*
Nauhyotl 1400–13	Xaltemoc 1390–98 (1408)	Tepolozmayotl 1393–1415	Ixtlilxochitl 1409–18	Chimalpopoca 1414–28
			Tepanec Tyrants Tezozomoc 1343–1427	Itzcoatl 1428–40
			Maxtla 1427–29	
			Texcocan Lineage *Resumed* Nezahualcoyotl 1418–72	Montezuma I 1440–69

1455–1507, Late Aztec III Period

Eastern Phase: Continued development of culture at Texcoco; growth of Chiconauhtla palace; elaboration of ceramics; Aztec IIIb pottery; cyclical dump at Chiconauhtla.

Western Phase: Political power of Tenochtitlan; extension of conquest over Mexico and Guatemala; reconstruction of great temple; increase in captive sacrifice; elaboration of ritual; diffusion of Aztec IIIb pottery; cyclical reconstruction at Tenayuca, Building V; cyclical dump at Nonoalco, Mexico City; seventh Aztec cycle counted, 1455–1507.

Culhuacan	Cuauhtitlan	Cuitlahuac	Texcoco	Tenochtitlan
unimportant	unimportant	unimportant	Nezahualpilli 1472–1516	Axayacatl 1469–81
				Tizoc 1481–86
				Ahuitzotl 1486–1503

1507–1519 (Conquest) Aztec IV

Eastern Phase: Growing friction between Texcoco and Tenochtitlan; last expansion of Chiconauhtla palace; Aztec IV pottery styles with good life forms. Conquest.

Western Phase: Tenochtitlan domination with coercion of Texcoco; maintenance of old conquests rather than success of new ones; cyclical reconstruction of Tenayuca, Building VI; Aztec IV pottery with many life forms; eighth Aztec cycle counted, 1507–59, incomplete with Conquest.

Texcoco	Tenochtitlan
Cacama 1516–19	Montezuma II 1503–20
	Cuitlahuac 1520 (4 months)
	Cuauhtemoc 1520–24 (murdered on way to Honduras)

states of the valley in a ferment of intrigue and oppression. Finally he murdered Chimalpopoca and also the chief of the neighboring town of Tlaltelolco, adding insult to injury, according to Indian thinking, by stepping up the tribute payments as well.

The people of Tenochtitlan were seething with indignation, and the small mainland town of Tlacopan (Tacuba) was sympathetic to the oppressed. Nezahualcoyotl,* the legitimate successor to the chieftainship of Texcoco, had taken to the hills after the defeat of his nation and was stirring up opposition to the enemy. He induced the Tenochcas under their new chief Itzcoatl† to attack Azcapotzalco through the back door of Tlacopan, while he rallied the Texcocans and their tributaries to assault the enemy with columns coming both by canoe and overland around the lakes. After a long war of several weeks the allies were successful. (See Plate 63.)

Nezahualcoyotl doubtless intended that his state should regain its position as the dominant power in the northern lake country. But he did not realize that when he formed the triple alliance for mutual defense and offensive profit he laid the foundation for a rival state which would surpass Texcoco. The Tenochcas and the Texcocans were each to receive two shares of all loot, the Tlacopans one, but the division was probably liberally interpreted by whichever chanced to be the strongest of the three allies. The Tenochcas gained land on the lake shore, which gave them a strong foothold for further conquest. Since this new territory was granted to the leading warriors, a caste of power and wealth was established. Thus outwardly the conquest brought the Te-

*Ne-za-wal-co'y-otl.   †Eet'z-co-atl.

nochcas from the condition of a feudal tributary to that of an independent state. Inwardly there was a change of feeling, a shift from an inferiority to a superiority complex. Itzcoatl, the fourth Tenochcan chief, expressed this attitude by ordering all the historical picture manuscripts to be burned, "as they were not appreciated by the ordinary people."[5]

From the time of Itzcoatl the state histories are in very close accord. Those written prior to his accession in 1428 exhibit considerable conflict, often resulting in discrepancies of a fifty-two-year cycle or more. I think this lack of agreement arose from the split in the tribal continuity at the time of the Chapultepec defeat in 1300. Part of the tribe refugeed to the islands in the lake and founded a town in 1325 or thereabouts, ruling it under a tribal council and a main chief. The other group was taken to Tizapan and became civilized according to Culhuacan standards. The founding of Tenochtitlan, from their point of view, did not take place until they joined the original colony on the lake where, as soon as possible, they erected ·stone temples and tried to found a dynasty.

Itzcoatl enabled the Tenochcas to assume Aztec civilization. His historical reforms doubtless coincided with ritualistic regulations as well, for he undertook the construction of temples and the ordering of a religious hierarchy. He ordained the ranks of the civil government and superintended the building of the city, constructing causeways to the mainland to ensure easy access. Systematically Itzcoatl began to mop up those independent Valley tribes not subject to Texcoco; he also won victories and acknowledgments of supremacy from the powerful Chalcas and Xochimilcas, tribes culturally allied more closely to the Puebla groups than to those of the northern Valley. To show his independence Itzcoatl had a brush with Nezahualcoyotl's Texcocans, and thereafter the peace between the former allies was somewhat precarious.

Montezuma* I, surnamed Ilhuicamina,† the Wrathy, succeeded Itzcoatl after his death in 1440. This chief, already marked as a leader in the wars of Itzcoatl, extended the domination of Tenochtitlan even further. He successfully fought the Chalcas, who detested the tribes of the northern Valley, and crossed the mountains to raid eastward into Puebla and Vera Cruz and southward to conquer towns in Morelos and Guerrero. A fairly close military co-operation must have existed between Texcoco and Tenochtitlan, for conquests claimed for Tenochtitlan by Tenochcan historians appear as gains for Texcoco in the Texcocan annals. Poor Tlacopan disappears from the scene, possibly independent still but certainly unconsidered in the division of pelf, a situation recalling that of Italy in 1918.

Under Montezuma I the cultural aspects of Tenochtitlan progressed mightily. He took measures to ensure the health of his people, building an aqueduct from the springs of Chapultepec to bring an abundance of sweet water to the city. Around the eastern rim of his capital he caused a great dike to be erected to dam off the spread of the lakes during the rainy season.

The conquests into Puebla brought the Tenochcas in touch with the highly developed religion of that area, so that many additional temples were built in honor of gods and goddesses which were revered by the conquered tribes. In times of relative peace he revived the War of Flowers, a

*Mon-tay-zo'o-ma.   †Il-wee-cah-me'en-a.

ceremonial contest between warriors of two tribes or groups
of tribes, in order that prisoners might be taken for sacrifice
without the economic dislocation of formal war. This practice was known long before in the Valley, the Tenochcas
participating in such struggles with the Chalcas in 1376–
84, but the Tenochcas had been so continuously at war
that they were accustomed to take their prisoners the hard
way.[6]

The crops failed from 1451–56, owing to severe storms
and frost. Many people died, and others, unable to support
themselves, adopted voluntary slavery in order to share the
bounty of the more fortunate. Usually a famine led to increased military activity to replenish the empty larders with
supplies exacted as tribute. But in this case the situation was
so severe and the Tenochcas so weak that they had to be
content with a War of Flowers.

Axayacatl* succeeded his father Montezuma I in 1469.
He extended Tenochcan domination over a still-wider area,
spreading west into the Matlatzinca country and south to
Oaxaca and Tehuantepec. He conducted a campaign into
the Tarascan territory and met with a dreadful defeat which
ensured the independence of these tribes of Michoacan up
to their conquest by the Spaniards. This was the only serious
Tenochcan military disaster until the grim days of 1519.[7]

Neither Axayacatl nor his successors was able to transform domination of a region into dominion. He did succeed,
nevertheless, in reducing the neighboring town of Tlaltelolco, killing its chief and denying its council the right to
meet with the Tenochcas in matters of tribal importance.
Tlaltelolco up to that time had maintained its independence

*Ash-ay-a'h-catl.

and had grown at the same rate as Tenochtitlan, aiding in many of the campaigns. It was famous for its merchants; and its market, even after its subjugation, was the greatest in Mexico. Local jealousy, however, did not lead to war until both towns competed in building temples to Huitzilopochtli, the War God. Apparently this competition for divine favor led to war, whereas economic conflict did not. Ridiculously enough the open break was induced by the insulting behavior of the Tlaltelolcan women, who flaunted their backsides at the enraged Tenochcan visitors.[8]

The religious arts reached their full development under Axayacatl. In his time was made the great Calendar Stone which weighs over twenty tons and is twelve feet in diameter. The block was quarried on the mainland, and the allied rulers sent help to drag this gigantic mass across the causeways. Designed to symbolize the Aztec universe, it is a masterly example of a pattern, the detail of which adds, rather than detracts from, the spaciousness of the concept.[9] (See Plate 52, top.)

In 1472, early in the reign of Axayacatl, the life of a great figure in American Indian history, Nezahualcoyotl, came to an end. This Texcocan chief had begun his manhood in political exile fleeing from Tepanec vengeance, but had fought and intrigued his way back into power. He even restored the fortunes of his people who, in the previous century, had rivaled the Culhuacanos in the formative years of Aztec civilization. Nezahualcoyotl had a broad judicial sense which enabled him successfully to elaborate the administrative structure of a far-flung realm. Since the Texcocans, before the Tepanec domination in 1419–28 already had a chain of tribute-paying vassals, this resumption of control in after years was not so much a conquest as the forceful exercise of due rights.[10]

He took a lively interest in the construction of temples and public buildings so that, for all its tattered decay today, Texcoco was one of the most imposing cities on the Central Plateau. His palace near by and his bath, hewn from the solid rock of Texcotcingo, are visible proof of the rich luxury of his life.

Nezahualcoyotl took a profound interest in religion and the arts. He transformed theological speculation into a philosophy of religion and worshiped a single god, the force through which nature manifests itself and from which the lesser gods derived their power and being. He encouraged the arts and in his own right attained great renown as a poet and orator. The lore of the stars fascinated him, and he had a deep knowledge of the astrological astronomy of his day and age. In contrast to the bleakly austere records of the Tenochca overlords, his career was a model of wise administration. Not the least of Nezahualcoyotl's achievements was his keeping the peace with his arrogant island ally, Tenochtitlan, which was ever ready by intrigue, murder or open warfare to add to its wealth and power.

Nezahualcoyotl was succeeded by his son Nezahualpilli,* who ruled until 1516. The length of his reign indicates the possession of an administrative skill equal to his father's. He successfully undertook a number of conquests, but they are not so dramatized as those of the Tenochcan chiefs.

Nezahualpilli had an interest in astrology, religion and necromancy, as would be natural in a chief whose religious obligations were as onerous as his civil and military duties.

*Ne-zoo-al-pe'el-li.

His later years were weighted with trouble with Tenochtitlan. He had married a sister of Montezuma II and, as she
was unduly free in granting favors to the young men of the
court, in 1498 he took advantage of his legal right to kill her.
The Tenochcas took this act as a gross personal affront and
directed every effort, short of war, to overcoming their
ancient ally.[11]

Axayacatl of Tenochtitlan died in 1479, while Nezahualpilli was young in his rule, and his brother Tizoc, who had
previously been the war chief, took his place. Tizoc's most
important act of office was to begin the reconstruction of
the great temple to Huitzilopochtli, the War God, and
Tlaloc, the Rain God. In commemoration of his conquests
he also had carved the so-called Sacrificial Stone. This mon-
strous-sized vessel for burning human hearts has a relief
on the edge, depicting Tizoc dressed as Huitzilopochtli seiz-
ing captives representing tributary tribes. Most of the towns,
unfortunately, must have been merely reconquered, since
their names appear in the previous conquest lists of earlier
rulers. It is not a complete surprise to read in some accounts
that Tizoc died of poison administered by chiefs disgusted at
his lack of military success.[12]

Ahuitzotl* succeeded his brother Tizoc in 1486. His first
task was to complete the great temple the others had begun,
in the dedication of which the gathering of sacrificial victims
played an important part. He invoked the aid of Nezahualpilli,
and the allies made a two-year campaign into northern
Oaxaca, amassing no less than twenty thousand victims, the
high point of the sacrificial cult in Mexico. At the start of
the dedication the captives stood in two rows, and Nezahual-

*Ah'-weet-zotl.

pilli and Ahuitzotl began the grisly work of tearing out the victims' hearts. Lesser dignitaries succeeded each other according to rank, until the awful immolation was completed.[13]

Ahuitzotl's military campaigns extended south into Guatemala and as far north as the Huaxteca in Vera Cruz. He was constantly engaged in putting down revolts, especially in Puebla, where the Tlaxcalans* and Cholulans had resisted Tenochcan domination. His capital, meanwhile, had grown so enormously that he had to construct another aqueduct, a fact which indicates that sheer pressure of population was an important cause for the military exploits of Tenochtitlan. An unusually disastrous flood beset the city in 1503, so that Ahuitzotl had to send to Texcoco for aid in restoring the dikes. While superintending these public works he received a head injury which proved fatal. Ahuitzotl's personality was strong and vicious. He was passionately fond of war, being a vindictive and relentless foe. Likewise he had those traits which so often accompany military character, lust for women and fondness for display.

The luckless Montezuma II, surnamed Xocoyotzin† (the Younger), son of Axayacatl, succeeded his uncle. Not only had he to keep the conquered tribes in order, but also he had constantly to provide captives for sacrifice. This bloody cult, which to the Tenochcan mind had brought such eminence, had to be maintained lest disaster ensue. He approached his uncle's piety on one occasion when twelve thousand captives from a rebel province in Oaxaca were delivered up to the War God.[14]

The last New Fire Ceremony took place in 1507. The years immediately preceding, with their threat of an ending

*Tlash-ca'-lans.   †Sho-coy-ot-se'en.

world, were especially ominous, since in addition to earthquakes and other supernatural portents word came in of
white strangers, propelled in odd craft, who were ranging
along the coast. But the ceremony took place, and the world
continued. (See Plate 29, top.)

Montezuma fought an unsuccessful war against the Tlaxcalans, but at the same time he succeeded in avenging himself
on his Texcocan allies for the death of his sister, by allowing
their force to be ambushed and wiped out. In 1516, at the
death of Nezahualpilli, he appointed his successor without
recognizing the choice of the Texcocan council. The ousted
candidate revolted and the already strained alliance was
broken.[15]

A year later Grijalva* reached Vera Cruz, and in 1519
Cortes started his march to Mexico. Montezuma died that
winter, stoned by his own people, according to Spanish accounts; strangled by the Spaniards, in the Indian versions.
Cuitlahuac succeeded him but died of smallpox in four
months, and the last of the free chiefs, Cuauhtemoc,† conducted the heroic defense of Tenochtitlan, only to be hanged
four years later on Cortes' march to Honduras.[16]

Thus ends the bare record of Tenochcan history, without
a description of the people, their government, their laws,
their gods or their arts. Lacking, also, is an account of the
clash between the two civilizations: Aztec and Spanish. The
records are abundant, and we can form a lifelike picture of
the time. Before we examine the nature of Aztec civilization
and the causes of its downfall, let us recapitulate briefly the
history of the valley tribes before the Conquest.

This chapter has covered the rise of the Tenochcas and

*Gree-ha'l-va.   †Kwow-ta'y-moc.

how they came to be the greatest example of Aztec civilization. Yet the events set forth show quite clearly that they did not originate this civilization or, beyond the sacrifice cult, contribute much to it. During their migration period, from 1168 to 1248, they were simple primitive folk. In their sedentary period, from the settlement at Chapultepec in 1248 to the election of Acamapichtli in 1376, they were busily absorbing the culture of their neighbors and overlords, especially that of the Culhuas. The tributary period, from 1376 to 1428, saw the Tenochcas under the control of the Tepanec, cautiously trying out the formal Aztec city-state organization. Not until Itzcoatl assumed the chieftaincy in 1429 did Tenochtitlan really advance, at which time the city took part in the general great rise of Aztec civilization.

On the other hand, Culhuacan was associated with the earliest phase of Aztec culture in the Valley and was contemporaneous with such distinctive styles as Coyotlatelco and Mazapan. The evolving Aztec culture in its ceramic aspect superseded and obliterated these earlier folk arts and was well established throughout the Valley at a date when the Tenochcas were nonentities. The historical position of Culhuacan closely paralleled the archaeological record, yet this early Culhuacan phase did not seem to be a spontaneous development so much as a derivative from Puebla and the Mixteca.

The availability of annals and the existence of competent excavations in sites like Tenochtitlan, Texcoco and Culhuacan have caused us to weight heavily the testimony of the people on the northern half of the lakes. Chalco and Xochimilco, to the south, whose annals have disappeared and whose sites are largely unexcavated, may have had a far more important part in the history of the Valley than appears here. Pueblan influence is far stronger in these southern city-states.

Aztec civilization, therefore, was a dynamic composite of many elements, some developed as an answer to tribal needs, others incorporated by contact with foreign peoples. Constant change took place, as in all other human societies, resulting from the continual adjustments man must make to fresh situations. Since individual men and women make up a community, let us in the following chapters begin with a single person and work our way through his social obligations and economics to his tribal organization and religion, finally reaching the Conquest and its aftermath.

CHAPTER VI

THE MAN AND THE TRIBE

*In which are set forth the basic ideas of Aztec educa-
tion, government, law and social customs*

THE SOCIAL ORGANIZATION of the Aztec tribes was in theory
completely democratic. An individual was a member of a
family which, in turn, belonged to a cluster of families or a
clan.* Theoretically twenty of these clans made up a tribe,
each of them regulating its own affairs but, in matters of
tribal importance, joining with the others in a council composed of all the leaders. The council appointed one chief to
control civil and religious affairs and usually a second for
war. Originally designed for simple farming communities
and presumably of an antiquity dating back to Middle Culture times, this organization later ramified into the governmental complexity of a populous and highly complicated
city-state.¹

The working of a community is best illustrated by the
position of the individual in it, a process which is described
in the third part of the Codex Mendoza. Immediately a child
was born it was washed and swaddled by a midwife. Since
the gods governed the fate of man on earth, the parents consulted a priest who looked in the *tonalamatl*,† or book of

---

*The term clan is used to mean a tribal division without connotation of
male or female descent.

†To'-na-la-matl.

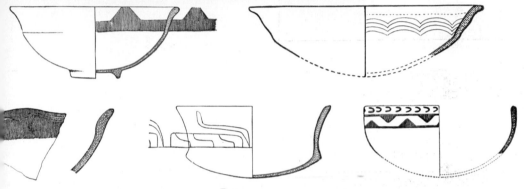

PLATE 17

LATE LOWER MIDDLE CULTURE POTTERY AND FIGURINES

Top: Figurines (Type A). Close scrutiny will disclose that this style is in a different tradition. The source may perhaps be Tres Zapotes, Vera Cruz. SECOND ROW: Red on yellow and incised black bowls. THIRD ROW: Fragment and bowls, incised red on white, etched black, red on white, distinctive forms defining this phase. BOTTOM ROW: Figurines (Type B) which are the survival of the local tradition, contemporary with Type A (*top*). Degeneration has set in, since the craftsmen's interest has shifted to the new style.

PLATE 18

UPPER MIDDLE CULTURES, OBJECTS AND ARCHITECTURE

Top: *Left:* Incense burner of lava, the oldest stone carving found as yet in the Valley of Mexico. The bowl rests on the back of a hunched human figure. *Right:* Earplug of carved baked clay. A collar at the rear was inserted in a perforation in the ear lobe. Bottom: View of platform of Cuicuilco. This oval structure of adobe faced with stone had fallen into decay before the lava (visible at upper left) flowed over the debris. At the left, circling the base of the platform, may be seen a parallel row of stones of unknown significance.

PLATE 19

POTTERY AND FIGURINES, UPPER MIDDLE CULTURES

Top: Three figurines (E) represent the early plastic art of this era. The bowl is polychrome and is ornamented with embossed birds. Bottom: The Type H figurines of the last phase of the Upper Middle Culture Era are covered with a white slip and painted. Their positions are lively and animated. The jar in the background is painted red on a brown background with a subsidiary pattern in black applied by the batik process. The small pot is of quartzite.

PLATE 20

POTTERY AND FIGURINES, UPPER MIDDLE CULTURE

Top: *Left:* This large seated figure of clay from Gualupita, Morelos, shows an individuality not found in the run of the sculpture. It belongs to the same school as the other figure (*right*), which appeared on Plate 3 in connection with "Olmec" sculpture. Bottom: These bowls from Ticoman show the standard shapes of this era. Note the elaborate tripod supports that distinguish these shapes from those of the preceding Lower Middle Culture Era.

PLATE 21

CHART SHOWING NATURE OF TOLTEC ARCHAEOLOGICAL MATERIAL

Top: Fresco from Temple of Agriculture, Teotihuacan, showing people taking
part in an offering ceremony. Second Row: Reconstruction of the ceremonial
precinct surrounding the Pyramid of the Sun. Third Row: Ceremonial vase,
Teotihuacan II, in champlevé; ceremonial vase, same period, with fresco decoration representing a butterfly; vase, Teotihuacan V, polished red ware, with de-
generate design. Bottom Row: Figurines representing the five stylistic stages of
Toltec culture. The last two figurines are moldmade.

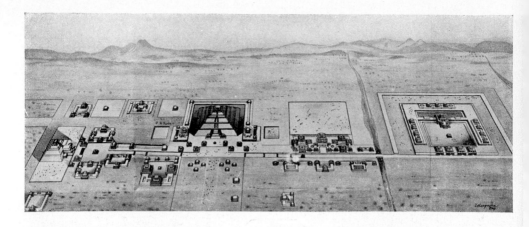

PLATE 22

TOLTEC ARCHITECTURE

TOP: Reconstruction of Teotihuacan by Gamio and Marquina. The long axis runs north and south and includes, beginning with the Temple of the Moon, the Plaza of the Moon, the Agriculture Group, the Group of the Columns, the Pyramid of the Sun, the Superimposed Buildings and the Citadel Group. Note the arrangement in terms of precincts and axes. BOTTOM: Air view of the Pyramid of the Sun, looking east. The adjacent buildings show the size of this monster temple foundation made of unfired bricks faced with stone.

PLATE 23

TOLTEC ARCHITECTURE

Detail from the Temple of Quetzalcoatl, which was later covered up to make the Citadel Group. The massive serpent heads had eyes of polished obsidian.

PLATE 24
TOLTEC ART

Top: *Right:* Mask of porphyry, showing a marvelous skill in reproducing their physical type. *Left:* This massive figure, ten feet tall, seems to be a water goddess. It is noteworthy for its monumental quality. Bottom: This offering scene is a fresco. The figures at either side suggest the Water Goddess. Flames shoot up from the altars in front of them, while tribesmen and long-robed priests bring their offerings of feathers, food, jade, shell and a bird. Note the speech scrolls.

PLATE 25

CHART SHOWING NATURE OF CHICHIMEC ARCHAEOLOGICAL MATERIAL

Top Row: Picture writings relating to this period. *Left:* Chichimec hunter from Mapa Quinatzin. *Center:* Tenochcas set forth on their wanderings and find their idol, from Codex Boturini. *Right:* The eight tribes who settled Central Mexico, from Codex Boturini (see Table VII). Second Row: The first three constructions at Tenayuca. Note the sloping walls of the Aztec-influenced Building III. Third Row: Diagnostic pottery styles of Mazapan, Coyotlatelco and the Culhuacan Aztec I. Fourth Row: Moldmade figurines, Coyotlatelco style. Bottom Row: Moldmade figurines, Mazapan style.

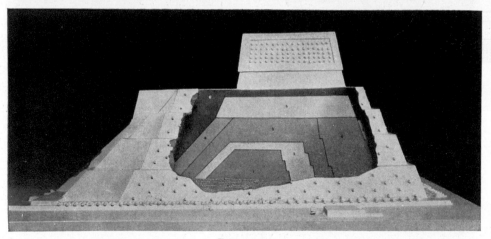

PLATE 26

POTTERY AND ARCHITECTURE, CHICHIMEC PERIOD

Top: Bowls of Aztec I–Cholula III type found at Chichen Itza, Yucatan. Middle: Temple of Cholula, Puebla. Note the large church resting on this ancient platform of adobe, which covers a ceremonial precinct of Toltec times. Bottom: Model of the Temple of Tenayuca, showing the original building and the five reconstructions, possibly corresponding to the cyclical ceremonies of 1299, 1351, 1403, 1455 and 1507.

PLATE 27

POTTERY, CHICHIMEC PERIOD

TOP AND MIDDLE: Design from a vase and another jar decorated in plaster cloisonné, from Jalisco. Vases ornamented in this technique were extensively traded in the twelfth and thirteenth centuries. BOTTOM: Jar in plumbate ware, a quasi-vitreous ware, made in Salvador and Guatemala, which was traded widely through Middle America in this period. The trade apparently ceased completely a century or so before the Conquest.

PLATE 28

POTTERY AND ARCHITECTURE, CHICHIMEC PERIOD

TOP: *Left:* Life-size figure, Mazapan Culture, fr[om]
Coatlinchan, Valley of Mexico. It represents the g[od]
Xipe dressed in a human skin. *Right:* Effigy va[se,]
Mazapan Culture, from a grave at the type site, [and]
seems to represent a dead man. These two figu[res]
indicate that the people of Mazapan had develop[ed]
clay sculpture into a major art. BOTTOM: Temple [at]
Teopanzalco, Cuernavaca. The remains of the la[ter]
stairs and walls may be seen in the foreground, w[ith]
the original temple and stair behind, and are larg[er]
than the first two Tenayuca buildings in the sa[me]
style. The later temple, to judge from the stair a[nd]
lower walls, had an architectural style as typica[lly]
Aztec as the last three Tenayuca temples on Pl[ate]
29.

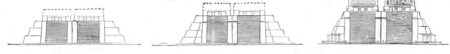

PLATE 29

CHART SHOWING NATURE OF AZTEC ARCHAEOLOGICAL MATERIAL

Top Row: Excerpts from historical picture manuscripts. 1. Arrival of the nations, in 1300, who brought a knowledge of writing (Mapa Quinatzin); 2. New Fire Ceremony of 1403; 3. New Fire Ceremony of 1455; 4. New Fire Ceremony of 1507 (2–4 from Codex Telleriano-Remensis); 5. The capture of Tenochtitlan in 1519 (Codex of 1576). Second Row: Last three constructions at Tenayuca, corresponding perhaps to the cyclical renovations ot 1403, 1455 and 1507. Third Row: *First three*, Aztec pottery, Types II, IIIa, IIIb, found respectively in the cyclical dumps for 1403, 1455, 1507, and a *fourth* type, IV, made from 1507 through the Spanish Conquest of 1520–21. Fourth Row: *First two*, Aztec figurines made prior to 1403. *Last four*, made between 1403 and the Conquest, representing Xochiquetzal, Xipe, Xochipilli and Tonantzin respectively.

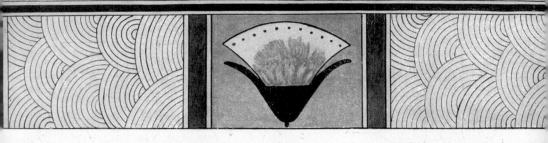

PLATE 30

TRADE POTTERY, AZTEC PERIOD

Vessels like these from Puebla and Tlaxcala were much prized in Central Mexico and obtained by trade or tribute. At the top, a design composed of a feather fan and concentric circles, taken from a hemispherical bowl. The middle cup utilizes a simple grecque pattern, while at the bottom the hieroglyph for the day Reed set against a black background decorates the neck of a vase, the body of which is painted a lustrous red.

PLATE 31

CEREMONIAL VASE

This vase from Mihuatlan, Oaxaca, is a masterpiece of Mixteca-Puebla ceramics. It represents the god Macuilxochitl (Five Flower), God of Games and Feasting. His dress, necklace and face painting are faithfully presented in polychrome, and above the left collarbone a turquoise bead has been inserted to indicate the god's heart. Jade and turquoise were precious, so also was the heart of a god. Therefore, there was no symbolic conflict in showing as green an organ which is red.

PLATE 32

AZTEC POTTERY

TOP: Design from bowl of the Aztec IV period, representing a marine worm, water plants and a fish. SECOND ROW: Trichrome vessels from the 1403 cyclical dump at Chiconauhtla. THIRD ROW: *Left:* Pentachrome trade bowl found in 1507 dump at Chiconauhtla; *Right:* Local trichrome bowl from the same dump. BOTTOM ROW: Bowl with orange-and-black design on red and two black-on-orange plates from the 1507 dump at Nonoalco.

fate, to see if the day of birth was lucky or unlucky. Four
days later the child's family held a feast both to celebrate
the birth and to name the child. If the day of birth proved
to be unlucky, custom sanctioned a religious fiction whereby the naming ceremony was postponed to a more favorable period. At the feast the guests sprinkled food and pulque
over the sacred fire, which had been kindled at the ac-
couchement as an offering to the Fire God, the Old God,
whose cult originated in the time of the Middle Cultures.
The child, if a boy, was shown toy weapons and tools
which the parents placed in his hands, guiding them in the
motions of use. If the child were a girl the parents made her
pretend to weave and spin with toy instruments. A name,
that badge of identity so important to man, was given to the
child at this time. A boy was often named for the date of his
birth, One Reed, Two Flower, Seven Deer, or for an animal,
like "Nezahualcoyotl" (Hungry Coyote), or for an ancestor,
like "Montezuma the Younger," or for some event at the
time of birth. Often the day name was given with an alternative animal title. Girls' names frequently were com-
pounded with the word for flower, *xochitl*.

Education began after weaning in the third year. Its purpose was to induct the child into the techniques and obligations of adult life as promptly as possible. A world in which
handwork is universal offers a child a chance to participate in
adult activities far earlier than in our heavily mechanized culture. Fathers supervised the training of sons, and mothers instructed their daughters. Up to six years of age the children
listened to frequently repeated homilies and advice, learned
the uses of the household implements and performed minor
household chores.[2]

The principal food was the tortilla, a flat cake of un-
leavened corn meal, which measured a good foot in diameter,
to judge from the size of the clay griddles used in cooking
them, in contrast to the modern tortilla which varies between four and six inches. At three the child received half a
tortilla a day; at four and five his ration was doubled; from six
to twelve a tortilla and a half were prescribed, and at thirteen
the allotment was two. Supplemented by beans and game, this
diet was filling and nutritious.

The Mendoza manuscript reflects the current Aztec ideas
on child psychology. Admonition was the chief method of
discipline up to the eighth year. From then on a rigorous corporal punishment awaited the recalcitrant child. This discipline ranged from pricking the hand with the maguey spine
to exposing the child to the chill rigors of a mountain night,
lying bound and naked in a mud puddle. In view of the almost
universal kindness which Indian parents show to their children, they probably seldom applied these extremely imaginative corrections for wrongdoing by the young.

This type of training, not unlike that of a modern farm
child, initiated him directly into the economic life of the
home. The satisfactions in playing a man's part by contributing
to the family welfare compensated the child for the heaviness
of his social obligation. At fifteen or sixteen most boys went
through a special training before assuming the full rights of
manhood; under certain conditions they were younger when
they received this special instruction. There were two types
of schools: the *telpuchcalli*, or house of youth, for standard training, and the *calmecac* of uncertain etymology, for
instruction in priestly duties. The *telpuchcalli*, maintained
by the clan for the children of its members, offered instruc-

tion in citizenship, the bearing of arms, arts and crafts, history and tradition and ordinary religious observance. The *calmecac* was in the nature of a seminary for special training ii priestly and chiefly duties, and several of them were maintained near the temples of important gods. The *calmecac* seems to have been an addition to ordinary training, required by the development of ritual, whereas the *telpuchcalli* carried on in special quarters instruction given in a simpler day by the old men of the clan. Other schools trained young women to be priestesses; they also learned to weave skillfully and to make featherwork for preparation of priestly vestments. (See Plate 39, top left.)

A youth was ready for marriage at twenty, and a girl was deemed mature at about sixteen. The parents arranged the marriage with the consent of the boy and girl. A priest was consulted to decide whether or not the fates of the couple were harmonious. Incest laws like our own prevailed with the further restriction that marriage must be outside the clan. Having satisfied these conventions, the father of the boy sent two elderly clanswomen with gifts to the girl's father, who, following custom, rejected the suit. The old ladies returned again to consult in earnest with the parents of the prospective bride. Such a discussion was necessarily intricate, since it involved the amount of the bride's dowry, which was to be balanced by the gifts of her suitor.

On the evening of the wedding one of the matchmakers carried the bride on her back over the threshold of the husband's house. Elaborate speeches were made by everyone, following which the mantles of the bride and groom were tied together, symbolizing the union. The old men and women gave tongue again in the form of long-winded homilies, and at last a feast, liberally lubricated with pulque, took place. The bride and the groom, after this merciless treatment, retired for four days of penance and fasting, and not until that period elapsed did they consummate their marriage.

As is often the case in a warrior nation which suffers from reduced man power, polygamy was prevalent. Yet the first wife took precedence over the others, and her children alone had the right to inherit. Concubines were permitted and there was, likewise, prostitution. Desertion was frowned upon, but a court would grant a decree of divorce under certain conditions. A man could obtain the right to cast out his wife if she were sterile, were subject to prolonged ill temper or neglected the household duty. The wife could be freed from a husband who failed to support her or educate the children or who ill-treated her in the physical sense, for the Aztecs had not invented mental cruelty. A divorced woman could remarry as she chose, but a widow had to marry a brother of her deceased husband or one of his clansmen.[3]

Women had definite rights, but they were inferior to those of men. They could hold property, enter into contracts and go to courts to obtain justice. In matters of sexual morality girls had to be chaste and wives faithful to their husbands. A man transgressed the rules of propriety only when his illicit relations involved a married woman. Otherwise his wife could not formally demand his fidelity. While the legal position of women was relatively low, judged by modern standards in the United States, personal influence was great, and there were several instances where a woman acted as regent when her son was too young to assume the office of chief. In matters of tribal alliance we have seen how the marriage of a chief's daughter or sister to another ruler cemented an

alliance. Moreover, marriages were carefully arranged between families, so that for a husband grossly to neglect his
wife's rights was a breach, if not of etiquette, certainly of
social contract. The priesthood may have offered a modest
field of influence and attainment to women. However, history records no mention of any advantage deriving from
temple service.

Men had the chief opportunities, and these lay in various
directions. The early chroniclers, conditioned by their
mediæval Spanish background, spoke of hereditary classes. In
all probability, judging from Indian communities as a whole,
there was *rank* but not *class* in the hereditary sense. As in our
own society, a man could attain high *rank* through his own
efforts, and through his eminence his children would consequently profit in their own social adjustment. Yet they could
not reach their father's position unless they earned it through
equivalent tribal service. *Wealth* did exist, and property in
the form of rights to use land, tools and other possessions
created a social and economic stratification. In theory and
practice Aztec society was democratic, and the communal
ownership of productive property was its economic base.[4]

A man attained rank through the measure of his tribal
service. The wise farmer, the wily hunter, the brave warrior
or the dexterous artisan gained admiration from his fellows
because of superior skill. If his wisdom and judgment were
conspicuous he might be elected as the clan representative to
the tribal council, or even as chief. Similarly an individual
who dedicated himself to learning the magic rituals to placate
the gods, could become a medicine man or priest. However,
in the populous and advanced city-states activities tended to
become specialized, and greater opportunity led to a more

finely graded scale of social eminence. (See Plates 33–36.)

A married man received a plot of land directly from the clan or else took over his father's fields if the latter were too old to work. Diligent husbandry, eked out by making stone tools, pottery or practicing some such craft for barter, could produce a good living. Unmarried men helped their fathers and were able to add to their prestige by taking part in the numerous military campaigns.

Since the capture of victims for sacrifice was the chief glory of war, an able soldier who could subdue his enemies and drag them to the rear received much honor. According to the number of captives taken, a warrior had the right to wear an increasingly elaborate costume. Consistently successful warriors could enter an order, like the Knights of the Eagle or the Ocelot (often referred to as Tiger), which performed special dances and rituals. Sometimes a warrior of unusual prowess received additional grants of land or more often obtained an increased portion of the clan's share of tribute. Having reached an established position by this means, he had a more important voice in clan councils and might attain a seat in the council itself. A special honorific, *tecuhtli* (grandfather), which corresponds to chief among the North American Indians, distinguished these men. The title signified high social, but not official, rank, and from these men who had distinguished themselves by probity, bravery and religious observance, high elective and appointive posts were filled.[5]

In this stratum there were many positions of honor and influence, which, like petty political offices in small North American towns, were held in connection with some other means of livelihood. There were officials who kept order in the markets and tribunals which settled disputes in clan affairs. Men of proven wisdom and experience taught the young in the *telpuchcalli*, or houses of youth. Others kept the records of tribute and wealth in the clan storehouses, superintended the distribution of this communal property and even went abroad to supervise its collection.

Each clan had its elected officers whose positions dominated the administration of the tribe. One official, the *calpullec*, performed the duties of secretary-treasurer and kept economic order within the kinship, drawing upon the members of the body for as much administrative assistance as his task required. Ranking with him, the *teochcautin* acted as sheriff, preserving social order and enforcing it. In wartime he commanded the military forces of the clan. Linking the clans to the tribe were the *tlatoani*, or "speakers," the supreme council, composed of a member from each clan and exercising judicial and directive functions. The wisest men and the most distinguished attained this post, for on them depended the well-being of the whole tribe. (See Plate 39, top right.)

Just as the clan had its executive officers, so this tribal body elected four officials who controlled the military forces of the four quarters, or phratries, into which the twenty clans were evenly divided. They maintained order among the clans and exercised tribal authority in disputes and crimes that could not be settled by the clan itself. Two were especially concerned with judicial matters; the third was an executioner, and the fourth acted as an intermediary between civil and military affairs.[6]

These four offices were the proving ground to test the abilities of the supreme chief and the religious leader. In Tlaxcala* it appears that they jointly exercised the executive

*Tlash-ca'-la.

leadership. In Tenochtitlan the supreme chief, *tlacatecuhtli*, "chief of men," was always chosen from the four and often occupied first the position of "Snake Woman," a name also given to an important fertility goddess, Cihuacoatl.* The functions of these high chiefs are difficult to interpret in terms of Western civilization. Roughly the "chief of men" may be said to have represented the tribe in its external affairs, like war and alliances. As such the office had highest significance to the Spanish observers who saw its holder as the leader of the tribe. The "Snake Woman" was the executive peak of the internal affairs of the tribe, where civil custom and religious demand governed almost every act. It is important to realize, however, that these chiefs could be deposed by the council at any time, if their services were unsatisfactory.

The continual election of such high officers from the same family or lineage, when democratic procedure obtained elsewhere, is harder to explain. Tradition is strong in primitive communities, and a family that produced one effective man might in the next generation produce another. The council in Tenochtitlan chose successive chiefs from a fairly wide range—brothers, sons, nephews and half brothers were scrutinized in the rigid proving ground of public service. Furthermore, a wise council, exercising its tremendous powers, could make a puppet "chief of men" seem effective as its representative in extratribal affairs. Even then, to be considered for election a person of privileged birth had to meet the long series of tests on which eminence was based.

Two other specialized fields were open to Aztec youth: trade and craftsmanship. Trade was a new development in

*Se'e-wah-co-atl.

a tribal economy which was based on living off the land. The opening up of intertribal contact through settlement and warfare and the growth of material and ritualistic wants, led to the establishment of a class, the *pochteca*, whose members traveled all over Mexico, exchanging local for foreign produce. They had their own god and apparently lived in a special quarter. From the valley they carried obsidian, cloth and rope, which in the hot country they exchanged for shells, tropical feathers, jade, cacao and other regional riches. In time they performed an important political function, spying out towns to conquer and reporting on the tribute which could be exacted. There is a very modern touch about the economic and political functions of these merchants who so often brought military conquest in their train.[7] (See Plate 38.)

Craftsmanship, with the growth of technique, must have attracted many men to whom straight agriculture seemed drab and unrewarding. Potters, jewelers, weavers and feather-workers came to pursue these crafts to the exclusion of other labor. The enormous elaboration of the religion called into almost continual activity sculptors, masons and painters. The market, still important in Middle American Indian communities, had a profound social significance, for there, in addition to bartering his products for those of others, an Indian could hear the news and widen his social and intellectual horizons. (See Plates 34–35.)

The priesthood offered a relentless sort of career. Religion penetrated into every part of daily life, and the individual participated in great and complicated rituals. Civic eminence depended greatly on religious observance, and chiefs led in the direction of ceremonies. Therefore, it is hard to recognize a priesthood completely separate from civil officialdom; both were mutually dependent. There was a priestly hierarchy, it is true, but it probably operated in conjunction with civil position. Permanent positions may have existed, but in the chapters on religion we shall describe more fully how completely the realms of Church and State coalesced among the people of ancient Mexico, in contrast to the cleavage between them in our own society.

Mexican society existed for the benefit of the tribe, and each member was supposed to do his part in preserving the community. However, the bane of working social orders as well as hypothetical social schemes are those unfortunates who, by mischance, maladjustment or just plain deviltry, do not do their part. The Aztecs, too, had this problem to cope with, and there developed a social class of people who had lost their civil rights and become slaves. This they might do voluntarily or because they were prisoners of war or were punished for crimes or were sold by their parents. Their treatment differed according to the circumstances of their enslavement.[8] (See Plate 38, bottom left.)

Military captives usually were sacrificed, but those who demonstrated some unusual skill were sometimes bought for domestic service or put to work on some communal enterprise. Criminal slaves lost their free status for such offenses as failure to denounce treachery, membership in a traitor's family, kidnaping for sale a free man, selling another's property without his consent, theft without restitution when over ten years old or hindering a slave from gaining the sanctuary of a chief's house. Penal slaves were privately owned, usually to make restitution to those whom they had injured.

Voluntary slavery was assumed by the poor and landless

who needed food, by the indolent who were too lazy to provide for their own support, by gamblers and by prostitutes who wanted finery. Parents often sold a child, to be replaced by a younger one when the first was old enough materially to contribute to the family welfare. Sometimes destitute people offered a bondsman in return for a loan from a more fortunate neighbor. If the bondsman died in service or the master took any property unlawfully the debt was discharged. To avoid this contingency the owner made the slave live at home and perform only personal services. Slavery, except in the case of war prisoners, was not too exacting. A slave could control his family, own property or even have slaves of his own. His children were always born free. What the slave lost was his eligibility for tribal office, which depended, as we have seen, on public service and was negated by his reliance on the bounty of others or his commission of antisocial acts.

An important aspect of the legal code of the Aztecs involved the loss of civil rights as a result of flagrant antisocial acts. In general, custom dictated and regulated human behavior. Membership in the community brought safety and subsistence. To break away or to be cast off meant death at the hands of foes or isolation as a solitary wanderer, a prey to marauding beasts. Competition for rank and renown existed in the field of public service rather than in the acquisition of wealth. Hence the antisocial behavior implicit in attaining many of our own higher grades or ranks was held to a minimum.[9]

Growth of the community to a size where none but the great were known to society at large probably tended to break down the sense of membership and participation, so that thefts and like petty crimes increased as mutual responsibility diminished. The increasing complication of tasks and manners of livelihood led to disputes and injustices. In a nation of warriors skilled in arms, personal animosity flared up into bloodshed. Thus the tribunals mentioned had to be set up to exercise their jurisdiction in affairs of clan and tribe and to reinforce the powerful influences of public approval and disapproval. (See Plates 35, 41.)

Religious crimes, like blasphemy or robbing temples, were rare, for the disfavor of the gods brought disaster on the community and on the individual as well. Religion, however, did not enter into the field of ethics, and no post-mortem punishment awaited the sinner. Special heavens existed for warriors and for women who died in childbirth and for people who died in certain specified ways, but this belief had to do with the favor of particular gods. It was not a carefully defined system of rewards and punishment.

Restitution for the sinned-against was the chief basis of dealing with antisocial acts, in contrast to our pattern of punishing the sinner. Exile or death was the lot of the evil-doer who endangered the community. A random sampling of crimes and punishment will show the tenor of Aztec law and why it was never necessary to resort to imprisonment as a means of enforcing expiation of a crime. Cages or detention pens, however, were used to confine prisoners before trial or sacrifice. (See Plate 34.)

Theft was punished either by slavery until restitution was made or by a fine of double the amount stolen, one part to the robbed, the other to the clan treasury. Highway robbery received the death penalty, and pilfering in the market place meant instant death by stoning, since that petty crime mili-

tated against the social advantages of the gathering. To steal
corn, the staple of life, when growing in the field, was a
serious offense, demanding the death penalty or slavery, but
a wayfarer might with impunity satisfy his hunger by pluck-
ing ears from rows adjacent to the road. To filch gold, silver
and jade, precious substances usually reserved for religious
ornaments, was also a mortal crime.

Murder, even of a slave, brought the death penalty. Rebels
and traitors received the same fate, but kidnapers were sold
into slavery. Drunkenness was a serious crime except at prescribed ceremonial occasions. Social disapproval, public dis-
grace, even death by stoning or beating, were penalties
suffered by the intemperate. However, the old of both sexes,
who had fulfilled their tribal obligations, were allowed great
latitude in their potations.

The witch or practicer of black magic was sacrificed, and
death was likewise the lot of him who impersonated a high
official. A slanderer had his lips cut off and sometimes his
ears as well. Brawling and fighting in the market place were
dealt with severely, but in an ordinary case of assault the
assailant paid for the cure of the assailed and for any damage
done. Adultery was punished with great severity, even death,
when committed outside the pale of the divorce laws. Hang-
ing was the usual penalty for violation of the incest laws,
and sodomy was punished with revolting brutality.

Thus reduced to cited instances, Aztec law was brutal.
Actually, from childhood on, the individual grew up into
correct social behavior; the violator of the code met with
serious consequences. All people had some kind of personal
property, but land belonged to the tribe and only its produce to the individual. Therefore, the elaborate legislation

surrounding our own property concepts was unnecessary.

There was little to harass the individual intellectually or economically. Existence was subject to divine favor, and a man fared much as did his fellows. Large as some towns were—Mexico City had three hundred thousand people—the sense of community was strong. Freedom of thought, individual liberty, personal fortunes, were nonexistent, but people lived according to a code that had worked well and continuously for centuries. An Aztec would have been horrified at the naked isolation of an individual's life in our Western world.

CHAPTER VII

ECONOMY

The Domestic and Tribal Economy of the Aztec People

THE AZTEC SOCIAL SYSTEM provided a means by which people could exist harmoniously together in considerable numbers. The domestic and tribal economy of the Aztecs offered the food, shelter, tools and clothing to which man largely owes his dominant position on earth. The measure of a human society may be gauged by the relationship between the organization of the people themselves and their use of materials to build houses and equip them. The Aztecs' economy had the same basic simplicity as had their social organization; likewise it had the same flexibility in expanding to meet the needs of a growing population.[1]

Agriculture was the basis of Aztec life, and corn, *zea mays*, was the chief food plant. The cultivation of plants ensured a food supply near at hand, which was not subject to the fluctuations of game and thereby enabled man to take thought for the morrow. The clan system, as we have seen, recognized that the fruits of the land supported the tribe. Therefore, it was only natural that the tribe should own and control the land which supported its members.[2] (See Plate 38.)

The tribal council divided the land among the clans, and

the leaders of each, in turn, apportioned its share among the heads of families justly and equitably. Sections were also reserved for the maintenance of the chief and the temple staff, for war supplies and the payment of tribute; these were worked communally, with some amount, no doubt, of slave labor. At the death of a tenant the land passed to his sons. If he died without issue the holding reverted to the clan for redivision, as was also the case if a tenant failed to cultivate his plot for a period of two years. Such a system could work equitably and profitably for all concerned so long as a society was relatively static and plenty of arable land was at hand. However, in the Valley of Mexico inequalities developed in the system.

The growing population of the Valley tribes used up all the available land, and families or clans had no way of adding to their farm holdings. A plot which produced ample supplies for a small family might yield a bare subsistence or less for a larger one. Normal variation in the richness of soil would result in similar injustices. Under such conditions the chiefs and priests who lived off the public lands would be far better off than the ordinary citizen whose holding, generation by generation, tended to diminish. Thus friction leading to foreign war and internal revolt was bound to result whenever a tribe could not expand its territorial limits to meet the needs of its population. The considerable migrations, like those of the Culhuas to Texcoco and Tenochtitlan or the Mixtec people to Texcoco years earlier, had their basis in a pressing economic necessity.[3]

The Tenochcas, who came late to the Valley, at a time when land was at a premium, had, we have seen, a difficult time in withstanding their hungry neighbors. Forced to retreat to islands in the lake, they met the land problem in the same ingenious way as did the Chalcas, Xochimilcas and the tribes to the northwest, in Lake Zumpango.

This method was to create *chinampas*, the so-called "floating gardens." The *chinampa* was, in reality, a small artificial island, made by scooping up mud from the marshy borders of the lakes and at first holding it in place by a re-vetment of reeds and later by trees whose roots bound the earth solidly together. Water flowed into the narrow pits, making them into canals. Fresh mud was always added be-fore planting, so that the fertility of the earth was constantly renewed. The Tenochcas and their neighbors thus con-verted great sections of otherwise unproductive marsh, flooded in the rainy season, into a grid of canals and fields, the fertility of which is equaled only by the river-flooded lands of the Nile Delta. *Chinampa* agriculture continues today in the districts of Xochimilco and Chalco, where most of the vegetables are grown for the modern metropolis of Mexico City. The inhabitants still use the Aztec language and occupy the same land as did their ancestors, renewing them each year by the same methods used in Aztec times. The outlines of former beds may be seen for a considerable distance round about, since the modern draining of Lake Texcoco has dried up much of the lake area of the Valley of Mexico.[4] (See Plate 37, bottom.)

When the Tenochcas moved into the lake they achieved living room. As the city grew it could incorporate the ad-jacent garden beds for house foundations, while the increase in population could be fed by building new *chinampas* on the outskirts of the farming area. Thus much of their suc-cess may be attributed to the freedom from internal strife achieved by the relatively unlimited possibilities of *chinampa* agriculture.

The Tenochcas supplemented their land hunger by another means. In conquered territories successful warriors received grants of land which were worked by members of the defeated tribe. Small colonies sometimes lived off this land to guard against revolt in the subjugated area. Such property passed from father to son, but if there were no heir it reverted to the tribal authority, not the clan in which the tenant had membership. Other such land must have been held for the benefit of the religious organization. Thus the central authority of Tenochtitlan, and presumably Texcoco as well, held considerable property to support the elaborate pomp of Church and State without straining the resources of the tribesmen. The relative fluidity of such real estate gave the tribal authority a wherewithal to adjust inequalities and dissatisfactions among the more ambitious tribal members. Naturally, as the Aztec peoples were less highly developed socially than ourselves, they did not attain our own elaborate system of rewards and adjustments by means of federal, state and municipal appointments.[5]

A powerful Aztec tribe had another source of support: tribute. The levies often consisted of foodstuffs and raw materials, both native and foreign to the Valley, and also included warriors' and priests' costumes, mantles, pottery and other articles of craftsmanship. Distributed throughout the community these goods enriched both communal enterprise and private convenience.[6] (See Plates 62, bottom right; 64.)

Manufacture and trade were beginning to play an important part in Aztec economy, although not to the extent of societies which have developed media of exchange, like money, and therefore emphasize personal wealth in the possession of such a commodity. Manufacture was in the handcraft stage, carried on as a supplement to the main business of raising food. Most households were self-sufficient, making whatever they required in the way of tools, utensils or clothing. However, certain towns had access to natural resources which others had not and developed special skill in exploiting them. A town might have a good clay bed, for example, and its pottery would be far superior to that of surrounding communities. Another village would be especially successful in growing peppers, while a third might have in its territory a good quality of obsidian or flint for making stone tools. Thus such products would be exchanged by one town for the produce of another and even redistributed by the same process. Shells from the Caribbean have been traded from hand to hand as far as the central United States; pottery vases from Salvador were carried to distant Tepic* in Mexico; gold ornaments from Panama appeared as votive offerings in the Sacred Well of Chichen Itza in Yucatan.[7] (See Plate 38.)

Such regional specialization was accompanied by the perfectly natural tendency of individuals to exploit what they made and produced with greatest aptitude. As technical knowledge grew specialization increased, and the market became an important institution. Each town held one at specified intervals to which people came from great distances. At Tlaltelolco the daily market was a wonder of the Western world, exciting by its lavish variety the admiring envy of the Spaniards. The importance of the market still persists in Indian communities, so much so that in Guate-

*Te-pe'ek.

mala the people travel miles to exchange their produce; and so important is the market as a social function that a merchant will not dispose of his produce except at that place, even though offered payment far in excess of its market value.[8]

Barter was the only means of exchange, and value was established by desirability and rarity. Money, an exchange medium of fixed value, did not exist. However, something had to be found which would balance an inequality of exchange by being not too valuable to use in adjusting small transactions and at the same time universally wanted. The cacao bean answered this requirement and was easily portable as well. The Aztecs were extremely fond of chocolate (the word itself is of Aztec derivation), so that beans were gladly converted into the national luxury drink. Quills of gold dust sometimes were used as an exchange medium, as were crescent-shaped knives of thin-beaten copper. These last had not the common acceptance or the utility of cacao beans, although they represented easily portable value.[9]

The most precious substance among the Aztecs was jade, or stones resembling it in texture and color. Both jadeite and nephrite occur in the New World, and the American variety is distinguishable from the Asiatic stone. Uncut stones are seldom seen today, for there is no lapidaries' market in modern Middle America or the United States, whereas jade is still extensively worked in China, so that men find it worth their while to search rivers in Burma for boulders of this rare substance. (See Plate 3.)

The testimony of the Conquistador Bernal Diaz is conclusive on this point of value. During the night when Cortes retreated from Mexico the leader, after taking off his share of treasure, turned the surplus over to his troops. Many,

burdened down with gold, drowned ignominiously in the
canals. Diaz, however, noted Indian usage and confined himself to four jades which he was able to exchange later and
which, in his words, "served me well in healing my wounds
and gathering me food."[10]

The Aztecs did not have our modern esteem for gold, so
the Spaniards had great difficulty in getting it at first. The
Mexican Indians responded to the invaders' demands for
objects of value by offering jade and turquoise, those substances most precious to themselves. Such misguided com-
pliance was highly irritating to Cortes and his men, who had
no ethnological training; nor, it is only fair to say, would
they have wanted such education, were it available. Gold
was valuable to the Aztecs only for the ornaments which
could be made from it, and silver may have had an even
greater value, since nodules were rare and the Indians had no
technique for smelting the ore.[11] (See Plates 46–47.)

Thus the Aztecs did not hold our ideas of value and
wealth. Yet they contributed much to our prosperity and
well-being, partly through being forced as slaves to work
the gold and silver mines, whose modern economic significance they so little understood, and even more through the
enrichment of the world's supply of foods. In addition to
corn of several varieties, the Aztecs developed many sorts of
beans, a very nutritive addition to human diet because of
the high protein content. Squash, gourds, *chia*, *camotes*,
green and red peppers, alligator pears and tomatoes were
products of the versatile Middle American farmer, enriching
the Aztec diet and that of the modern world. Trade with
southern Vera Cruz brought chocolate, vanilla and pine-
apples to the Aztec larder.[12]

The maguey plant, or agave, was important to household economy for its sap, which was fermented to make a kind of beer. Not only was this pulque used both as a tipple and a ceremonial intoxicant, but it had an important nutritive effect as well in counterbalancing the lack of greens in the Mexican diet. The plant itself had many other uses. Its fibers could be twisted into twine or rope and woven into containers or even clothing. The thorns were excellent needles and had a more lugubrious use as instruments for mortifying the flesh in religious penances. The leaves as a whole sometimes were employed in constructing shelters or roofing huts. Small wonder that the maguey and the corn plants were symbolized as goddesses and worshiped accordingly.

The Aztecs cultivated cotton in many varieties. Tobacco they smoked for the most part in hollow reeds as a sort of cigarette. Late in their history they also used elbow-shaped pipes, probably for some ceremonial purpose, much as our modern Pueblos restrict pipe smoking to rain-inducing rituals. They consumed quantities of copal gum as incense during religious ceremonies and obtained rubber from Vera Cruz and the south, as well as from the dwarf guayule plant found in northern Mexico. The Aztecs, like us, found this material indispensable to their culture, for balls in their ceremonial game, *tlachtli*, and as a gum to fix feathers and other adornments to costumes. Bitumen, which came from the oil seepages in Vera Cruz, had its function as an adhesive and as a body paint. In western Mexico the Indians prepared a serviceable lacquer which they used to coat gourds and wooden trays. This incomplete list of plants and substances cultivated and exploited by the Aztecs and their neighbors gives an idea of our deep indebtedness to these past civilizations. The original inventors and innovators are lost in the black obscurity of American history, but the fruit of their ingenuity plays an important part in our modern economy.

As opposed to this wealth of plants, the Aztecs were poor in domesticated animals. They had several varieties of dog, one of which was bred for food, but they never used this animal for transport as did Indians of our Northern plains. The turkey was their chief domesticated fowl, although there is some evidence that they bred geese, ducks and quail also. In plantations of the nopal cactus they carefully tended the cochineal bug for the rich crimson dye it yielded when crushed. A second insect, the maguey slug, still retains its place as a delicacy of the Mexican table, served with another typically Aztec dish, *guacamole*,* a thick mixture of tomato, alligator pear and chile.

Hunting, when possible, produced food, but as early as Upper Middle Culture times the deer were nearly all killed off. The seasonal migrations of the birds, which still visit the lakes of Mexico, offered a profusion of geese, ducks and other wild fowl. Small fish, netted or speared with a trident, were sometimes consumed, and the eggs which a certain fly lays on the lakes were made into a paste still eaten in Mexican communities. The high functionaries, since they were supported by the community, kept a much better table than the poor, who lived meagerly off the produce of their own fields; the daily repast of Montezuma was described by the Spanish conquerors as the height of Lucullan luxury.[13]

Tools showed relatively little variation from Middle Culture to Aztec times. The *coa*, or digging stick, was the chief farming instrument, and the *metate* and *mano* even now re-

*Wah-ca-mo'-lay.

duce the kernels of corn to flour. Stone tools still persisted for cutting and grinding, and cold, beaten copper was beginning to find favor as a material for needles, axes and ornaments. The volcanic glass, obsidian, because of its sharp edges and its abundance, was as satisfactory as most of their edged metal tools. The simple loom and the weighted spindle were sufficient equipment for the weavers, and pottery had a variety of uses in the storage and service of food. The bow, throwing stick, lance and club were the chief weapons. By and large, mechanical inventiveness was not conspicuous in Aztec culture, although craftsmanship, through the superior use of simple tools, was developed to a high degree, as we shall show in the next chapter. (See Plates 35, bottom left, 38.)

The great cities of the Aztecs had their origin in the simple villages of sedentary tribesmen. Just as in their social organization and economy, there was a simple base, comparable to the settlements of some of our sedentary North American tribes. The houses on the outlying *chinampas* represented the primitive state of Aztec housing. These were huts with thatched roofs resting on walls of wattles smeared with mud, a type of shelter probably in use in Middle Culture times and persisting two thousand years later in the Indian villages of present-day Mexico. (See Plate 42.)

More imposing establishments graced the older portions of the city, where generations of successive residents had brought care, renovation and innovation to domestic architecture. Each house rested on a raised platform faced with stone, which gave some protection against floods. Rooms for social purposes, sleeping, cooking, storage and quartering slaves were arranged in a rectangular plan about a central court. The house walls had stone bases and, according to the wealth or taste of the owner, were finished in stone or adobe. The roof was constructed by covering crossbeams with small poles tightly fitted together and spreading a layer of lime plaster over the whole. As there were no windows, the houses had to be shallow. To admit light and air the buildings were usually two rooms deep and prolonged according to taste and wealth. The back room, which contained a hearth for cooking, was completely enclosed save for the door to the outer chamber which was left largely open on the patio side, columns or short wing walls supporting the rafters. Two-story houses probably did not exist before the Conquest, but there are cases where, to have light and circulation of air, a rear court with its surrounding rooms was elevated on a platform to the height of the roofs of the rooms around the patio in front.[14] (See Plate 41.)

Recent excavations in the palace of the chief of Chiconauhtla, a fief of Texcoco, revealed interesting data on the growth of a chiefly establishment. This palace was continually being rebuilt and expanded to meet the demands of a growing population and richer economy. Patios were arranged at different levels, according to the plan described above. The earliest rooms had the congested quality of a Teotihuacan plan, but the later chambers were more spacious and open to sun and air. Each renovation called for more space, so that allowing a family of five to each hearth, the entourage of the chief more than trebled in a century and a quarter.[15] (See Plate 43.)

The plan of an Aztec town tended to have a rectangular form, since the division of the land among the clans usually followed a more or less orderly rectilinear pattern. A central plaza was essential for communal gatherings; the market and the principal structures, like the main temple and the chief's quarters, were situated at this point. In Tenochtitlan, which was reported to have sixty thousand fires or hearths, or figuring on the same basis as above, three hundred thousand people, additional centers existed for each clan and for the four larger districts into which the city was divided for administrative purposes.[16] (See Plate 37, top.)

We have been left a description of an Aztec city in 1524 from a Spanish monk, Fray Toribio de Benavente, called by the Indians "Motolinia," or "poor," in reference to his Franciscan simplicity of life. His firsthand observations have a fresh reality:

"They called these temples *teocallis,* and we found all over the land that in the best part of the settlement they made a great quadrangular court, which, in the largest pueblo, was one crossbow shot from one corner to another, while in the smaller places it was not as large. This court they enclosed by a wall, many of which enclosures were with battlements; the entrances looking towards the chief highways and streets, which all terminated at the court, and even, in order to still more honor their temples, they led their roads up to these in a straight line from two and three leagues' distance. It was a wonderful aspect, to witness from the top of the chief temple, how from all the quarters and the minor places, the roadways all led up in a straight line to the courts of the *teocallis,* . . . the devil did not content himself with the aforesaid *teocallis,* but in each pueblo and in each quarter, as far as a quarter of one league off, there were other small courts containing, sometimes only one, sometimes three or four *teocallis.* . . ."[17]

The streets of Tenochtitlan were the canals bordered by footpaths, and frequent bridges allowed easy access to all parts of the town. Three great causeways led north, west and south to the mainland, touching it respectively at Tepeyac, now Guadalupe, Tlacopan, now Tacuba, and Coyoacan. Canals paralleled these main roadways where they entered the city proper, following them as far as their terminus at the main plaza. Two aqueducts also joined the city to the mainland. The one to Chapultepec seems to have been constructed exclusively to carry water and had two channels, so that when one was being cleaned or repaired the other could remain in use. The Coyoacan aqueduct, built later by Ahuitzotl, may well have followed the great southern causeway. The problem of sanitation must have been serious, but boats were tied up at strategic points for public use, and when filled their contents were sold to fertilize the fields. Pottery vessels were kept in the houses to preserve urine, which the Aztecs used as a mordant in dyeing cloth. Hence sunlight and these simple methods for getting fresh water and disposing of offal kept down the pestilence that beset the city in Spanish times when the ancient methods of sanitation were abandoned.[18]

A city so advantageously situated had no need of fortifications, and formal military architecture was rare. The temples, which dominated the city, were natural strong points; indeed, the hieroglyph for the capture of a town was the burning of a temple, an indignity to which no people would submit unless driven from this last rallying point.

The temples had stone or rubble walls surmounted by a high roof, the construction of which consisted of a cribwork of logs, either thatched with straw or covered with plaster.

Each temple usually had a chamber and an antechamber, and in some cases two or even three shrines rested on the same platform. This platform or substructure gave height and mass to the temple. The usual practice was to lay up rough stone, set in adobe or lime, into a truncated pyramid, the sides of which were broken up by three narrow setbacks and by a steep ramp leading to the top. The surface was of veneered cut-stone slabs, and additional blocks were laid along the ramp to make the stair. Wide balustrades bordered the staircase and often ended in gigantic serpent heads. Aztec construction was the simplest type of engineering, but imposing architectural effects were gained by the consummate artistic sense and superb craftsmanship of the builders.[19] (See Plates 50–51.)

The adequate, even imposing, housing of the Aztecs and their gods by no means eclipsed their dress. Clothing, besides protecting man from the weather, has an important social function. It is a guide to the sex, age, group, occupation, rank and even character of its wearer. The simple and standardized clothing of our modern society performs the same service, and with a moment's observation one can tell much about a stranger from his clothes. The Aztecs, like many peoples of the world, strove by their dress to accentuate the social differences between people, and pomp and panoply dominated their costume. On the barbaric splendor of high civilian dress was superimposed the fantastic garb of the priests and priestesses in their impersonation of the complex and ornately represented divinities in their pantheon.[20]

The *macehual*, or ordinary tribesman, left his head uncovered, his hair long, and customarily wore a *maxtli*, or loincloth, a mantle knotted over one shoulder, and sandals of leather or woven maguey fiber in cold weather. Women wrapped about their loins a finely woven cloth, which they sustained with a narrow belt. A sleeveless slipover, or *huipil*, completed their costume. They plaited their hair into braids, sometimes interlacing them with ribbons, and these they wrapped around their heads. This woman's costume may still be seen in many parts of Indian Mexico. (See Plates 33–36.)

The poor made their garments of maguey fiber or coarse cotton. The rich wore the same clothing fashioned from finer textures and decorated with elaborate embroidery. The many names given to the different kinds of mantles show their interest and importance to the wearers. Wool was almost never made into cloth, since dog hair was all they had, but feather cloaks were highly esteemed. Chiefs wore a fillet of leather from which hung two tassels, and administrative chiefs had a sort of diadem of gold or jade and turquoise as a badge of office.

The warriors frankly gloried in their costumes. Rich mantles and ornate feather headdresses were not enough for some, who carried on their shoulders a harness of wicker supporting an elaborate structure in feather mosaic. Others wore costumes modeled on the appearance of an ocelot or an eagle. On specified occasions the priests assumed the dress of the gods and goddesses, whose costumes were sumptuous and ornate and defined by exacting ritualistic marks of identification. (See Plate 61.)

Jewelry consisted of ornaments of copper, gold and silver, shell, various-colored stones, like jade, turquoise, emeralds, opals or moonstone, and mosaics laid on a backing of clay, wood or reed. Large plugs were inserted in the ear lobes of men and women alike. Men often wore ornaments passed through the septum of the nose or suspended from a slit in the lower lip. Elaborate necklaces and pendants, armlets and leg bracelets, gave brilliance to a costume for state occasions. Cosmetics were not used to touch up nature, as with us, but instead a lavish application of face and body paints in red, blue, yellow, green and black enhanced with prismatic richness the softer tones of their brown flesh. (See Plates 46–47.)

It is obvious that the Aztecs were no pitiable craven savages. They lived upon variegated and delicious foods and dwelt in houses that were comfortable and airy. Their dress stimulated the exercise of merited self-satisfaction, not to be confused with the compensations of vanity. Their manner of life enabled them to take advantage of their personal aptitudes and exchange the products of their own creation for whatever they lacked. Articles for daily and ceremonial use were made with the loving care of master artisans, and rare indeed was the object that did not have the impress of some little decorative touch that makes a pleasant possession of a drab utensil. Their crafts deserve to themselves a complete chapter.

CHAPTER VIII

CRAFTSMANSHIP

A consideration of how the Aztecs attained a high degree of skillful craftsmanship with relatively few mechanical aids

CRAFTSMANSHIP allows an exercise of the creative impulse, satisfying the individual through his domination of the raw material. In our modern mechanized age most of us suffer from the lack of opportunity to create, since almost everything we use comes machine-made, and not even the skilled mechanic feels that his ingenuity and craftsmanship alone have produced a useful and attractive object. The ordinary modern floats like Mohammed's coffin, without contact with the earth on which he lives or the universe of which he is an infinitesimal part. The Aztec, however, lived in the most intimate contact with nature in its finite and infinite manifestations. Because his conscious being was set in terms of the group mind, he seldom felt that sensation, common to the Western intellect, of having cut himself from the tree of natural existence with the saw of his own reason.

The home production of articles for daily use gave an impetus to craftsmanship, since wealth and prosperity lay in a man's possessions, not in the abstract ownership of rights to the work of others. Thus a successful man had a well-made house, finely fashioned and decorative clothing, care-

fully worked utensils and tools and well-tended and productive fields, while an unsuccessful man had a small and
miserable equipment. Yet except for the intervention of
natural disaster the differential was largely due to the ability
of a man and his household to produce with their own hands
the symbols of his wealth or to exchange his specialized
product for equivalent superior equipment made by others.
The entrepreneur and broker had small place in the undertaking of production and its distribution.[1]

The gods also stimulated good craftsmanship. Every home
had an altar, and every act was accomplished through the
favor of some deity. Ceremonies to appease these custodians
of natural force were of frequent occurrence. Thus the use
of symbols, referring to the god whose favor was sought,
came to exercise an important influence on design. Since a
man does reverence with his most esteemed social attitudes
and his best material possessions, each household must try
to surpass its previous efforts to honor the gods. The temple
equipment, therefore, tended to represent the cream of local
craftsmanship.

Work in stone, the most durable natural substance available,
is a common gauge of human ability. Since the tools last
forever, it is possible to compare the technical abilities of
peoples over an enormous span of human history. However,
for basic equipment like projectile points, axes, grinding
stones, and the like, satisfactory forms are reached fairly
early and do not change in proportion to cultural advances
in other directions. Thus the arrow or the dart points of
Aztec times were not technically better than those used by
the Middle Culture peoples. However, the technical demands
of the sacrificial cult called for a heavy broad-bladed flint

that could tear through human flesh at a single stroke, and this type of knife, not found in earlier horizons, was produced commonly with the extra care in chipping which is to be expected in a ceremonial object. (See Plate 60.)

The three-legged *metate*, or grinding stone, was not better made in Aztec times than before. In Middle Culture and Toltec times it had an edge, so that the *metlapil* (son of the *metate*, i.e., *mano*, or grinding stone) was beveled and fitted within the confined space. The Aztec *metate* was flat, and the *mano* had swollen handles, projecting on either side of the grinding surface of the *metate*. I have never had the misfortune to break my back grinding corn in a *metate*, so that I have no way of knowing whether this represents a technical advance or a mere change in style.

The demands of ritual necessitated stone boxes for burning and storing human hearts. These boxes were pecked out of lava and lavishly decorated inside and out with reliefs, referring symbolically to the gods for whom the sacrifice was made. Some of these eagle vases (cuauhxicalli*) fall into that area of superior craftsmanship we designate in our own culture by the term "fine art." The great circular cup, ordered by Tizoc and miscalled the Sacrificial Stone, eight feet in diameter and two and one half feet thick, attained the stature of a monument. Stone incense burners, often in the form of the Old God, were common in Toltec and rare in Upper Middle Culture times. The quantity of religious sculpture, produced chiefly in late Aztec times, to judge from the style, did not detract from the quality of the workmanship, so strong was the control of religious and social factors.[2] (See Plate 55, bottom right.)

*kwow-shee-ca'lli.

Obsidian must have had important economic value for the Valley peoples, and since volcanic glass is portable and very useful for its sharp cutting edge, it was widely traded to the tribes of nonvolcanic regions. Techniques were established early in the Middle Culture, and the art of polishing this stone was known to the Teotihuacan Toltecs, who utilized it as eyes for the idols of the Temple of Quetzalcoatl. Ceremonial bloodletting called for a constant supply of thin blades (made by pressure flaking), some of which are exquisitely long and narrow. Yet scalpels of comparable fineness were made in Toltec and Mazapan times as well. Indeed, the principal innovation of the Aztecs was in fashioning vases from obsidian, a formidable task, owing to its hardness.[3]

The making of mirrors called much ingenuity into play. They are so rare that they must have been used solely for ritualistic magic. Blocks of obsidian were sometimes polished to produce an eerie and mysterious reflection. However, iron pyrites, burnished and shaped, were more common; and rarer examples had thin pyrite flakes laid in a mosaic and glued to a background of wood or shell. In another technique used on the coast the artisan detached a surface of pyrites in its matrix of slate, burnishing one side and carving the other to fashion a mirror with a carved back. One example, at least, is known of a mirror of marcasite with its surface so ground as to produce a magnified reflection.[4]

Stone sculpture we shall consider more conveniently under art, but the mass production of dressed stone for building must have required patience and skill to accomplish. Stoneworking throughout Middle America was achieved without metal tools. Flaking and chipping for the hard stones, pecking and hammering for the softer ones, were the preliminary steps in every case. A final polishing with some simple abrasive like water and sand often completed the process. Some hard stones seem to have been detached from their matrix by applying the abrasive and sawing with a cord of rawhide or a tool of harder stone. The Middle American people also developed tubular drills of bone and reed, which, rotated by a bow and aided by an abrasive, could hollow out vases or bore out places that were otherwise inaccessible to the clumsy tools of the time.[5]

Save for descriptions and drawings, the destruction of time and man has left us only a few examples of the weaver's art. Weaving of some kind is very old, and no people, however primitive, exist in the world today who do not make at least some kind of basketry. Textiles are made as a rule by higher groups, but they are found in the American continent as part of the material equipment of peoples who had not yet learned how to make pottery. An early example of cloth, combining threads of cotton with some fiber like yucca, was found in the Lower Middle Culture horizon of Zacatenco.

The long practice of weaving must and did have a significant effect on decoration, for the rectangular patterns, to which the weaver is confined, influence all of Indian art in Continental America. Design and the arrangement of elements are more important than form in Indian art. While many geometrical patterns appear in pictures of Aztec clothing, fine embroidery could produce the effect of curvilinear designs or even naturalistic patterns drawn from the regional flora. Batik and tie dyeing also enriched the decoration of Aztec clothing. Other processes produced the effect of velvet and brocade, and some garments even imitated in texture and pattern the skins of animals. Judged on a visual basis, the designs on Aztec clothing were by no means inferior to those of the celebrated textile art of Indian Peru. However, we have no positive evidence that technical development of Aztec weaving was equal to Peruvian, for those ancient South American weavers knew and practiced every method known to man and even a few unique to themselves.[6] (See Plates 33–36; 62, bottom right; 64.)

Feather mosaic is probably an old craft, since evidence seems to show that it was known to the Upper Middle Cultures. Feather- and the technically allied fur-cloth appear in primitive horizons in North America. The process consisted in tying the stems of feathers into a fabric during the weaving process. Featherworkers adorned shields in this way, dispersing the feathers to represent animals or else purely decorative designs. They made cloaks, too, and created sumptuous insignia worn on the head or harnessed to the body. In these objects the blending of colors was so delicate and perfect as to rival paintings. As late as the nineteenth century, although the art had declined, the Mexicans still depicted landscapes and scenes from daily life in this medium, and today they make charming pictures for the tourists with cardboard, feathers and glue.[7] (See Plate 45.)

Feather mosaic had an early counterpart in stone and shell; we found a turquoise mosaic in a Lower Middle Culture grave. The wooden handles of sacrificial knives were sometimes ornamented in this way, as were masks, shields and even small gold ornaments. A *tour de force* of the mosaic worker is a wooden shield from the Mixteca, on which little pieces of turquoise were fitted together in a relief sculpture depicting a religious scene.[8] (See Plates 48; 60, bottom left.)

Mosaic workers utilized stones of different colors and shells of various kinds. Pure designs were common, but elements representing the costume or the body paint were shown when the mosaic covered a figure in wood or stone. An application of mosaic on a larger scale was frequent in architecture, a veneer of cut stone being applied to the rubble of a platform or building. The temples of Mitla, Oaxaca, influenced by the same Mixteca-Puebla culture to which Aztec civilization owed its origin, are masterpieces of this technique, for individual blocks have their surfaces carved to fit together in an intricate geometric design.[9] (See Plate 11, bottom.)

The woodworkers, owing to the impermanence of their medium, have left little to exhibit their prowess, but the few surviving masks, idols, drums and *atl-atls*, or throwing boards, bear ample witness to their superb craftsmanship. The very fact that they had to work wood with stone tools makes their achievement noteworthy. Their copper tools were dull and unserviceable in cutting even the softer woods, and these implements came into use relatively late in Aztec times.[10] (See Plate 54, bottom.)

Wood was used extensively in buildings for roof beams and doorjambs. A beam in the palace at Texcoco was ninety feet long and five feet thick, so that its preparation and transport must have been an arduous task. There was probably little use of planks in Aztec building, since it would be difficult to prepare them with the rudimentary equipment at Aztec disposal, and adobes and plaster were easier to make and just as serviceable. Wooden canoes, however, were essential for life in the lakes. Some were dugouts hollowed out by fire, but others, to judge from the type used by the Xochimilcan

Indians today, were flat-bottomed punts, constructed of planks which were probably tied together in Aztec times rather than pegged, as they are today. The portable bridges used to cross the canals were also simple combinations of planks, or planks resting on beams. (See Plate 35, bottom left.)

Furniture, which in European culture has done much honor to the woodworker, was little used in Mexico. Mats sufficed for beds and seats. High dignitaries sat on a sort of wooden throne which had legs and often a back and was called *icpalli*, from which the Mexican word *equipale* for a modern wickerwork and leather chair is derived. Mention is made of screens and chests and ornamental sheathing for room interiors, but no examples are left for us to judge their craftsmanship. (See Plate 39, top right.)

The wooden drums, on which musicians beat out ceremonial rhythms, were handsomely carved, as befitted their religious use. There were two types, a vertically cylindrical drum (*huehuetl**), which had a skin head, and a horizontally cylindrical drum (*teponaztli†*), the top of which was slotted to form two tongues. While the notes differed, there was usually the same interval between the resonant sounds emitted when the tongues were struck. The task of reaching the pitch must have been excessively difficult, for the wood had to be hollowed by fire and then chiseled to a nicety. At times the artist fashioned these drums to represent a crouching man or animal. Masks were often used in temple ceremonies when a god was impersonated, and ceremonial staffs were part of this equipment. So, also, were the throwing boards, or *atl-atls*, with which a warrior flung a javelin, the lengthen-

*way-wa'ytl.   †te-po-na'z-tli.

ing of the arm thereby giving the missile an increased propulsive force. Some of these *atl-atls* were most delicately carved and represent the best of Aztec design. (See Plate 54, bottom.)

Metallurgy was in its infancy. Copper was cold-hammered; the art of adding alloys to make bronze had not reached Mexico from the south, but the gilding of copper and mixing of gold and copper were adopted by Mexican goldsmiths. Copper was cast into bells and ornaments, and the process, used also for gold, was the cire-perdue, or lost-wax, method. The desired shape was modeled in clay, over which was dusted finely ground charcoal, followed by an even layer of wax. This coating was also dusted with charcoal and the whole enclosed in clay, which was perforated at the top and bottom. The molten metal was poured in at the upper hole after the wax was melted and the lower orifice plugged. When the metal cooled the cast was broken and the finished object removed.[11] (See Plates 46–47.)

Although most of the native goldwork found its way to the Spanish melting pot, a few lovely ornaments survived; in 1932 the quantity was more than doubled by Dr Alfonso Caso's discovery of the undisturbed tomb of a high Mixtec official. The design and shape of these necklaces, earplugs and rings, by their sheer intricacy and bulk, make one realize that the Spanish descriptions of Cortes' loot understated the rich ability of the Aztec goldsmiths.[12]

Metalworking, without much question, had its origin in Ecuador or Peru, and various techniques were transmitted up the Pacific coast to Panama and Costa Rica, where important goldworking industries were founded. Although the intervening area produced little metal, another center was

established in Oaxaca in Mixtec times. The Oaxacan ornaments, although deficient in some of the southern technical
developments, surpass in design and workmanship the best
of the older goldwork of Peru and Ecuador.[18]

Metallurgy seems to have arrived late in Mexico, certainly
not before the eleventh century. Mentions of copper in Toltec times refer more probably to the Dynastic Period than
to that of Teotihuacan. I know of neither copper nor gold
which comes from the early or middle periods of the great
Middle American civilizations, although some hollow clay
bells from the late Toltec occupation of Azcapotzalco tan-
talizingly suggest metal prototypes. Toward the close of the
Independent Civilization phase, and more especially during
the domination of Mixteca-Puebla culture, there are con-
sistant occurrences of metal objects.

Mining methods were rudimentary. Gold was collected
in nugget form or panned as dust; copper also was mined
as nodules or nuggets; silver, which seldom occurs pure in
nature, was for this reason rarely converted into ornaments.
The melting furnaces were heated with charcoal and their
draft forced by a man blowing on the embers through a
tube. The casting we have already described. This work in
gold, one of the great wonders of the Conquest, was achieved
by the same simple methods of all Aztec handiwork and was
another triumph of sheer skill, unassisted by technical aids.

Pottery making was the greatest New World craft, and
probably no other continent has such a complex range of
form and design. The pliability of clay made it easy to
work, and firing was simple, so that pottery products were
an important part of Indian craftsmanship. In the Valley of
Mexico we have no trace of people before the introduction

of pottery, and in the chapters in Indian history we have seen how every tribe, almost every village, had its own particular style, which changed gradually through slow shifts in the popular taste as time wore on. In the absence of written records the archaeologists fortunately have been able to rely on pottery styles to peg out in time and space the relationships of these ancient and forgotten tribes and thus lay a basis for New World history.[14]

The Aztecs, like all the other New World peoples, did not use the potter's wheel but built up their vessels with strips of clay, relying on their keen eye and sensitive fingers to achieve the desired shape. They did not use molds to form their vessels, as was occasionally done in late Teotihuacan times; nor, apparently, did they make use of the *kabal*, a block on which Yucatecan potters rested their vessels and which they turned with their feet in shaping the raw clay.

The Aztecs had an abundance of finely textured clay, orange after firing, from which they fashioned vessels for the storage and service of food. The potters of Culhuacan used this ware first, making plates with flat bottoms resting on cylindrical legs.[15] On the floors they painted curvilinear designs which were sometimes faintly naturalistic. In the second period, when the manufacture of this ware became popular all over the northern Valley, the vessels were made more coarsely, and the hollow legs degenerated to thick, elongated cones.[16] The decoration was converted into an abstract combination of curvilinear *motifs* that had the quality of European script writing. In contrast to the usual rectilinear quality of Middle American design, it may be more than a coincidence that the introduction of this style at the beginning of the fourteenth century was contemporaneous with the traditional date of the diffusion of picture writing by the peoples from the Mixteca. (See Plate 29, third row.)

The third phase of this style, made during the fifteenth century, saw a gradual conversion of the linework into crude, continuous patterns, but the construction of the vessels proper was much finer.[17] A few potters rejected this slovenly manner and drew elaborate geometric designs. The closely parallel lines in some of these patterns were done freehand on the curved interior surfaces of the bowls, revealing extraordinary control in draftsmanship. Perhaps in trade, perhaps in tribute, many foreign vases were introduced at this time and stimulated the local potters to develop new styles of their own.

In the fourth period, during the chieftaincy of Montezuma, the potters broke away from these extremes of concentrated meticulousness and slovenly linework. Naturalism found favor, with birds, fish and plants used as designs and executed with that careless finesse of brushwork which characterizes Japanese sepia drawing. After the Conquest draftsmen accustomed to working in this style were able to copy accurately such elements of Spanish design as the double eagle of Charles V and the coats of arms of nobles.[18] (See Plate 32, top.)

Polychrome pottery was made locally, usually consisting of a red slip, or wash, adorned with a geometric design in black and white. Coarse construction with painfully careful, if crude, draftsmanship characterized the fourteenth-century ware. In the fifteenth century the hands of the potters loosened so that they were able to paint more sophisticated designs on vessels as thin and delicate as any pottery ever made in the Americas. Trade wares were rare at first and emanated chiefly from Puebla, but in the fifteenth century the quality and quantity increased, indicating the effects of trade and tribute. The historical reports that Texcoco was culturally superior to Tenochtitlan are borne out by archaeology; the Texcocan wares, although following the same styles as the Tenochcan, were better made and had a greater variety of design. Also there is evidence of more trade with foreign tribes.[19] (See Plates 30–32.)

Goblets were made for pulque; graters were made for grinding chilis, and clay vessels were made for every conceivable use; one form was a small oval platter with a special compartment for sauce, resembling the "blue-plate special" dishes of our modern restaurants. The circular roaster or griddle for cooking tortillas came in with Mazapan culture and continued to be popular through Aztec times. The bottoms of griddles were roughened so that heat would penetrate rapidly and evenly to the dough on the smoothed upper surface.

Clay utensils had their use in weaving. The Aztec spinner rested the end of her distaff in exquisite little cups, often charmingly ornamented. Her spindle weights were also made of baked clay. In the fourteenth century these were heavy and had holes large enough for a heavy spindle. Often their burnished black or red surfaces were cunningly adorned with stamped or incised designs representing conventional patterns or human and animal figures. In the fifteenth century the spindle weights became much smaller, so that at times it is hard to distinguish them from beads. This reduction in size perhaps indicates the spinning of more delicate cotton threads.

The spindle weight, or whorl, has an important bearing

on discussions as to whether or not the Aztecs knew the
wheel. The weight had the function of a flywheel in accel-
erating the rotation of the distaff. The explorer Charnay
apparently mistook spindle whorls for wheels which might
have been attached to toy clay animals. His ingenuous explanation is not seriously considered today, for later research
has proved the existence of jointed dolls both in Toltec and
Aztec times. These had holes in their bodies through which
strings were passed, attaching the arms and legs, which were
similarly perforated. In 1940 Dr Stirling discovered some
clay animals which rested on rollers, tubes of clay probably
connected by wooden axles, socketed to holes in the legs.
This knowledge does not seem to have been put to any
efficient use. In the history of invention there are several
similar cases, notably the Chinese discovery of gunpowder.
They used it to make a noise in ceremonies, but not until
the Europeans took over the substance did its application
have any practical purpose.

In Aztec times stone sculpture was the usual medium used
in reproducing the human form. The figurine cult, which in
Middle Culture and Toltec times manifested the chief development of the plastic arts, became insignificant. The use
of the mold did not induce superior craftsmen to fashion
even the originals. Yet in these dull reproductions of gods
and goddesses there still lurks that ability to capture the
spark of essential vitality so characteristic of this field of art
in earlier times. Curiously enough, the goddesses, more
kindly and less ridden with abstract virtues than the gods,
usually awoke a response in these ancient idol makers that
resulted in perfectly charming little figures.[20] (See Plate 29,
bottom row.)

Pottery was not confined to household chattels; great roof ornaments of baked clay were made to adorn the temples. Sun-dried adobes were commonly used for general house construction. However, they were sometimes fired into bricks which formed the back walls of fireplaces or were substituted for dressed stone in the corners of buildings. A temple at Tizatlan carries brick construction in the pillars before the altar, but rubble faced with cut stone was preferred as a general building material for temples. Before the great temples, braziers the height of a man combined ritualistic usefulness with architectural ornament. Cones of baked clay were used as studding to keep the plaster from slipping off the temple walls and to serve as a decorative element as well.[21]

The Mexican crasftsman had at hand an abundance of good pottery clay, which from the earliest times provided a medium for plastic experiment and experience. Work in clay created the background for that sureness and security in creation that stands out in the later Mexican sculpture in stone and wood. According to our Western standards, clay is a substance inferior to wood or stone for plastic expression. However, the ancient Mexicans, like the old Chinese, considered it fit for the finest examples of their arts and crafts.

Mexican craftsmanship, whatever the tribe and whatever the era, was superb in that it answered the necessities and ideals of both the time and the people. There is little evidence of a wide gap between superior and inferior workmanship, as in our Western civilization, where there is less need or opportunity for high-grade handwork. In unindividualized societies the general skills of the tribesmen, so far as can be judged by their work, follow a more even course than in

elaborated and specialized groups. To turn such craftsmanship into art required a mere flick of the switch of social
demand. The arts, as considered in the next chapters, were
just projections of the craft background.

The measure of Aztec civilization cannot be gauged solely
by its technical achievements. The arts and crafts transcend
the products of Old World peoples at the same mechanical
level. The spirit of the Aztec people, as exemplified in their
religious art, soared to the lofty heights attained by the creators of all those ancient civilizations, like Egypt and Mesopo-
tamia, whose monuments reflect the glory of their builders'
religious devotion.

CHAPTER IX

THE FINE ARTS

*A consideration of those aspects of Aztec craftsman-
ship which we segregate as Fine Art*

THE AZTECS did not have a term for "fine arts," nor did
they speculate about aesthetics nor make objects to be con-
templated for their beauty alone. They had none of the
socially sterile attitudes toward art which we adopt in our
own culture. Instead, they recognized the value of superior
workmanship and used its products to honor the gods who
were intermediaries between man and the infinite power of
the universe. Aztec art, in this respect, is no different from
the great traditions ancestral to our modern aesthetic. Religion
has always evoked man's best in thought and deed so long as
human society believed that religion was essential to its
survival.[1]

Aztec art was powerful in architecture and sculpture,
weak in painting and drawing. The dance was more advanced than music, and literature, in the absence of an effective method of writing, was confined to the evanescent out-
put of oratory. The years and the elements have left us only
such examples as could survive the ravages of time, and we
have no way, except by analogy with living groups, to ascertain the Aztec attitude toward their creations in those fields
of endeavor which we moderns dignify as art.

The most impressive expression of architecture was in religious building. Houses might have a fortuitous beauty of proportion, but the main consideration was adequate shelter. Public buildings of a secular character, like the clan house or the chief's quarters, were large-scale projections of the domestic architecture. The addition of many apartments for attendants and concubines, a swimming pool and a menagerie, such as composed the palace of Montezuma, did not alter structurally or in basic plan the scheme of rectangular rooms set about a patio.

The temple architecture, on the other hand, achieved real majesty. The great gods lived in the sky, so that their shrines and images were very naturally elevated above the level of worldly affairs. The climate contributed indirectly to the conversion of religious requirement into an impressive art form. It was not necessary to house the congregation or protect it from the weather. The altar or shrine alone needed to be elevated, and the worshipers stood in the plaza below. Thus the temple capped the substructure and was the culmination of a harmonious series of ascending planes, calculated to increase the illusion of height by emphasizing the effects of mechanical perspective.[2]

Such aesthetic canons were probably not laid down as laws but were reached after centuries of experimentation had produced a standard procedure. The earliest temple found in the Valley was Cuicuilco, of Upper Middle Culture date, where the altar was exposed upon a massive oval mound.[3] There is no trace of temple walls, and the use of fire precluded a canopy. However, at Teotihuacan, in the classical Toltec period, the temple had replaced the open altar, and in all probability it housed a representation of a god in wood or stone. In the whole of Mexico there is no more harmonious treatment of gigantic mass and planes than the substructure of the Temple of the Sun.[4] (See Plates 18, bottom; 22, bottom.)

The floors of the temple survive, though the roof and walls were destroyed long ago, but the illusion of infinite height and space still remains. The planes between its terraces are so cunningly calculated that the observer standing at the foot of the great staircase cannot see people at the top. He is conscious only of the massive ascent disappearing into space. When the stair was used by a religious procession, in all its pomp and color, the effect must have been stupendous. The elaborate hierarchy of a great civilization moved upward to meet, at a point unseen by the beholders, the infinity of the heavens, concentrated aloft in the god's image.

The plan of the sacred city of Teotihuacan was calculated to maintain the illusion of mass and height. The buildings were laid out in groups along a north-south axis, broken laterally by several precincts oriented to the east and west. From whatever angle one approached Teotihuacan the eye was led toward a point of interest, guided by the arrangement of the planes and masses. Thus the diminishing effect of distance was avoided. Within each precinct the surrounding walls insulated the observer from the rest of the city and emphasized the mass and height of the principal precinct temple. Not even the Pyramids of Egypt present so carefully calculated a plan to dominate the individual with the sheer weight of supernatural power. The modern visitor to Teotihuacan, now in ruins, cannot escape the ancient association of ideas that the greater his temple, the more powerful a god must be. (See Plate 22, top.)

Teotihuacan was probably the result of the co-operation of communities scattered over a large part of the Valley. Its scale and vastness could not have been achieved by a single resident community. In Chichimec times, when there was no central authority, each community built its temple or temples as best it could, and few survived. Tenayuca still has a temple of this period, the platform walls of which ascend almost vertically. Apparently shrines to two gods rested on the summit. At this same time, across the mountains in Puebla, the Cholulans were piling sun-dried brick on sun-dried brick to make a man-made mountain. So huge is this structure that the priests' quarters as well as the temple were located on top of one of the platforms. A large colonial church founded on the pyramid has obliterated evidence of the ancient temple proper, which tradition dedicated to Quetzalcoatl. It would seem logical to assume that the priests' houses were on a lower level than the shrine, since the tenets of Aztec religious architecture required a dominating position for the earthly residence of the god.[5] (See Plate 26.)

However, in the Valley of Mexico the communities prospered and their peoples multiplied. As resources and man power increased, the temples became larger and more numerous. Yet so complete was the destruction by the Spaniards and their Indian converts who transformed many a temple on its platform into a large parochial church, that the modern visitor finds little to suggest the architecture of the past. Archaeology has abundantly confirmed, in fragmentary form, the amazed descriptions of the conquerors.

The last two reconstructions at Tenayuca bear witness to the excellent proportions and dramatic principles of Aztec architecture. Excavations in the hill above the railway station at Cuernavaca revealed a temple intact in all except its roof. The temple of the Tepozteco, perched high in the hills over Tepoztlan,* is another nearly perfect example of Aztec architecture on a small scale. A pit sunk in a vacant lot across the street from the cathedral in Mexico City reached the corner between the stair and the western wall of the great temple of Huitzilopochtli, War God of the Aztecs, and the massive size and ornate decoration prove that the startled descriptions of the Spaniards did less than justice to this tremendous monument. A recent excavation in a cliff overhanging Malinalco, near Tenancingo, state of Mexico, brought to light a temple complex, largely hewed from living rock, which thrusts the famous Egyptian rock tombs of Abu-Simbel into the limbo of provincial opera-house scenery.[6] (See Plates 28, bottom; 37, top; 50–51.)

The Aztec temple had a platform, the sloping sides of which were generally broken by three terraces. A steep, broad stair flanked by balustrades, occasionally with a third dividing it into two, gave access to the top. Carved stone blocks, projecting in rows from the sides of the platform, represented snakeheads, skulls or some other symbolic form of the cult. At the foot of the balustrades huge serpent heads with gaping jaws added to the architectural design and created awe in the beholder. The stair rose broad and steep, focusing the attention on the sacrificial block at the top, over which victims were stretched to await the searching knives of priests.

Behind the block stood the temple or temples, which generally had a back room for the idol and an antechamber for the priests. The walls were usually of dressed stone and

*Te-pos-tla'n.

sometimes ornamented with carving or relief. The roof,
which was thatched in poor or primitive temples, in important shrines was made of beams laid like a corncrib, growing smaller toward the top. Plaster laid on twigs or poles
sealed the roof against the rain and was carved with designs
symbolic of the god inside. The interiors were noisome
places, coated with blood and smoke, for incense was burned
in profusion, as were the hearts of sacrificed victims. The
proportions of terrace to terrace, temple to platform, stair
to façade, were maintained irrespective of size, producing
an effect of height and mass which yet in no way detracted
from either the platform or the temple. This sense of proportion extends into every aspect of Aztec art and craftsmanship.

Some temples were cylindrical and rested on square or
circular platforms.[7] These were dedicated to Quetzalcoatl,
often represented as Ehecatl,* God of the Wind, to whose
passage a rounded surface offered no obstacle. Sometimes
the door of such a temple was fashioned in the form of a
serpent head, while the circular building suggested its body.
A superb temple of this type is part of the Malinalco group
mentioned above, which is hollowed out of the living rock.
The door is carved at either side in low relief to suggest a
serpent head in profile, while the whole also can be visualized
as a snakehead in full face, of which the open mouth constitutes the door. A bench circles around the walls within,
and the *skins* of eagles and ocelot, emblematic of the rising
and setting sun, are carved in relief as if they hung from the
wall to drape over the bench. An altar in the center of the
room represents another eagle. This elaborate concept is

*Ay'-hay-catl.

carved from the solid rock cliff and is a marvelous blend of architectural design and sculptural skill.[8]

The Aztec sculptors worked in relief and in the round, in heroic and in miniature size, and were equally able in symbolic and naturalistic conceptions, which they could execute in whatever medium was available. Our modern appreciation of their work is hampered by the prominence of religious *motifs*, which often detract by crowded detail or grotesque fantasy from the clean lines of their basic proportions. Aztec art, we have insisted, was never completely secular. Yet, in compensation, the Aztecs allowed a lively appreciation of natural elements to enter purely religious conceptions wherever possible.

From the time of the Middle Cultures the Mexicans used baked clay extensively for sculpture and worked out in it their artistic standards. The few surviving examples of wooden sculpture suggest that this medium was carved in accordance with stone techniques and did not, as in Egypt and Greece, serve as a training ground for standards later transferred to stone. If anything, the plastic methods of Mexico had their origin in a long and continuous handling of clay. Both media entail an emphasis on surface and contour; and the technical process of reducing stone by pecking and polishing, if more laborious, is not, in the last analysis, very different from the final smoothing and finishing of a work in clay. Thus the sculptors achieved a delicate appreciation of the contours and lines of the human form.

Partly owing to the past tradition and partly because the images of the gods were set in the temples, the Aztec artists showed their figures in passive attitudes, more often seated than erect. The austerity of their life led the Aztecs to attribute similar attitudes to their gods, and, as a result, the soft emotionalism so characteristic of European art is almost totally absent. Thus Aztec sculpture is even more forbidding and gloomy than other Middle American arts, which have at first a depressing effect on observers accustomed to Old World aesthetics.[9] (See Plates 40, 49, 52–56.)

The same sense of proportion so evident in Aztec architecture produced a monumental quality in their sculpture. The smallest piece has the same dignity that attends the most massive temple carvings. A photograph reveals no impression of the original scale, and in one case the head of a goddess was carved identically in a small piece of jade and a four-foot block of basalt, with no loss of plastic or monumental values to either.[10]

In relief sculpture the forming of the object and the disposition and subordination of details show the mastery of design inherited by eyes trained in centuries of weaving. The vast block of the thirteen-foot Calendar Stone is carved with as delicate an appreciation of the relative values of space as similar designs painted on pottery vessels or graven on jade. (See Plate 52.)

The finest Aztec sculpture, to the Western eye, reproduces the young gods and goddesses that presided over the crops. Thus the Aztec body, long of trunk, short of limb, softly rounded in its well-fleshed strength, is simply and accurately portrayed with passive grace. The patient and resigned features were perfect subjects for the sculptor and his medium. Some gods could assume the guise of animals, and the sculptors took full advantage of their close observation of nature to carve a coyote with ear atilt or to dignify a red basalt grasshopper with the armored malevolence of an insect

in heroic scale. The serpent, emblem of Quetzalcoatl, symbol
of time and the year, representative of mystery and power,
was frequently carved. The sinuous curves ending in the
savage symmetry of the head offered a challenge which the
sculptors accepted with a success that evokes the mysterious
horror of the Aztec universe. (See Plates 53, 56.)

The grotesque gods are abstract and horrible to our modern eye. Coatlicue,* the "Lady of the Serpent Skirt" and
mother of Huitzilopochtli, was thought of as powerful and
awesome, so the task of the sculptors was to transmute those
qualities into stone. The great statue in Mexico, whose head
is twin serpents, whose necklace human hands and hearts,
whose feet and hands are viciously armed with claws and
whose skirt is a mat of writhing snakes, brings into a dynamic
concentrate the manifold horrors of the universe. A smaller
carving, simpler and less detailed, produces this same effect,
implying that the very essence of fear was honored and worshiped. An altar of red lava, dug up in the street behind the
cathedral, is grimly adorned with ranked skulls, but the design
is so harmonious that death becomes an abstraction, part of a
distant universe of fear, and not the imminent individual disaster which besets us moderns. (See Plates 54–55.)

The Calendar Stone embodies a finite statement of the
infinity of the Aztec universe. In the center is the face of
the Sun God, Tonatiuh, flanked by four cartouches which
singly give the dates of the four previous ages of the world
and together represent the date of our present era. The
twenty names of the days circle this central element, and
they, in turn, are ringed with a band of glyphs denoting jade
or turquoise, which give the idea of being precious and sym-

*Co-at-le'e-kway.

bolize the heavens and their color. This strip is girdled by
the signs for stars, through which penetrate designs emblematic of the rays of the sun. Two immense Fire Serpents,
symbolic of the Year and Time, circle the exterior to meet
face to face at the base. Boring back through these forms to
the significance behind them, we have a grandiose conception of the majesty of the universe.[11] (See Plate 52, top.)

In recent years, under the Presidential Palace in Mexico
City, a monolith over a meter high was found, which represented a platform and a stair crowned at the top by a similar
solar disk. Reliefs on the sides show Huitzilopochtli, God
of War, and Tezcatlipoca, God of the Smoking Mirror,
symbolizing the sacred war between night and day. Probably
the Calendar Stone was set up in much the same manner,
and it is tantalizing to think of the lost reliefs which explained and ornamented the great disk when it was in
position.[12] (See Plate 52, bottom.)

The historical accounts record that the Calendar Stone
was made in 1479 and the great eagle vase of Tizoc during
his rule from 1481 to 1486. A trough, extending from the
basin to the edge of the vase, has been explained as a drain
for blood to run out. However, the design is not keyed to
this drain, and the purpose of the basin is to burn hearts,
not to receive blood. Therefore, the furrow was probably
made by the Spaniards, who sought either to use the vase
as a nether millstone or tried unsuccessfully to smash it as
an example of idolatry.[13]

The dates of these two monuments indicate that this was
the time when Aztec civilization burst into flower. It is a
tribute to Aztec artists that, originally fettered by the more
lowly tasks of handicraft, they could accept the tremendous

economic, social and religious stimulation of their sudden rise to power as a license to convert craftsmanship into great religious art.

The Aztecs did not create their art forms or their religion, which seems to have seeped in from the Mixteca-Puebla country. There the religious manuscripts and the ritualistic concepts hewn in stone and painted on vases were more complex and better drawn than their Aztec equivalents. Unfortunately, as yet, archaeological investigation has not extended to more than a sampling of this potentially rich area of Mexican civilization. However, the Valley people, given the opportunity, eagerly accepted these forms and created their own versions of the parent art.[14] (See Plates 57, top; 58, 59.)

The same elements portrayed in stone monuments appeared in smaller objects. Wooden drums and *atl-atls* had relief carvings the equal of the temple ornaments in all except scale. The same divinities were graven in bone against a background of turquoise mosaic. The goldworkers reproduced in miniature the images of the gods and goddesses and the symbols of their cult, carrying out in costume ornament the elements of the ritual in which they were used. Lapidaries succeeded in reducing jade, obsidian, rock crystal, opal, moonstone and amethyst into tiny sculptures which carry the same emotional authority as the grand-scale art. The bulk of first-rate material is enormous. It would seem that the products of tribal craftsmanship had been raised en masse into arts. Virtually overnight a cluster of primitive villages had transformed themselves into great creative centers.[15] (See Plates 45–48; 55, bottom left.)

Painting and drawing did not reflect this transmutation.

True, we have recovered a few examples, but they come from sources which produced fine sculpture. The surviving frescoes at Tizatlan and Malinalco are in no way superior to the drawings in the codices or manuscripts. The use of color is lavish, but the drawing is crabbed and conventional, confining itself to correct delineation of ceremonial elements rather than to the combination of composition, perspective and color values into a significant emotional experience. Apparently the finer workers devoted themselves to sculpture, while drawing and painting, subordinated in the outward expression of ritual, fell to less skillful hands. Yet design was a requisite in a work in two dimensions, and, considered on this basis, the symmetrical disposition of the figures renders less serious the anatomical flaws and rigidity of presentation.[16] (See Plate 57, top.)

The pictographic annals often exhibit an engaging charm in the little historical scenes recorded. The humor cannot be entirely fortuitous. There is something inherently fascinating about drawing little men that impels a draftsman to humanize his figures with a resultant and welcome loss to their dignity. Even the supremely competent draftsmen who decorated the Egyptian tombs in the Fourth Dynasty could not resist a casual impishness. Aztec drawing was hardier than the sculpture and was able to survive until the close of the sixteenth century. The Indians copied old records, and some annals were carried on in the same style until 1560. The friars used Indian artists to illustrate reports on indigenous affairs, and there are several manuscripts in which Indian and European drawing methods are inextricably and delightfully mingled. Pictured history has always had its appeal, to which emphasis of the essential and the suppression of the irrelevant, implicit in drawing, largely contribute. In our present day, with all the superb methods of photographic recordings and reproductions, the comic strip has a vogue unparalleled in our history.[17] (See Plates 62, 63.)

Aboriginal music has largely disappeared. The friars quickly adapted the chants and dances of Europe to Indian needs and substituted Christian for Indian ritual practices, using song and dance as formulas easily understood by primitives. To judge from the instruments, Aztec music was strong in rhythm but lacking in tone. The two-tone and one-tone drums could emit sonorous rhythms, but the bone and clay flutes pipe pitifully and are not gauged to a fixed scale. The conch shell could be blown with varying notes, according to the intensity of the blast, although it was more suitable for summoning people than for making music. Whistles, rattles of clay and gourds, bells and shell tinklers enhanced the effect of carefully regulated rhythms. Notched bones, often human, were rasped with a stick and produced quite pleasant sounds. A strange type of drum, which seems to have been indigenous, had an amazing resonance attained by beating an inverted gourd floating in a large container of water.[18] (See Plates 39, bottom right; 61, middle right.)

The dance was highly important, but native steps seldom persist except in the most primitive outlying districts, for they were transformed by the friars into Christian patterns. The chroniclers describe dances of many types in which masses of people participated. It is impossible that the Aztecs, with their profound sense of design and form, should not have had elaborate rituals in which great bodies of people moved in complex patterns to complicated rhythms. Song was used to reinforce the ceremony, and the words of some chants survive without, alas, the musical notation. These dancers, acting out mythical events pertaining to the lives of the gods, must usually have been highly theatrical. Thus as with other peoples of the past, religious service fulfilled the function of the drama.[19] (See Plate 62, bottom left.)

The pictographic writing of the Aztecs was too simple to record a literature. However, the many references to oratory and the wealth of allusions and synonyms referring to the gods and goddesses give a picture of rich fantasy and poetic imagination. The emphasis on the spoken word, the complex background of the religion, the closeness of the supernatural world, would not have produced lean, accurate prose. Rather a semipoetic, highly symbolic verbiage came from the practice of oratory and the chanting of prayers. Thus a rhythmic and rich verbosity existed as a form of polite address that, given a system of writing, might have been transmuted into literature.[20]

These activities, which we sanction in our own culture under the terms of arts and letters and to the practitioners of which we assign honor as creative artists, were existent in Aztec society. The status of these practices, however, was very different from their position in our own culture. Much of that area of our own life divided up into the infinite gradation of commercial, legal and governmental pursuits fell within the span of the individual Aztec's normal social life. That energy and activity which we exhaust in religion, art, belles-lettres and science were combined by the Aztecs in the observance of their religious requirements. An understanding of the nature of their religion and its position in Aztec life and social practice is fundamental to a realization of the nature of their culture.

CHAPTER X

RELIGION

A brief survey of the Aztec universe and the unpro-
nounceable gods and goddesses who presided over it
and ruled men's fate

Aztec religion, in purpose and practice, tried to attract those natural forces which are favorable to human existence and repulse those which are harmful. Ethical control and spiritual perfection fell within the province of social custom, so that the moral goals of our own religion were largely absent; the Aztec religion had no Savior of mankind, no heaven or hell to reward or punish the consequence of human behavior.[1]

The Aztecs and their forebears believed that the forces of nature acted for good or evil very much as does mankind, so that it was logical for them to personalize the elements as gods or goddesses. The process of worship entailed offering presents, uttering prayers and performing symbolic acts to induce the divine powers to operate for the public benefit. The tribal intellect was mobilized, as it were, to sort out the processes of nature, find out how they acted and devise magical procedures or rituals to win them to action favorable to man.

Nature operates in series of recurrences which give the effect of rhythms. Birth, maturity and death follow relent-

lessly in human life; night succeeds day; the stations of the
year rotate endlessly through spring, summer, fall and winter; the planets move in eternal sequence through the sky.
Thus to discover what those rhythms were and follow their
complicated but regular beat would, in Aztec philosophy,
ensure the happy survival of the community. There was
little thought of the perfection of the individual when vast
powers hovered close, ready to destroy the whole tribe if
it ceased its vigilant watch on nature. Thus rhythm and form
become an essential part of worship and found their outlet
in ritual and religion, art, philosophy and science.

The growth of civilization, with the resultant ramification
of social function and material equipment, led likewise to a
more complex perception of the universe, expressed in the
stratification of gods and goddesses and a specialization of
their functions. This result led to a more intense observance
of ritual, which consumed a great part of the material and
intellectual product of the tribe.

Aztec religion was an outgrowth of the recognition and
fear of natural forces and the attempt to constrain them. The
process by which man defines these forces and grades them
in order of importance is as much a part of the evolution
of culture as art, mechanics or social organization. The
Aztecs developed a conception of the relationship of the
supernatural forces to the universe that, given the precision
of our method of thought, could have been developed into
an imposing philosophy.

According to Aztec belief, the world passed through four
or five ages, or Suns. Details differ, but the record on the
great Calendar Stone may be taken as the official version in
Tenochtitlan. The first era, Four Ocelot, had Tezcatlipoca

as the presiding god, who, at the end, transformed himself into the sun, while jaguars ate up the men and giants who then populated the earth. Quetzalcoatl was the divine ruler of the second era, Four Wind, at the expiration of which hurricanes destroyed the world and men were turned into monkeys. The Rain God, Tlaloc, gave the world light in the third epoch, Four Rain, brought to a close by a fiery rain. Chalchihuitlicue,* "Our Lady of the Turquoise Skirt," was a Water Goddess who presided appropriately over the fourth Sun, Four Water, wherein a flood came, transforming men into fish. Our present age, Four Earthquake, is under the control of the Sun God, Tonatiuh, and it will be destroyed, in time, by earthquakes.[2] (See Plate 52.)

While the versions vary from place to place, we seem to have a recapitulation of the great disasters from flood, volcanic eruption, hurricanes and earthquakes that beset the communities of ancient Mexico. Also there is a reflection of the order in which the gods attained prominence in the local worship. In the history of the Mexican tribes there are references to struggles within single towns between the devotees of two cults, as to which would have the mastery.[3]

The universe itself was conceived in a religious rather than a geographic sense and was divided horizontally and vertically into areas of religious significance. The horizontal universe, possibly the older concept, recognized five directions, the four cardinal points and the center. The Fire God, old and fundamental in Mexican religion, controlled the central zone. The east was assigned to the Rain God, Tlaloc, and the Cloud God, Mixcoatl (Cloud Snake), and was a region of abundance. In this idea geography was combined with

*Chal-chee-we'et-le-kway.

ritual, since the intensely fertile Vera Cruz coast plain is the actual source of the seasonal rains caused by the condensation of warm air when the Gulf of Mexico is exposed to the chill winds of the Central Plateau. The south was considered evil, possibly because of the arid zones south of Morelos and Puebla, but had as presiding deities gods associated with spring and flowers, Xipe (the Flayed One) and Macuilxochitl* (Five Flower). The west, however, had a favorable significance, being the home of the planet Venus, the evening star, which was associated and even identified with Quetzalcoatl (Feathered Serpent), the God of Knowledge. The north was a place gloomy and awful, presided over by Mictlantecuhtli† (Lord of the Dead), who, in one of those contradictions so frequent in Mexican theology, was sometimes connected with the south as well.[4] (See end papers.)

The vertical world was divided into heavens and hells which had no moral significance, being merely overworlds and underworlds. The number of heavens varied up to thirteen and represented the dwelling places of the gods, according to their rank in the hierarchy, the original creator living in the topmost heaven, and so on down the scale. One of these heavens belonged to Tlaloc, who received those who died by drowning, lightning or other causes connected with water. One school of thought divided the heavens into east and west, according to the passage of the sun. The east was the home of warriors, whose death in battle or sacrifice nourished the sun, and the west the home of women who died in childbirth, thus sacrificing themselves in the bearing of potential warriors.[5] (See Plate 57, bottom right.)

The rest of the dead passed to Mictlan, the underworld.

*Ma-kweel-sho'-chitl.   †Meek-tla'n-tay-coot-li.

PLATE 33

PROCESSION OF NOTABLES, DOING HONOR TO MONTEZUMA

This drawing by Keith Henderson, in the Henry Holt Edition of Prescott's *Conquest of Mexico*, was adapted from native picture records. The artist reconciles the crabbed fidelity of the Indian drawing with our own representational standards.

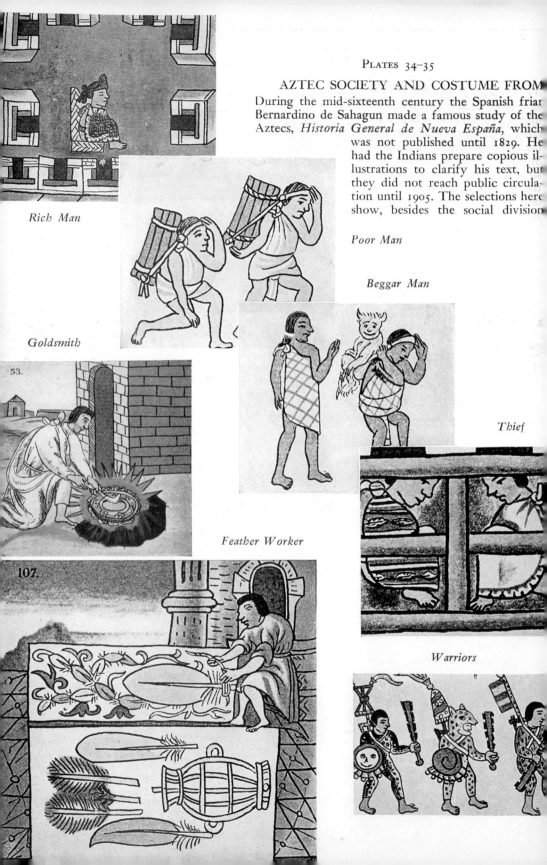

Rich Man

AZTEC SOCIETY AND COSTUME FROM

During the mid-sixteenth century the Spanish friar
Bernardino de Sahagun made a famous study of the
Aztecs, *Historia General de Nueva España*, which
was not published until 1829. He
had the Indians prepare copious illustrations to clarify his text, but
they did not reach public circulation until 1905. The selections here
show, besides the social division

Poor Man

Beggar Man

Goldsmith

Thief

Feather Worker

Warriors

THE CODEX FLORENTINO

expressed in our nursery rhyme: "Rich man, poor man . . ." various other activities, caught with a fresh and humorous eye. Although some of the background details indicate that Spanish influence was already strongly felt a generation after the Conquest, the general details disclose a strong persistence of the Aztec way of life.

Chief

Lawyer

Merchant

Women

Doctor

Sailor, beware

Ant Bite

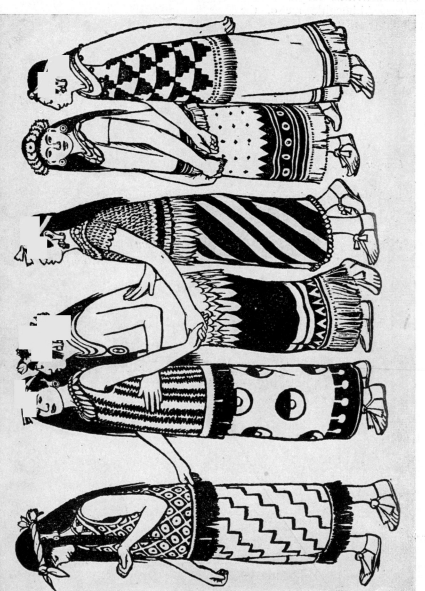

PLATE 36

AZTEC WOMEN

Rich embroidery enlivened the simple dress of Aztec women, as shown in this drawing by Keith Henderson. The measure of this artist's accuracy may be taken by comparing this plate and Plate 33 with the Codex Florentino paintings on Plates 34–35.

PLATE 37

THE AZTECS' MEXICO

TOP: Ignacio Marquina's reconstruction of Tenochtitlan as it was in 1519. The reader looks slightly southeast. At the left looms the great temple; at the right stands the skull rack; in the foreground is the northern canoe basin. Left and right of the great temple may be seen the palaces of Axayacatl and Montezuma. The sacrificial stone, and behind it a round temple to the Wind God, Ehecatl-Quetzalcoatl, occupy the middle distance. BOTTOM: The "floating gardens" of Mexico are much the same today as in pre-Conquest times. Xochimilco, where this picture was made, is occupied by the same Aztec-speaking people who lived there before the Tenochcas ever entered the Valley.

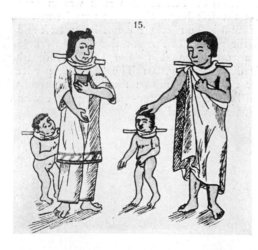

PLATE 38

AZTEC ECONOMICS AS SEEN IN THE CODEX FLORENTINO

TOP ROW: A farmer plants his corn, using a digging stick, and later he and his wife store the harvest for the winter. Basic farming methods still persist among the modern Indians. MIDDLE ROW: *Left:* A produce market, which recalls the neatly arranged wares of a modern Indian vendor. *Right:* King Ahuitzotl receives produce of the coast: shells, jaguar skins, plumage, jade and cacao. BOTTOM ROW: *Left:* Members of a slave family wearing bars across their necks as a sign of bondage. *Right:* A merchant from the coast chaffers for such Highland products as cloth, gold ornaments, copper, obsidian tools and maguey-fiber rope.

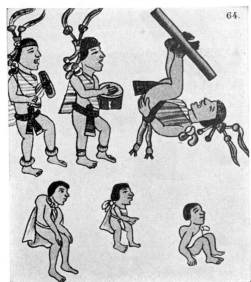

PLATE 39

SOCIAL OBLIGATIONS, RE-WARDS AND PUNISHMENTS

TOP: *Left:* Boys are taken by their fathers to the school or *Calmecac.* These people are of the poorer classes. *Right:* Four chiefs sentence criminals to death by noose and clubs for outrageous crimes. MIDDLE: *Left:* Warriors of proven worth engage in ceremonial combat. They wear the costume of warriors' orders or of chiefs. *Right:* A tribal ruler invests two leading men with badges and trappings of rank. BOTTOM: *Right:* Montezuma had professional entertainers, hunchbacks, jugglers and musicians.

PLATE 40

EAGLE KNIGHT, NATIONAL MUSEUM

This head represents the ideal warrior, steadfast, hardy and devout. The "very parfit gentle knight" of the Middle Ages would meet his peer in this noble Aztec. *Photograph by Sunami.*

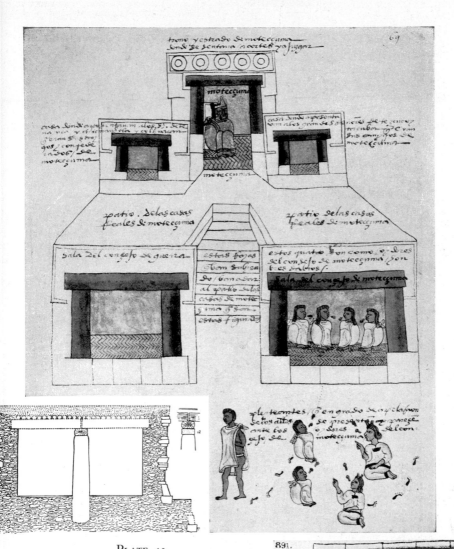

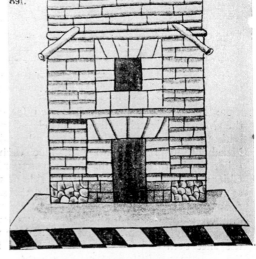

PLATE 41

AZTEC ARCHITECTURE

Top: Montezuma's palace, from the Codex Mendoza. His apartments are on a platform reached by a stair. At right and left are rooms for allied chiefs, such as the rulers of Texcoco, Culhuacan, Chiconauhtla, Tlacopan and Tenayuca. The left-hand room on the first floor is reserved for the war council and the quarters at the right are for the judges, who may be seen settling a case between several litigants. Middle: *Left:* Section through a temple at Mitla showing details of Aztec construction. Bottom: A two-story house of probable post-Conquest date. The palace above with ascending platforms shows the customary Aztec method of elevating rooms.

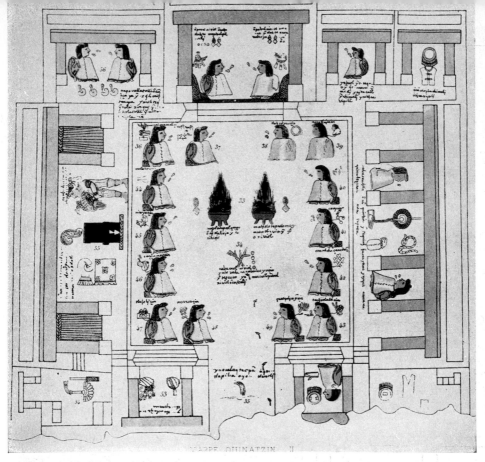

AZTEC ARCHITECTURE

TOP: An Aztec palace at Texcoco from the Mapa Quinatzin, drawn in elevation without perspective. Nezahualcoyotl and Nezahualpilli, father and son, face each other in the throne room. In the courtyard sit vassal chieftains, including the chief of Chiconauhtla (No. 46). The right side of the court is walled by storehouses for tribute; at the left is a temple, designated by the scribe as a hall of science and music. The top rooms are for the judges (*left*) and the arsenal (*right*). The bottom rooms house the war council and visiting ambassadors. BOTTOM: *Left:* House of wattle and daub, still used in Mexico. *Right:* A chief's house with adobe walls on stone foundations, wooden pillars for the anteroom and fresco painting on the façade.

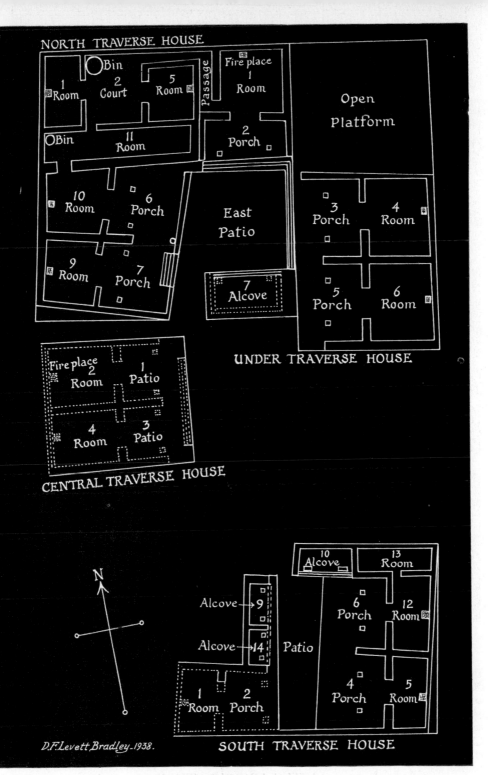

NORTH TRAVERSE HOUSE

UNDER TRAVERSE HOUSE

CENTRAL TRAVERSE HOUSE

SOUTH TRAVERSE HOUSE

D.F.Levett Bradley.1938.

PLATE 43

AZTEC ARCHITECTURE

Palace at Chiconauhtla. Note how closely the plan resembles that of the Texcocan palace on Plate 42.

PLATE 44
AZTEC ARCHITECTURE

The Lienzo Chalchihuitzin Vasquez shows the chief and the founder of his line in the central house. The topmost row of figures discloses his descent, and the smaller houses joined to his palace by roads are those of his subjects. The people in the two large houses at lower right and left are allies. Post-Conquest painting on cloth.

PLATE 45

AZTEC FEATHERWORK

Top: Nineteenth-century survival of a famous Aztec craft of which few examples have resisted the ravages of time. Bottom: Montezuma's headdress, now in the Vienna Museum. Cortes sent it to the Emperor Charles V, who gave it to his nephew.

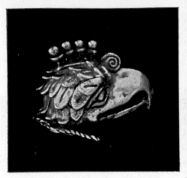

PLATE 46

AZTEC GOLDWORK

TOP ROW: Small gold ornaments from Oaxaca reveal exquisite workmanship. MIDDLE: A buckle representing the god Xipe has a strong sculptural quality. BOTTOM: *Left:* A gold worker from the Codex Florentino makes a mosaic ornament like that at right, in which turquoise mosaic enhances a gold reproduction of the shield and arrows, constituting the sign for war.

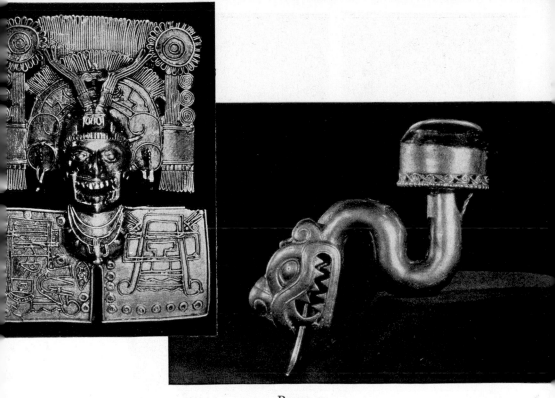

PLATE 47

AZTEC GOLDWORK

Almost all Aztec goldwork went into the Spanish melting pot. Most surviving examples come from Oaxaca, where the supply was doubled by Caso's discovery of Tomb 7 at Monte Alban, represented by upper left and bottom and opposite-page middle. The lip ornament (*upper right*) has a movable tongue that makes a very lively serpent indeed. These few examples give an idea of the range of form and skill of the Aztec goldsmith.

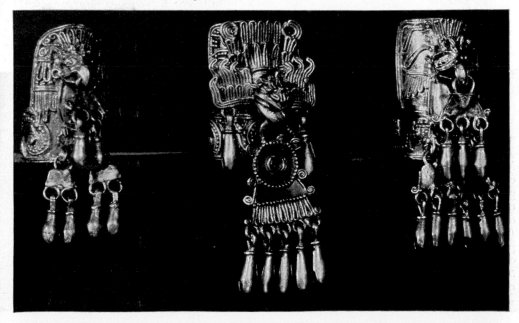

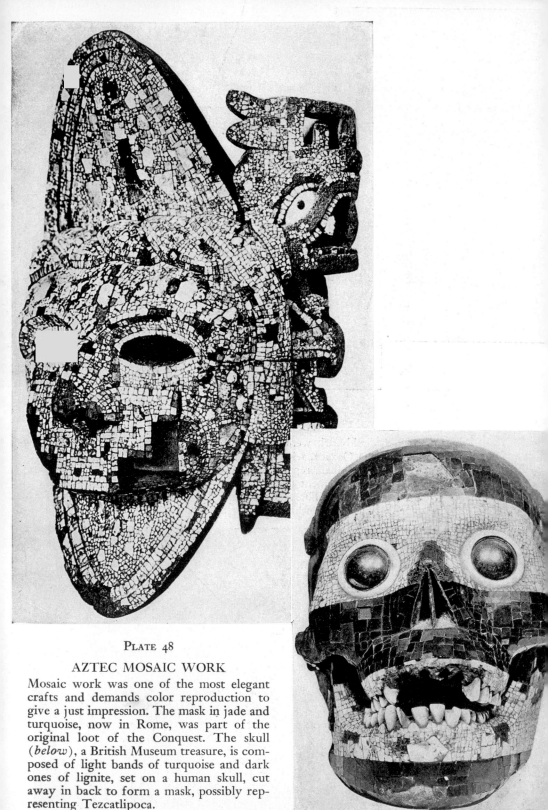

PLATE 48

AZTEC MOSAIC WORK

Mosaic work was one of the most elegant crafts and demands color reproduction to give a just impression. The mask in jade and turquoise, now in Rome, was part of the original loot of the Conquest. The skull (*below*), a British Museum treasure, is composed of light bands of turquoise and dark ones of lignite, set on a human skull, cut away in back to form a mask, possibly representing Tezcatlipoca.

They had to overcome several hazards before they could take up their life there, so they were equipped with charms and gifts for the journey, which took the sacred number of four days. The wayfarer had to travel between two mountains which threatened to crush him, avoid first a snake and then a monstrous alligator, cross eight deserts, surmount eight hills and endure a freezing wind which hurled stones and obsidian knives upon him. Then he reached a broad river which he crossed on the back of a little red dog, sometimes included in the grave furniture for the purpose. Finally arriving at his destination, the traveler offered gifts to the Lord of the Dead, who assigned him to one of nine different regions. Some versions make the dead spend a probationary period of four years in the nine hells before they take up their life in Mictlan, which was, like the Greek Hades, devoid of moral significance.[6]

The Aztecs, as we have said, conceived of their universe as extending horizontally outward and vertically upward and downward. The world, as horizontally divided, implied the association of divine powers with the phenomena of geography and climate. This significance of direction is a familiar religious concept. The vertical arrangement of the heavens had rather more to do with rank and order than with a realization of natural phenomena. The hierarchy of the Christian saints, with its implicit recognition of position and authority, approaches closely to the point of view with which the Aztec peoples regarded their gods. Aztec and ritualized Christian worship have much the same attitude toward distinctions between philosophy and practice, and between the point of view of the instructed theologian and the humble worshipers.

At the head of the Aztec pantheon, in a theological sense, was a supreme and ineffable god, Tloque Nahuaque; but an active cult in his honor seems to have been restricted to a single temple, at Texcoco, which became a center of religious philosophy under the stimulus of the great chief, Nezahualcoyotl. Ranking below this abstraction of divine power and far more widely recognized was a supreme couple, Tonacatecuhtli* and Tonacacihuatl,† "Our Lord and Lady of Subsistence." These gods were theologically important and fulfilled the functions of parenthood and origin for other divinities. They were not extensively worshiped, since their control of nature was remote. An equivalent being, Ometecuhtli,‡ "Lord of Duality," occupied an analogous position, resulting from priestly speculation as to the ultimate origin of the gods who controlled man's destiny. The Sun God, Tonatiuh, who also discharged the functions of a heavenly overlord, was, however, more closely associated with the active expression of Aztec religion. The daily appearance of the celestial orb, so infinitely important to the existence of all life, made sun worship an essential part of the Aztec religion.[7]

There were several gods who intervened in human affairs and were venerated above all others. Usually one of this group was the tutelary spirit of a community and had arrogated to him supreme powers. Such a god was honored by the principal temple, synthesized the abstract position of the gods invented by the theologians and partook of all the supreme powers exerted by the chief god of other commu-

*To-na-ca-tay-co'o-tli.   ‡O-may-tay-co'o-tli.
†To-na-ca-se'e-watl.

nities. This group, without exception, was composed of sky gods.

Tezcatlipoca, the "Smoking Mirror," sometimes appeared on the scene as an adversary of the Toltec divinity Quetzalcoatl, the "Feathered Serpent." He was widely worshiped, and his powers were shared by other chief gods. His attributes, as depicted in the sacred manuscripts, showed him to be protean, and they were often assigned to the tribal divinities of other places. A Mixtec manuscript, which emanates from the probable center of the Tezcatlipoca cult, shows the same divinity presiding over the four directions but with a different color in each instance. The powers and dress of this great god passed to local tribal divinities with the spread of Mixtec religion and the Tezcatlipoca cult to the Valley of Mexico. (See Plates 57, top; 61, top.)

The red Tezcatlipoca of the west took the name of Xipe, or Camaxtli, the tutelary god of Tlaxcala. Huitzilopochtli, the great War God of the Tenochca, assumed the functions and dress of the blue Tezcatlipoca of the south and was a Sun God as well, but his adversary and opposite divinity of the night retained the name Tezcatlipoca and was shown as the black Tezcatlipoca of the north. Quetzalcoatl was sometimes depicted as a white Tezcatlipoca, associable with the east as a morning star and the west as an evening star. Under the name "Feathered Serpent" but with the attributes and powers of Tezcatlipoca, he presided over the destinies of Cholula. Tezcatlipoca, as god of a favorable region, as surrogate of the sun and as the chief god of the original cult, was the chief divinity worshiped at Texcoco.

Tlaloc, the Rain God, is an ancient god, going back to Toltec times. His eye rings, his fangs and the volute over his lips render him an easily recognized figure in the Mexican pantheon. At Tenochtitlan he shared the great temples with Huitzilopochtli, and his control of rain made the attraction of his powers essential to survival on the Mexican plateau. (See Plate 59, top left.)

Quetzalcoatl, the "Feathered Serpent," God of Civilization and the planet Venus, seems to have been widely venerated but under different guises. In contrast to Tezcatlipoca, whose functions and appearance were assigned to tribal gods with different names, Quetzalcoatl had several forms shared by distinctive divinities. The sculptures of Teotihuacan and Chichen Itza show that a feathered snake was honored, and the local records mention Quetzalcoatl and Kukulcan, Nahuatl and Maya names having the same meaning. At Tenochtitlan there is ample evidence of a feathered-serpent cult, but the records refer to Xiuhcoatl,* "Fire Snake," as well as to the standard sacred variety. The term Quetzalcoatl applies as well to a bearded god with a projecting mask, also called Ehecatl, the "Wind God." In parts of the Mixteca-Puebla area and the Valley, as we have seen, there is evidence that the "white" Tezcatlipoca had the name "One Reed," the date name synonymous with Quetzalcoatl.[8] (See Plates 23, 53; 59, top right.)

In addition to this confusion over Quetzalcoatl, the God of Civilization, the annals and myths tell of Quetzalcoatl, the great king, who civilized the Toltecs and left for the east to return again. The friars seized upon this myth as evidence that St Thomas the Apostle had visited Mexico and converted its inhabitants, who later slid back into pagan ways. Therefore, the friars, to justify the Conquest, made

*She'e-oo-co-atl.

much of a blond god who, after taking leave of his people, promised to return from the east by sea. Yet the Quetzalcoatl of the Valley of Mexico manuscripts was never blond but usually black in beard and face paint, when he was not shown as the masked Wind God, Ehecatl.

As if the confusion between a man and a god of many guises were not baffling enough for the historian, we find to our dismay that the title Quetzalcoatl not only was given to the rulers of the Teotihuacan Toltecs but also was borne at Tenochtitlan by the chief priests who exemplified the learning of the time. Distinguished authority has supported the hypothesis that a Mexican named Quetzalcoatl went to Yucatan where he attained high office and absorbed the civilization of the Maya. Later he returned to Mexico and taught a version of the calendar, as well as many other useful arts, to the peoples of the plateau. Others, more romantic, see in Quetzalcoatl an Irishman, Norseman or even Atlantean, who popped into Mexico and spread sweetness and light. I, personally, believe that the introduction of superior culture elements and the creation of local arts as well might not only lead to the invention of a God of Civilization but also endow individual innovators with the name of that god. The conflicting data suggest to me that the name and concept did not originate in any one person but resulted, rather, from the experience of many peoples over a long period of time in explaining and honoring the introduction of those benefits which ensured their corporal and spiritual well-being.

The great gods of the sky played an important part in the duality of the Aztec world in which an eternal war was fought symbolically between light and darkness, heat and cold, north and south, rising and setting sun. Even the stars were grouped into armies of the east and the west. Gladiatorial combats, often to the death, expressed this idea in ritual; and the great warrior orders, the Eagle Knights of Huitzilopochtli and the Ocelot Knights of Tezcatlipoca, likewise reflected the conflict between day and night. This Sacred War permeated the ritual and philosophy of Aztec religion.[9] (See Plates 39, middle left; 40.)

While the great gods, the chief deities of the tribe, tended to be associated with the heavens, there were many others who controlled growth and fertility. Often these gods had goddesses as wives or companions, as if the idea of reproduction of the male and female principles were dawning in Aztec theology. Tlaloc, the Rain God, held sway over growth and vegetation, and his companion Chalchihuitlicue, (Our Lady of the Turquoise Skirt), presided over lakes and rivers. This goddess was the center of an important cult and is represented as a charming young girl beautifully dressed. Xipe (the Flayed One) symbolized spring, and his distinctive costume, a human skin, represented the new covering of vegetation with which the earth clothes itself each year. His priests, at the ceremonies in his honor, carried this symbolism into their costume by donning the skins of freshly flayed captives. (See Plates 28, top left; 59, top left; 61, middle left.)

The corn goddesses were young and lovely and probably derived from the old cult of the Middle Culture goddesses. Chicomecoatl,* (Seven Snake), was the Goddess of Crops and Subsistence, represented by corn, the staple food. Xilonen,† "Young Corn Mother," and Xochiquetzal,‡ "Flower

*Chee-co'-me-co-atl.   ‡Sho-chee-kay-tza'l.
†Shee-lo'-nen.

Bird," were the embodied spirits of young growth and, by analogy, youth and the games. These had as male counterparts such gods as Cinteotl, "Maize God," Xochipilli,* "Flower Prince" and Macuilxochitl, "Four Flower," whose functions, identified with growth, youth and games, are almost synonymous. (See Plates 31; 56, top left; 57, bottom left.)

About the maguey plant revolved another cult embracing the goddess Mayauel, who represented the plant and whose four hundred sons were associated with pulque. According to some accounts, the various styles of drunkenness were recorded in terms of these gods or their associated animal, the rabbit. Four hundred rabbits stood for complete drunkenness, while fifteen or twenty suggested mere conviviality. The chief of these pulque gods was called "Two Rabbit," after his day in the almanac, and another, Tepoztecatl, was the tribal god of Tepoztlan, honored by a temple placed high in the mountains of Morelos.

The gods of the earth and death were highly important, since growth takes place in the earth and the dead are received there. The sun on rising seems to be born in the earth and at its setting to be hidden by it, thus passing apparently to the world of the dead. The gods and goddesses associated with the earth had significance for the solar cults as well as for growth and fertility.

Tlaltecuhtli, "Lord of the Earth," was depicted as a male monster of horrifying aspect, partaking of the attributes of a toad and an alligator. His open mouth could consume even the sun, since the setting sun passed into the earth, according to Aztec astronomical ideas. The goddesses, however, seem

*Sho-chee-pe'e-ly.

to have been worshiped more extensively, and the clay images made in their honor also continued in unbroken line the tradition of the Middle Culture figurines. Coatlicue (Our Lady of the Serpent Skirt) was the mother of the gods in their stellar aspect but also was honored as the mother of Huitzilopochtli. The measure of her importance may be gauged by the great statue of her in Mexico which is a masterpiece of sacerdotal art and undoubtedly had a temple to itself. Coatlicue was also represented as a mother carrying a child in her arms. In this guise her function as a mother goddess brought her image into almost every home in the valley. Tonantzin (Our Mother), which may have been an aspect of this same goddess or of Cihuacoatl (Snake Woman), had a temple at Tepeyac, now the site of the shrine to the Virgin of Guadalupe, and her cult was transferred to the Virgin by the early missionaries, an act exemplifying their intelligent procedure in evangelizing the Aztecs. A goddess, Tlazolteotl (Eater of Filth), was extensively worshiped and was also synonymously known as the "Mother of the Gods." Primarily an earth-goddess, she, alone of the goddesses, had a moral significance, since in eating refuse she consumed the sins of mankind, leaving them pure. A rite of confession developed in her cult. (See Plates 54–55.)

Standing out from the numerous divinities associated with death were Mictlantecuhtli and Mictlancihuatl,* (Our Lord and Lady of the Region of Death). They wore masks made from human skulls, and their ornaments were either human bones or representations of them. They presided over the northern regions and also ruled the hells below the earth. Theirs was no punitive function, for all who died, save in

*Meek-tlan-se'e-watl.

war or sacrifice, childbirth or drowning, passed upon death to their domain. (See Plate 55, bottom left.)

This incomplete description of the gods and goddesses who thronged the Aztec pantheon gives an idea of their variety of purpose and character, outlined more fully in Table X. For an individual to try to do honor to so many gods could result in an insupportable situation. Yet even the modern Navajos pass a third of their time in ceremonial activity, and they do not have half the economic wealth of the Aztec peoples. While the ancient Mexicans extended their ceremonialism to greater lengths than do the most ritualized Christian sects, yet the relationship between the Aztecs and their gods and the Christians and their saints is not so very dissimilar, different as are the ultimate concepts of the two religions.

The priests gave guidance and prescribed the ceremonies, and the worshipers gave heed to those especial divinities upon whose patronage their life directly depended, much as a devout Catholic selects certain saints for veneration above the list of those whose days are recorded on the calendar. In the same way the Aztec tribal god has his counterpart in the patron saint of country, town or craft. The Aztec, however, thought of his gods as having strong material powers, but their spiritual aspect counted little with him.

The ritual of Aztec religion was as complex as the theology. The organization of the priesthood followed the pyramided structure of the social order, but the ceremonies were worked out in accordance with the ritualistic requirements of the calendar and the seasons. In the following chapter we shall describe the priesthood, the ceremonies and also the Aztec methods of counting, recording and using time.

TABLE X

PRINCIPAL MEMBERS OF THE AZTEC PANTHEON, THEIR CHARACTER, AND SPHERES OF WORSHIP

	Month	Week	Day	Day Hour	Night Hour
GREAT GODS					
Huitzilopochtli, Hummingbird Wizard, War and Sun God, chief god of Tenochtitlan	5* 9 15				
Tezcatlipoca, Smoking Mirror, chief god of pantheon, solar attributes, chief god of Texcoco	5 12		13 8	10	
Quetzalcoatl, Feathered Serpent, God of Learning and of Priesthood, chief god of Cholula, frequently shown as Ehecatl, the Wind God		2	2	9	
CREATIVE DEITIES					
Tloque Nahuaque, Lord of the Close Vicinity, creative spirit, theological abstraction					
Ometecuhtli, Lord of Duality, like Tonacatecuhtli and his wife					
Tonacatecuhtli, Lord of Our Subsistence, Creator God, chief of the gods		1	1		
Tonacacihuatl, Lady of Our Subsistence, wife of the above					
FERTILITY GODS					
Tlazolteotl, Goddess of Dirt, Earth Mother, worshiped under many synonyms	11	13	14	5	7
Teteoinnan, Mother of the Gods, synonym of Tlazolteotl					
Ixcuina, Four Faces, synonym of Tlazolteotl					
Toçi, Our Grandmother, synonym of Tlazolteotl					
Chicomecoatl, Seven Snake, Corn Goddess, ancient goddess dating from Middle Culture times	4 11				
Cihuacoatl, Serpent Woman, Earth Goddess, ruling childbirth and death thereby					
Tonantzin, Our Mother, synonym of Cihuacoatl					
Coatlicue, Serpent Skirt, Earth Goddess, associated with spring, mother of Huitzilopochtli					
Cinteotl, Corn God, son of Tlazolteotl, husband of Xochiquetzal, important				(12) (7)	4
Xochiquetzal, Flower Feather, Goddess of Flowers, of Craftsmen, important		19	20	(13)	
Xochipilli, Flower Prince, God of Pleasure, Feasting, Frivolity			11	(3) 7	
Macuilxochitl, Five Flower, synonym of Xochipilli					

*The numbers refer to the *Tonalamatl* of the *Codex Borbonicus*. Those in parentheses refer to variations found in the *Tonalamatl Aubin* and the *Codex Telleriano-Remensis*.

182

TABLE X (*Continued*)

	Month	Week	Day	Day Hour	Night Hour
Xipe, Our Lord, the Flayed One, God of Seedtime and Planting, the red Tezcatlipoca, highly important	2	14	15	(11) (4)	
Xilonen, Young Maize Mother, Goddess of the Young Corn	8				
Ilamatecuhtli, the Old Princess, a goddess of ancient times, related to corn and the earth	17			13	

GODS OF RAIN AND MOISTURE

	Month	Week	Day	Day Hour	Night Hour
Tlaloc, He Who Makes Things Sprout, Rain God, very important	6 13	7	7	8	(8) 9
Tlaloques, minor rain gods, children or brothers of Tlaloc, a plural synonym	3 1 16				
Chalchihuitlicue, She of the Jeweled Robe, Water Goddess, very important	1	5	5	3	6
Huixtocihuatl, Salt Woman, Goddess of Salt and of the Dissolute	7				
Napatecuhtli, Four Times Lord, one of the Tlalocs					
Ehecatl, Wind, Wind God, a frequent guise of Quetzalcoatl					

FIRE GODS

	Month	Week	Day	Day Hour	Night Hour
Xiuhtecuhtli, Lord of the Year, Fire God, a divinity of ancient times, important	18 10	20 9	9	(7) 1	1
Huehueteotl, Old God, a synonym of Xiuhtecuhtli					
Chantico, In the House, goddess associated with the hearth and volcanic fire		18	19		

PULQUE GODS

	Month	Week	Day	Day Hour	Night Hour
Mayauel, She of the Maguey Plant, Goddess of the Maguey and also of Fertility		8	8		
Patecatl, He from the Land of Medicines, God of Medicine, husband of Mayauel		11	12		
Tezcatzontecatl, Straw-Covered Mirror, an important pulque god, identifiable with the Chac Mool figures in stone					
Centzon Totochtin, Four Hundred Rabbits, the many pulque gods					

PLANETARY AND STELLAR GODS

	Month	Week	Day	Day Hour	Night Hour
Tonatiuh, the Sun, Sun God with intimate connections with Huitzilopochtli and Tezcatlipoca				4	
Piltzintecuhtli, Young Prince, synonym of Tonatiuh					3
Metztli, the Moon, Moon God, sometimes identified with Tezcatlipoca					
Tecciztecatl, He from the Sea Snail, synonym of Metztli		6	6		(5)
Mixcoatl, Cloud Serpent, God of Stars and of Numbers	14				
Camaxtli, god of Tlaxcala, synonym of Mixcoatl, a War God					

TABLE X (*Continued*)

	Month	Week	Day	Day Hour	Night Hour
Itzpapalotl, Obsidian Knife Butterfly, stellar and also agricultural goddess		15	16		
Tlahuizcalpantecuhtli, Lord of the House of Dawn, Venus, the morning star, variant of Quetzalcoatl		9		(1) (12)	
Coyolxauhqui, Painted with Bells, Moon Goddess, sister of Centzon Huitznaua					
Centzon Huitznaua, 400 Southerners, star gods of south					
Centzon Mimixcoa, 400 Northerners, star gods of north					
Tzitzimime, Monsters Descending from Above, stellar gods					
GODS OF DEATH, EARTH					
Mictlantecuhtli, Lord of Region of Death, God of Death		10	10	11	5
Mictlancihuatl, Lady of Region of Death, wife of Death God					
Tepeyollotl, Heart of the Mountains, Mountain God, Jaguar God		3	3		8
Tlaltecuhtli, Lord of Earth, earth monster, personification of earth in contrast to sun				2	
Teoyaomiqui, God of Dead Warriors, a specialized Death God				6 (6)	
Huahuantli, the Striped, synonym of Teoyaomiqui					
VARIANTS OF GREAT GODS					
Itztli, Stone Knife, a surrogate of Tezcatlipoca in guise of sacrificial knife.		20			2
Itzlacoliuhqui, Curved Obsidian Knife, another variant of Tezcatlipoca		12	(13)		
Paynal, the Hasty, messenger of Huitzilopochtli					
Yacatecuhtli, Lord Who Guides, God of Traveling Merchants	15 12				
Chalchiuhtotolin, Jeweled Fowl, variant of Tezcatlipoca		17	(18)		
Yaotl, Enemy, synonym of Tezcatlipoca				(5)	
OTHER GODS					
Xolotl, Double, Monster God, twin of Quetzalcoatl		16	17		
Ixtlilton, Little Black Face, God of Health and Cures from Ills				(2)	
Cihuateteô, Goddesses, witches, spirits of women dead in childbirth					
Huehuecoyotl, Old Coyote, backbiter or mischief-maker, god of Otomi		4	4		

CHAPTER XI

RITUAL

*In which are Summarized the Nature of the Religious
Organization, the Feasts, and the Relationship between Ritual, Calendar and Writing*

RELIGION was a general group activity necessary for the
social and economic safekeeping of the tribe, and the priesthood was a highly important force in the direction of the
communal life. In the early simple societies there were two
executive chiefs, one for war and one for religious affairs.
We do not know whether the priesthood comprised laymen
who performed the ritual acts of specific ceremonies or
whether it was an established group whose whole life
was devoted to religious ends. It is probable that selected
individuals originally carried out the religious duties of the
tribe in addition to their civil obligations, but as Aztec culture became more elaborate, the complexity of their functions molded them into a body of permanent officials.[1]

In Tenochtitlan the Chief of Men and the Snake Woman
had double duties in respect to civil and religious affairs, the
former actively leading the services and the latter supervis-
ing the temples, the form of the rites and the internal affairs
of the priesthood. Two high priests directed cult activities
in honor of the War God, Huitzilopochtli, and the Rain
God, Tlaloc, the chief divinities worshiped in this city. They

were called *Quetzalcoatl-Totec-tlamacazqui** and *Quetzal-coatl-Tlaloc-tlamacazqui*. The name Quetzalcoatl was given them perhaps as an honorific title in memory of the God of Civilization and Learning, who was the archetype of the priestly ideal. The second names refer to the gods of the respective cults, and the third word means priest. Ranking below these two officials was a third, *Mexicatl-Teohuatzin*, who, like a vicar-general, supervised general religious business in the city-state and conquered towns. Two assistants looked after the instruction in the schools for citizen-warriors and for priests, and other officials supervised the pulque ceremonies.[2]

Next in rank were the priests who were in charge of the worship, temple and ritual of each specific god or goddess and who, in the ceremonies, assumed the dress of the divinity, impersonating him on earth. They, in turn, had a host of assistants who were supplemented by aspirants to the priesthood, the bottom of the hierarchical scale. There seem to have been priestesses as well, and schools for their instruction were established in connection with certain temples. As might be expected as an accompaniment of a highly ritualized religion far above the comprehension of the masses, there was an active practice of magic carried on by male and female witch doctors. Undoubtedly many of these unsanctioned rites were rooted in the more primitive stages of the Aztec development; and in modern times, although the formal Aztec religion has been almost completely eradicated, the indigenous population continues many of the old magico-medical practices.

The priests, however, directed the intellectual life of the

*Kay-tz'al-co-atl-To'-tec-tla-mah-ca'z-kee.

tribe. They elaborated cult ritual and so instilled the realization of the power and proximity of the gods into the minds of the people that even their arts were dedicated chiefly to religious expression. The complicated astronomic and mathematical computations that kept the solar and religious calendars in harmony with the passage of the seasons were also the province of the priesthood. The priests arrayed the dancers, who, depicting mythological events, performed a type of mass drama. Aztec life under hierarchical direction became a pattern of rhythmic ritual, and this continued ceremony served the more firmly to establish the priests as interpreters of the divine order. One has the impression that the priests never overtly showed their temporal power. Situated as they were, with the instruments for interpreting the divine will in their own hands, they had to follow the exactions of ritual far more exigently than did the masses. Were one to choose a single word to describe Aztec government, it would be theocracy. The gods ruled; the priests interpreted and interposed, and the people obeyed, not the priests, but the rhythm of action whereby the gods lived. (See Plate 58, middle.)

At the core of the religion stood the calendar, which was arranged in two divisions: a ritualistic succession of days, the *tonalpohualli* (Tables XI–XVI), and a solar calendar (Table XVII), divided into eighteen twenty-day months and a five-day unlucky period, in which the months' names related to crops and indicated the agricultural origin of this time count. A combination of the two systems permitted the numbering of years, which were counted not on an infinite scale, as with us, but in terms of a fifty-two-year cycle.[3]

The *tonalpohualli*, sometimes erroneously referred to as

TABLE XI

DAY NAMES AND NUMBERS OF THE AZTEC MONTH

1 Cipactli (Mythical Water Monster, Crocodile, Alligator)	
2 Ehecatl (Wind)	
3 Calli (House)	Year Name
4 Cuetzpallin (Iguana Lizard)	
5 Coatl (Snake)	
6 Miquiztli (Death's-Head)	
7 Mazatl (Deer)	
8 Tochtli (Rabbit)	Year Name
9 Atl (Water)	
10 Itzcuintli (Dog)	
11 Ozomatli (Howling Monkey)	
12 Malinalli (Grass)	
13 Acatl (Reed)	Year Name
1 Ocelotl (Ocelot)	
2 Cuauhtli (Eagle)	
3 Cozcaquauhtli (Vulture)	
4 Ollin (Motion, Earthquake)	
5 Tecpatl (Flint Knife)	Year Name
6 Quiauitl (Rain)	
7 Xochitl (Flower)	
8 Cipactli	
9 Ehecatl	
10 Calli	Year Name
11 Cuetzpallin	
12 Coatl	
13 Miquiztli	
1 Mazatl	
2 Tochtli	Year Name
Etc., etc.	

TABLE XII

Tonalpohualli: Sequence of Day Names, Numbers, and Weeks

Day													
	I												
Crocodile	[1]	8	2	9	3	10	4	11	5	12	6	13	7
											XVIII		
Wind	2	9	3	10	4	11	5	12	6	13	7	[1]	8
										XV			
House	3	10	4	11	5	12	6	13	7	[1]	8	2	9
								XII					
Lizard	4	11	5	12	6	13	7	[1]	8	2	9	3	10
						IX							
Serpent	5	12	6	13	7	[1]	8	2	9	3	10	4	11
				VI									
Death's-Head	6	13	7	[1]	8	2	9	3	10	4	11	5	12
		III											
Deer	7	[1]	8	2	9	3	10	4	11	5	12	6	13
													XX
Rabbit	8	2	9	3	10	4	11	5	12	6	13	7	[1]
											XVII		
Water	9	3	10	4	11	5	12	6	13	7	[1]	8	2
									XIV				
Dog	10	4	11	5	12	6	13	7	[1]	8	2	9	3
							XI						
Monkey	11	5	12	6	13	7	[1]	8	2	9	3	10	4
					VIII								
Grass	12	6	13	7	[1]	8	2	9	3	10	4	11	5
			V										
Reed	13	7	[1]	8	2	9	3	10	4	11	5	12	6
	II												
Ocelot	[1]	8	2	9	3	10	4	11	5	12	6	13	7
											XIX		
Eagle	2	9	3	10	4	11	5	12	6	13	7	[1]	8
										XVI			
Vulture	3	10	4	11	5	12	6	13	7	[1]	8	2	9
								XIII					
Motion	4	11	5	12	6	13	7	[1]	8	2	9	3	10
						X							
Flint Knife	5	12	6	13	7	[1]	8	2	9	3	10	4	11
				VII									
Rain	6	13	7	[1]	8	2	9	3	10	4	11	5	12
		IV											
Flower	7	[1]	8	2	9	3	10	4	11	5	12	6	13

tonalamatl, after the book in which it was recorded, was a sacred almanac. It covered a period of 260 days, the significance of which may have been magical or possibly of an astronomical origin, as yet unexplained. It was composed of the twenty day names of the Aztec month, combined with the numbers one to thirteen (Table XI). Whenever the sequence of numbers ended, the series was repeated, and the same arrangement held true for the list of days. Thus the fourteenth day of the twenty in the list received the number one, and so on up to seven for the twentieth day. Then when the series of day names recommenced the first name was numbered eight. By this means within the 260-day period every day was distinguished by the combination of one of twenty names with one of thirteen numerals. At the close of each period another began immediately, as is shown on Table XI.

This sacred period was further divided into twenty weeks of thirteen days each (Table XII). Every week began with the number one and the day name which came up according to the rotation of the sequence. Thus within the *tonalpohualli* period no day in one week could be confused with that of another, since the name and associated number precluded repetition.[4]

A god or goddess presided over each of the list of twenty days (Table XIII) and over each of the twenty "weeks" (Table XIV). The gods of the weeks followed the same order as the day gods, with this exception, that the god of the eleventh day was dropped from the list, moving the remainder in order up one place each. The resultant vacancy in the twentieth week, was filled by two divinities who exercised joint control. Sometimes there was a further re-

FIG. 1. AZTEC DAY SIGNS FROM CODEX

Cipactli Crocodile	*Ehecatl* Wind	*Calli* House	*Cuetzpallin* Lizard	*Coatl* Serpent
Miquiztli Death's-Head	*Mazatl* Deer	*Tochtli* Rabbit	*Atl* Water	*Itzcuintli* Dog
Ozomatli Monkey	*Malinalli* Grass	*Acatl* Reed	*Ocelotl* Ocelot	*Cuauhtli* Eagle
Cozcaquauhtli Vulture	*Ollin* Motion	*Tecpatl* Flint Knife	*Quiauitl* Rain	*Xochitl* Flower

finement whereby the nine gods and goddesses succeeded each other in governing the nights of the *tonalpohualli*, or sacred period (Table XVI). Finally thirteen of these gods influenced the thirteen stations of the Aztec day (Table XV), and nine held sway over the night hours (Table XVI). The names and characters of these divinities are set forth in the accompanying tables.

The array of gods had to be placated and honored at the appropriate time by the priesthood; but the individual, before embarking on an undertaking, could find out the proper

TABLE XIII

DAY GODS OF TONALPOHUALLI

Day	God	Name and Nature
1 Crocodile	Tonacatecuhtli	Lord of Our Subsistence, a Creator God
2 Wind	Quetzalcoatl	Feathered Serpent, Sky God, God of Learning
3 House	Tepeyollotl	Heart of Mountains, an Earth God
4 Lizard	Huehuecoyotl	Old Coyote, Mischief-Maker
5 Snake	Chalchihuitlicue	Lady of the Jeweled Robe, Water Goddess
6 Death's-Head	Tecciztecatl	He from the Sea Snail, Moon God
7 Deer	Tlaloc	He Who Makes Things Sprout, Rain God
8 Rabbit	Mayauel	She of the Maguey Plant, Pulque Goddess
9 Water	Xiuhtecuhtli	Lord of Year, Fire God
10 Dog	Mictlantecuhtli	Lord of Region of Dead, Death God
11 Monkey	Xochipilli	Flower Prince, God of Spring and Flowers
12 Grass	Patecatl	He from the Land of Medicines, God of Medicine
13 Reed	Tezcatlipoca or variant like Itzlacoliuhqui	Smoking Mirror, a Great God, cf. Gods of Weeks Carved Obsidian Knife
14 Ocelot	Tlazolteotl	Goddess of Dirt, Earth Mother
15 Eagle	Xipe	Our Lord, the Flayed One, God of Seedtime
16 Vulture	Itzpapalotl	Obsidian Butterfly, a Stellar Goddess
17 Motion	Xolotl or variant	Double, Monster God
18 Flint Knife	Tezcatlipoca or Chalchiuhtotolin	Smoking Mirror, Great God, Jeweled Bird, a Week God
19 Rain	Chantico	In the House, Goddess of Hearth Fire
20 Flower	Xochiquetzal	Flower Feather, Goddess of Flowers

TABLE XIV
GODS OF TONALPOHUALLI WEEKS

Week Beginning	God	Name
1 Crocodile	Tonacatecuhtli	Lord of Our Subsistence, a Creator God
1 Ocelot	Quetzalcoatl	Feathered Serpent, a Sky God
1 Deer	Tepeyollotl	Heart of the Mountains, an Earth God
1 Flower	Huehuecoyotl	Old Coyote, Backbiter, old Otomi tribal god
1 Reed	Chalchihuitlicue	Lady of the Jeweled Robe, Water Goddess
1 Death's-Head	Tecciztecatl	He from the Sea Snail, Moon God
1 Rain	Tlaloc	He Who Makes Things Sprout, Rain God
1 Grass	Mayauel	She of the Maguey Plant, Pulque Goddess
1 Snake	Xiuhtecuhtli	Lord of the Year, Fire God
1 Flint	Mictlantecuhtli	Lord of the Region of the Dead, Death God
1 Howling Monkey	Patecatl	He from the Land of Medicines, God of Medicine
1 Lizard	Itzlacoliuhqui	The Carved Obsidian Knife, God of Cold
1 Motion	Tlazolteotl	Goddess of Dirt, Earth Goddess
1 Dog	Xipe Totec	Our Lord the Flayed One, God of Seedtime
1 House	Itzpapalotl	Obsidian Butterfly, a Stellar Goddess
1 Vulture	Xolotl	Double, Monster God
1 Water	Chalchiuhtotolin	Jeweled Fowl, variant of Tezcatlipoca
1 Wind	Chantico	In the House, Goddess of Hearth Fire
1 Eagle	Xochiquetzal	Flower Feather, Goddess of Flowers
1 Rabbit	Xiuhtecuhtli and	Lord of Year, Fire God
	Itztli	Stone Knife, God of Obsidian Knife

TABLE XV

GODS OF THE DAY HOURS AND THEIR ASSOCIATED BIRDS

Day Gods	Name	Associated Bird
1. Xiuhtecuhtli	Fire God	White Hummingbird
2. Tlaltecuhtli	Lord of Earth, the Earth Monster	Green Hummingbird
3. Chalchihuitlicue	Water Goddess	Falcon
4. Tonatiuh	The Sun, Sun God	Quail
5. Tlazolteotl	Earth Mother	Eagle
6. Teoyaomiqui	Warrior Death, Death God	Screech Owl
7. Xochipilli	Flower Prince, God of Flowers	Butterfly
8. Tlaloc	Rain God	Striped Eagle
9. Quetzalcoatl-Ehecatl	God of Learning	Turkey Cock
10. Tezcatlipoca	Great God	Horned Owl
11. Mictlantecuhtli	Death God	Guacamaya
12. Tlahuizcalpantecuhtli	Lord of the House of Dawn, Venus God, variant of Quetzalcoatl	Quetzal
13. Ilamatecuhtli	Old Princess, ancient Earth Goddess	Parrot

TABLE XVI

GODS OF THE NIGHT HOURS AND THEIR ATTRIBUTES IN DIVINATION

Night Gods		Significance
1. Xiuhtecuhtli	Fire God	Good
2. Itztli	God of Obsidian Knife	Bad
3. Piltzintecuhtli	Lord of Princes, Sun God	Good
4. Cinteotl	God of Corn, Corn God	Indifferent
5. Mictlantecuhtli	Death God	Bad
6. Chalchihuitlicue	Water Goddess	Indifferent
7. Tlazolteotl	Earth Mother	Bad
8. Tepeyollotl	Earth or Jaguar God	Good
9. Tlaloc	Rain God	Good

divinity to appease on the date of that undertaking. It is improbable that the ordinary communicant daily honored each god any more than a Catholic layman prays daily to each saint in the calendar. He did reverence in terms of his own spiritual and actual necessity.

A number of the *tonalamatl* have survived. These reference books for priestly guidance are made of paper beaten from the bark of the amate or wild-fig tree, although some post-Conquest copies were composed of European paper. An ancient book consisted of a long paper strip which was prepared and coated to take paint and subsequently folded screenwise to permit easy handling. Occasionally only one but usually the two open pages were devoted to each week. A large colored drawing depicted the divinity controlling the week, and other figures represented subsidiary gods and objects connected with their worship, such as thorns, incense burners, altars, and the like. The rest of the space was ruled off into squares, in which were painted the requisite thirteen day names and numbers, the gods and goddesses associated with each and occasionally their *nahuals*, the bird or animal forms which the divinities could assume. Obviously only the initiate could make use of this information, which existed in the form of pictures without an explanatory text. However, it is the great good fortune of Mexicanists that some of the friars after the Conquest annotated a few of these manuscripts according to the explanations of Indian informants.[5] (See Plate 59, bottom.)

The great Aztec ceremonies, however, took place in accordance with the solar year, composed of eighteen months of twenty days and a five-day period which was considered unlucky (Table XVII). The months had names having to do

TABLE XVII

THE SOLAR YEAR, THE EIGHTEEN MONTHS, AND CEREMONIES

Months, seasonal character, approximate Gregorian dates, presiding gods and chief ceremonies

I Atlcoualco (want of water), ceasing of rain [Feb. 12–Mar. 3]. Chalchihuitlicue and Tlalocs. Ceremonies for rain; child sacrifice; Xipe sacrifice with blunt weapons.

II Tlacaxipeualiztli (boning of men), seedtime [Mar. 4–Mar. 23]. God Xipe. Impersonation of Xipe by priests wearing skins of captives; dances by priests wearing human skins; agricultural dances.

III Tozoztontli (short fast), rain desired [Mar. 24–Apr. 12]. Coatlicue and Tlalocs. Child sacrifice to Tlalocs to bring rain; end of Xipe rites which sometimes held over a month.

IV Huei Tozoztli (long fast), worship of new corn [Apr. 13–May 2]. Centeotl and Chicomecoatl. Ceremonial bloodletting; decoration of house altars with corn plants; young girls' ceremony with blessing of seed corn.

V Toxcatl (dry or slippery), rainy season begins [May 3–May 22]. Tezcatlipoca and Huitzilopochtli; god-impersonation ceremonies for either or both great gods (p. 202); scarification of children.

VI Etzalqualiztli (bean porridge), rain desired [May 23–June 11]. Tlalocs. Ceremonial robbing; rain ceremonies; fertility rite, drowning boy and girl in canoe filled with hearts of sacrificial victims.

VII Tecuhilhuitontli (little feast of princes), rain desired [June 12–July 1]. Huixtocihuatl. Ceremony of salt-workers, who leeched product from lake; women's dance with sacrifice of priestess impersonating goddess.

VIII Hueitecuhilhuitl (great feast of rulers), adoration of ripening corn [July 2–July 21]. Xilonen. Feast for Goddess of Young Corn; eight-day feast; women wear hair loose as sympathetic magic; sacrifice of slave girl impersonating goddess; after sacrifice people can eat new corn.

IX Tlaxochimaco (birth of flowers), first flowering [July 22–Aug. 10]. Huitzilopochtli. Feasts on turkeys and corn-meal cakes in honor of the god; great dance with both sexes taking part and men even touching the women; merchants' feast, honoring their patron god Yacatecuhtli.

X   Xocotlhuetzi (fall of the fruits), heat for ripening [Aug. 11–Aug. 30]. Xiuhtecuhtli (Huehueteotl). Furnace sacrifice (p. 202); competitive climbing of high pole by young men to win special insignia at top.

XI   Ochpaniztli (month of brooms), refreshment of Earth Mother [Aug. 31–Sept. 19]. Tlazolteotl or Teteoinnan (Toçi). Sacrifice of woman impersonating Goddess of Ripe Corn; efforts to avoid sorrow by buffoonery, sympathetic magic to avoid rains at harvest; review of warriors and distribution of insignia of rank; drills and mock combats of Eagle and Ocelot Knights.

XII   Teotleco (return of the gods), harvest [Sept. 20–Oct. 9]. Tezcatlipoca. Ceremonies honoring the return of the gods to the earth; Tezcatlipoca first to come; two absent, Xiuhtecuhtli, too old to travel, Yacatecuhtli, merchant wandering off beaten track; ceremonial drunkenness and furnace sacrifice.

XIII   Tepeilhuitl (feast of the mountains), rain [Oct. 10–Oct. 29]. Tlalocs. Ceremonies for mountain rain gods, an aspect of Tlalocs; use of wooden snakes and figurines covered with amaranth paste; sacrifice of four women and a man with subsequent ceremonial cannibalism.

XIV   Quecholli [bird, quail(?)], rain [Oct. 30–Nov. 18]. Mixcoatl. Making of weapons; general penance of four days; licensed old people abstain from liquor and husbands from their wives; ceremonial hunt with sacrifice of game and ceremonial feasting on the hill.

XV   Panquetzaliztli (feast of the flags), winter solstice [Nov. 19–Dec. 8]. Huitzilopochtli. Festivals honoring War God; mock or staged combats; imprinting of hand impressions by captives.

XVI   Atemoztli (fall of the waters), rain [Dec. 9–Dec. 28]. Tlalocs. Vigils and offerings to household gods; winter solstice at time of conquest; erection of poles with paper streamers coated with rubber.

XVII   Tititl (severe weather), season of serenity [Dec. 29–Jan. 7]. Ilamatecuhtli. Sacrifice of woman impersonating goddess; sympathetic magic to bring rain by weeping, through children crying on first day of month and men and children beating women with straw-filled bags to make them cry.

XVIII   Izcalli (resuscitation), toasting of corn supply [Jan. 18–Feb. 6]. Xiuhtecuhtli. Ceremonial hunt; killing of captives every four years; killing of birds and arrow sacrifice at Cuauhtitlan.
Nemontemi (five unlucky days) [Feb. 7–Feb. 11].

with farming, and the days of the month were distinguished by numbers, in addition to their *tonalpohualli* name and number described above. Years were identified in terms of the two methods, since they were named for the *tonalpohualli* day on which the year began.[6]

Only four of the twenty day names could begin the year, as a simple mathematical calculation will prove. Three hundred and sixty-five (the number of days in a year) divided by twenty (the total of the day names) leaves a remainder of five. Thus of the twenty day names only four can begin the year. House, Rabbit, Reed and Flint Knife must always recur as New Year's Day, since they are the third, eighth, thirteenth and eighteenth days in the list, thus being separated from each other by five numbers. In that thirteen, the quantity of numbers available, divides into 365 with a remainder of one, the number of the day increased by one each new year. Thus the years were numerically distinguishable— 1 Rabbit, 2 Reed, 3 House, 4 Flint Knife, 5 Rabbit, and so on, until the thirteen numbers and four day names began to repeat themselves, which occurred after fifty-two (13 × 4) years. This is the mathematical reason for the Aztec cycle or major time unit, and in the Valley of Mexico they did not go further and distinguish between cycles except indirectly. In consequence there is the same sort of confusion in referring to events as would result were we to designate years within the century without distinguishing the number of centuries before or after Christ. Thus the discovery of America would be recorded as 92 and the Declaration of Independence as 76, and only a detailed knowledge of history would enable us to fix the events in their proper relationship to the fifteenth and eighteenth centuries. (See Plates 62, top left; 63.)

The lag between the calendric and the solar year, for which
we compensate by adding a day every four years as the
twenty-ninth of February, was difficult to adjust by Aztec
standards since so much of the time count hinged on the
orderly mathematical sequence of days. Some authorities believe that the Aztecs let the calendar drop behind, others
that compensation was made during the unlucky period of
five days. A third suggestion interprets the celebration of a
feast held every eight years as a sign that a dateless day was introduced, unrecognized in the *tonalpohualli* of the year but
honored with special rites.[7] (See Plate 58, middle.)

However the matter of the leap year was settled, the close
of one cycle and the beginning of a new one was celebrated
with great pomp each year Two Reed chosen as the first
day of each cycle for some ritualistic reason. In the Mixteca-
Puebla area the *tonalamatls* show evidence that the priests
observed the planet Venus and took note of a Venus Year of
584 days. At the end of two cycles (104 years) there was a
tremendous ceremony of great ritualistic significance, for at
the same time as the beginning of a Venus count, a solar
count, a fifty-two-year cycle, and a *tonalpohualli* all coincided. That four mystical rhythms, affecting such diverse
aspects of the universe and the gods that dwelt therein, could
meet must have produced great satisfaction and occasioned
the utmost rejoicing among people for whom pattern and
form had such great significance.[8]

Although the Valley of Mexico Aztecs did not use the
Venus count they celebrated the cyclical change with the
utmost ceremony. They thought of the change from one
cycle to another as the death of one life and the beginning of
a new one. The realization that nature could withhold the

continuance of their existence endowed the ritual with profound solemnity. The New Fire Ceremony was symbolized by the extinction of the old altar fire, which had burned perpetually for fifty-two years, and the kindling of a fresh one in token of the new grant of life.[9] (See Plate 29, top row.)

During the five useless days (*nemontemi*) of the final year the people let their fires go out and destroyed their household furniture. Fasting and lamentation were the order of the day while the populace awaited catastrophe. Pregnant women were shut up in granaries, lest they be changed into wild animals, and children were marched up and down and kept awake, for fear that sleep on that fatal evening would result in their turning into rats.

At sunset the priests, in solemn panoply, representatives of the whole array of the Aztec pantheon, ascended the Hill of the Star, anciently known as Huixachtecatl. This extinct volcanic crater rises abruptly from the Valley floor and is visible from almost every quarter of the Valley of Mexico. From the temple on its summit the priests anxiously scanned the heavens as the night wore on, awaiting the hour when a certain star or stars, Aldebaran or the Pleiades, reached the center of the heavens and gave the sign that their world would continue.

At the very moment when these stars passed the meridian the priests seized a wooden fire drill and kindled a new fire in the open breast of a victim freshly slain for the purpose. The populace—priests, chiefs and commoners—thrilled to a great happiness. Runners lit torches from the new fire and rekindled the altars in the temples of every town and hamlet, whence the people bore the flames to their hearths. Like fireflies the darting torchbearers sped through the night, bringing the promise of a new life to every man, woman and child.

With the dawn, more than ever gracious in its fulfillment of a nations' piety, the populace rallied, renovating their temples, refurbishing their houses and making new utensils for temple and household use. There was feasting on special food, and sacrifice both by personal bloodletting and the immolation of captives betokened the measure of popular gratitude.

Another striking ceremony fell on the day Four Earthquake (or Motion), the sign of the present age, and symbolized the passage of the sun through the heavens. At dawn a captive dressed as the Sun God, Tonatiuh, ascended the platform where the Calendar Stone was set. Four priests spreadeagled the victim, and a fifth opened his breast to tear out the heart as an offering to the god. The populace then feasted until noon, gashing their ears and parts of their bodies with blades of obsidian. In the afternoon the Eagle and Tiger Knights, votaries of the solar cult, took part in a dance dramatizing the sacred war wherein the sun is slain, to be reborn the following day. The dance culminated in a gladiatorial sacrifice. Selected Eagle and Tiger Knights, armed with real weapons, slew a captive warrior, chosen for his military distinction, who was tethered to a circular stone representing the sun's disk and who defended himself with dummy weapons only.[10] (See Plate 60, top right, bottom.)

A curious type of sacrifice took place in connection with the worship of the god Xipe and may be the origin of the arrow sacrifice which is performed in honor of the morning star by the Pawnee of our Western plains. In the Mexican rite the victim was lashed to a scaffold, and priests, using bows or *atl-atls*, shot him to death.[11]

The Aztecs performed a hideous ceremony in honor of the Fire God, Huehueteotl. Prisoners of war and their captors took part in a dance in honor of the god, and the next day the captives ascended to the top of a platform, where a powder, *yauhtli* (Indian hemp), was cast in their faces to anesthetize them against their ghastly fate. After preparing a great fire, each priest seized a captive and, binding him hand and foot, lifted him onto his back. A macabre dance took place around the burning coals, and one by one they dumped their burdens into the flames. Before death could intervene to put an end to their suffering the priests fished out the captives with large hooks and wrenched the hearts from their blistered bodies.[12]

In contrast to the callous brutality of the fire sacrifice, the ceremony in honor of the god Tezcatlipoca was strikingly dramatic, tinged with the pathos with which we view the taking of a life. The handsomest and bravest prisoner of war was selected a year before his execution. Priests taught him the manners of a ruler, and as he walked about, playing divine melodies upon his flute, he received the homage due Tezcatlipoca himself. A month before the day of sacrifice four lovely girls, dressed as goddesses, became his companions and attended to his every want. On the day of his death he took leave of his weeping consorts to lead a procession in his honor, marked by jubilation and feasting. Then he bade farewell to the glittering cortege and left for a small temple, accompanied by the eight priests who had attended him throughout the year. The priests preceded him up the steps of the temple, and he followed, breaking at each step a flute which he had played in the happy hours of his incarnation. At the top of the platform the priests turned him over the sacrificial block and wrenched out his heart. In deference to his former godhood his body was carried, not ignominiously flung, down the steps; but his head joined the other skulls spitted on the rack beside the temple.[13] (See Plate 61, top.)

Every one of the great monthly sacrifices had a dramatic significance, and a list of the principal feasts, the gods they honored and the month of their occurrence is set forth on Table XVII. Several authors have availed themselves of Friar Sahagun's matchless descriptions to set forth the elaborate rituals which we have lightly sampled here. The elements of time, training and elaborate preparation of costume, it can be readily seen, must have absorbed a large part of the resources of the tribe. The tentacles of ritual extended throughout the tribal activities, so that even games and sports were transformed into acts of religious meaning, although the participants undoubtedly derived a great deal of fun from their performance.

The ball game, *tlachtli*, was such a game, played in a court shaped like the capital letter *I*. Walls extended on either side of the stem of the *I*, and in the middle of each a stone or wooden ring was set vertically, in contrast to the horizontal position of a basketball hoop. The players tried to pass through this ring a hard rubber ball, which they could only strike with their elbows, hips or legs. There must have been some other method of scoring than by goals alone, since these, very naturally, were of rare occurrence—so much so that, in the event of one, players and backers had the right to snatch the wearing apparel of their adversaries. The game was played far and wide, courts having been found from the Republic of Honduras to southeastern Arizona. It has a special interest for us in that the first description of rubber, so important in our modern economy, was when Oviedo, in the sixteenth century, wrote of the game and the ball used by its players.[14] (See Plate 57, bottom left; Fig. 3.)

There were also games of chance which were played with a semisacred significance. One such game, *patolli*, utilized a board shaped like a cross, with spaces ruled in the arms, not unlike a version of the old-fashioned parchesi of our childhood. Macuilxochitl, Five Flower, the god of all games, was sometimes portrayed in connection with players of *patolli*.[15]

Another important entertainment involved the erection of a high pole at the top of which a movable platform was socketed. Men dressed as gods or the birds into which the gods transformed themselves, and, fastened by ropes wound around the platform, leaped off into space. As they did so the ropes, unwinding, rotated the platform and gave the effect of flight to the circling performers. Each turn brought the birdmen nearer to the ground, and they were wont to alter their center of balance and adjust their wings, producing the effect of the rise and fall of soaring birds. This modest application of the principle of gliding must have created a spectacle of color and beauty. The ceremony is still performed in parts of Mexico, and the Volador, or flying place, of Tenochtitlan was, until very recently, the site of the "Thieves' Market" in Mexico City.[16]

The application of human sacrifice to the most simple ceremonial act of thanksgiving offers a grisly contrast to the spirit in which these rituals were carried out. However, social and religious behavior are calculated to preserve human existence and ensure man's well-being, regardless of how warped the methods may become. It follows that the idea of sacrificing precious possessions to attain such ends would lead to the offering of the most precious gift of all, human life, since that is what man most ardently strives to keep intact. Thus instances of human sacrifices keep cropping up in the world's religious systems, and we preserve in our own culture the concept of martyrdom, achieved by voluntary or involuntary means, as an act of virtue. The very beautiful example of the Saviour transmutes to the highest spiritual plane this idea of sacrifice for the good of humanity.

The Aztecs did not reach this spiritual level, but the symbolism of their sacrifice has, nonetheless, its own barbaric beauty. They reasoned that for man to survive, the gods who permit his existence must also live and wax strong. These gods, however, received their best nutriment from the most precious of offerings, the hearts of men. Thus a vicious circle became established which led to sacrifice on an increasing scale. The gods manifested their favor and their strength to the Aztecs by letting them prosper, but the Aztecs, on their part, had to sacrifice hearts to the gods to maintain their good will. A good part of the tribal prosperity emanated from military success, so that the most acceptable sacrifices were the hearts of adversaries, which were the hardest to acquire since prisoners could not be taken without military victory. A martial success, on the other hand, could only be achieved through the exercise of divine favor. Thus sacrifice led to war and war back to sacrifice, in an unending series of expanding cycles. The effect that this practice had on foreign affairs we shall describe in the next chapter. (See Plate 60, top.)

War captives were the most esteemed offering, and the braver and higher in rank, the more valuable they were. Slaves were killed for minor ceremonies, and in rare instances women and children were slain in fertility rites to ensure growth in plants by the powers of sympathetic magic. Ceremonial cannibalism was sometimes practiced, in the belief that the eater can absorb the virtues of the eaten, but this rite cannot be considered a vice. The letting of one's own blood was another way to ensure divine favor, and people did horrible self-penances such as mutilating themselves with knives or drawing through their tongues a string on which were threaded maguey spines. The higher the social position of the individual and the more he consequently knew of ritualistic observance, the more arduously he performed the fasts, penances and tortures imposed by the religion. The priests, therefore, were strongly cognizant of their social responsibility and by the rigor of their own lives strove to ensure the well-being of the tribe.[17] (See Plate 61, bottom right.)

The picture writings of the Aztecs take human sacrifice and penance as a matter of course but seldom indicate the quantity of victims. Indeed, only one such manuscript records the monthly ceremonies, and a post-Conquest copy of another reveals a sacrifice of twenty thousand people at the dedication of the enlarged great temple of Mexico.[17] The Spanish accounts and those of the educated Indians agree, but whether Christian piety induced exaggeration, and how much, it is difficult to ascertain at this time and age. The Conquistador who counted thousands of skulls on the skull rack in Tenochtitlan apparently confirms these other statements, which the great humanitarian and Indian lover, Las Casas, discounted in his special pleading for decent treatment of the indigenous population of New Spain.[18]

The priesthood, beside performing these bloodcurdling acts, had other more pacific duties; they also instructed youth in the mysteries of writing and keeping records. Aztec writing was pictographic and was arriving at the stage of syllabic phonetics, which is an important part of the hieroglyphic writing of Egypt. There was no alphabet, but a picture of an animal or thing could be combined with the picture of another animal or thing to give a third meaning in terms of its sound value, much like our method of rebus writing. We could write: "I can be hospitable," in terms of the sounds given to pictures of an eye, a tin can, a bee, a horse, a hole in the ground and a table. The Aztecs wrote the name of their capital by drawing stone *tena* from which sprouted a nopal cactus, *nochtli*, or the town Pantepec, by drawing a flag, *pantli*, on a conventionalized hill, *tepec*. Color, position, puns and abbreviations all contributed to recording sounds by this means. Conventionalized signs, like footprints to show travel or movement, a shield and club for war, a bundled corpse for death, gave simple connotations of action.[19] (See Fig. 2.)

Aztec writing offered no way of making general statements or expressing abstract ideas. Yet the full accounts of historical events, set down after the Conquest in Spanish or Nahuatl, indicate that oral traditions, possibly learned as a chant or saga, supplemented these ideographic records.

Their numerical system was vigesimal. The Aztecs counted by twenties where we count by tens. They indicated quantities up to twenty by the requisite number of dots, although in the Mixteca this method was abridged by using bars to represent groups of five. The Aztecs used a flag to indicate twenty, repeating it for quantities up to four hundred, while a sign like a fir tree, meaning numerous as hairs, signified four hundred (20×20). The next unit, eight thousand ($20 \times 20 \times 20$), was indicated by a bag, referring to the almost innumerable contents of a sack of cacao beans. (See Fig. 2.)

FIG. 2. AZTEC NUMBERS AND METHODS OF ENUMERATION

a. one, a dot or finger　　b. twenty, a flag　　c. four hundred, a sign denoting hairs　　d. eight thousand, a bag　　e. ten masks of precious stone
f. twenty bags of cochineal dye　　g. one hundred bags of cacao　　h. four
hundred bales of cotton　　i. four hundred jars of honey of tuna　　j. eight
thousand leaf-bundles of copal gum　　k. twenty baskets each containing
one thousand six hundred ground cacao nibs　　l. four hundred and two
cotton blankets of this type

A post-Conquest manuscript shows devices that may not
have been of native origin but European adaptations of the
Aztec system. For example, fractions are shown by blacking
in segments of a quarter, a half or three quarters of a disk.
Similarly fives and multiples of five are indicated by coloring
the requisite spaces in the flag of the sign for twenty, and
hundreds by showing the proportionate lines in the four-
hundred symbol.[20]

Aztec histories consisted of annals of ancient times, contemporary events, year counts, accounts compiled yearly,
specific records for each year, books of each day and
day-by-day counts or diaries.[21] Some of the ancient and
contemporary histories have been published, but none of

the shorter records have reached print, even if they survive in some library. These histories followed two main
styles. One, exemplified in the Mapa Tlotzin and Codex
Xolotl, sets forth events, the people or tribes involved and
the places, each designated by its hieroglyph. Year names
were appended to give the dates. These Texcocan records
are highly complicated to follow, but fortunately some have
glossaries appended after the Conquest.[22] (See Plate 25, top
row.)

The other style recorded the succession of the years, one
after the other, for the whole time covered by the history.
Events, like conquests or the death of chiefs, were appropriately drawn near the proper year sign and sometimes were
connected by a line. This type of history seemed largely confined to Tenochtitlan. Since Tenochcan history is much
more accurate after 1400 A.D. than before, one wonders
whether the destruction of the books, ordered by Itzcoatl,
did not really pave the way for a new style of writing.[23] (See
Plates 62, top; 63.)

In addition to the histories and the sacred almanacs tribal
records were kept. These are most useful to the modern
student, for the names of the towns are inscribed in one
column, while the rest of the page records the amount of
gold, ornaments or cloth that was paid in as tribute. Since
the geographical location of most of these towns is known,
the chief products of each area can be determined. Other
records showed lines of descent, lands occupied and other
data essential to family economics.[24] (See Plates 62, bottom
right; 64.)

Fortunately, after the Conquest the Spaniards utilized the
native methods of writing as well as their own in civil records,

such as tax rolls, lawsuits, and the like, so that the Indians could understand the Spanish legal code and present their complaints.[25] Friar Nicolas Tester even made an attempt to shift the picture writing over to syllabic writing—the effect of the Lord's Prayer in Aztec glyphs is startling.[26] This was too cumbersome a plan and was soon abandoned for the recording of Nahuatl words in Roman characters. However, it is due to this usage of Aztec pictographs that so much survives of the records, many of which, with their oral accompaniment, were copied into Roman characters both in Spanish and Nahuatl. From these we derive such knowledge as we have of Aztec history and customs. (See Plate 44.)

The drawback of picture writing is its rigidity and its uselessness for the expression of abstract ideas. The cyclical count created great confusion as to the particular cycle in which an event took place. Exact and careful drawing was essential for the glyphs, and a slurred line might result in a totally different reading. However, the worst feature of Aztec history is its provincialism, for the scribes saw things only in terms of the tribe and took no heed of internal events in other communities. The picture writings show how communal interests extended vertically, as it were, from the tribe to the pantheon. There is no reflection of a horizontal interest outward to the lives and occupations of other peoples. The attitude of the Aztec communities to foreign affairs merits a chapter in itself.

CHAPTER XII

FOREIGN AFFAIRS AND WAR

The relationships of Aztec tribes to each other in peace and war, the nature of the Aztec domain and methods of military organization and warfare

THE COMMUNITY or tribe was the center of the political and economic life of the Aztecs. Existence depended on the favor of the gods, who participated directly in the tribal fortunes, so that the degree of elaboration of the ceremonial structures was an accurate gauge of tribal prosperity. A man's position in the civil life of the community had a corresponding level in the hierarchy, since conspicuous fulfillment of civil obligations entailed an equal attainment in piety and observance of ritual. The basic design for living was a communal agriculture. The early tribal existence sought to achieve this pattern by avoiding other peoples and finding new land to settle. There is an essential affinity between agriculture and political isolation, just as commerce and manufacture require successively broader political contacts.[1]

In the early history of the Valley of Mexico there appears to have been a series of small isolated settlements which carried on a vague process of exchange. The Toltec civilization seems to have attained uniform development over a wide area spread by a population which gradually filled up unoccupied territory. There was little to suggest war or conquest at first. Later civil disintegration caused the Toltec decline, and the character of the Valley was transformed. Formerly, tribes had slowly grown in numbers until dense occupation of a previously unpopulated territory took place. But in the Chichimec period men were driven from their home territories by various factors, of which overpopulation may have been one, vague unrest another, and set out in search of new land. While the goal of each group of immigrants may well have been to settle and farm in peaceful isolation, the very process of movement must have brought war and consequent readjustments in the social organization.

Throughout Chichimec times and into the Aztec period as well, the political unit was a tribe, dwelling in its own village, supported by its own land. Even though a tribe might grow to thousands of members, the village become transformed into a city-state, and the communal lands cease to support the population, no real shift in political organization took place. No leader developed the concept of empire so successfully applied by the Incas of Peru. The group experience of the Indians was to colonize new land but, with perhaps the sole exception of Peru, never to incorporate, through conquest, weaker communities into their own tribe.

However, when the tribe became too unwieldly to migrate en masse, an adjustment had to be made between population and food supply. One method was for part of the population to break away and join another community whose economic resources were relatively unexploited. As an illustration we have the case of the Chimalpanecs and the Culhuas, who joined the nascent community of Texcoco to the vast benefit of its material and intellectual culture.[2] (See Plate 29, top row, Fig. 1.)

The more usual means of adjusting food supply to population was the exaction of tribute from richer and weaker neighbors. Quinatzin of Texcoco instituted the system first in the northern Valley in the early fourteenth century, and it is an interesting point to speculate as to whether or not the Chimalpanec immigrants suggested this as a practice found successful in their homeland. Quinatzin, by force of arms or by persuasion, induced a number of towns to turn over to him supplies of various sorts. The local chiefs recognized him as an overlord but maintained a complete political independence. He, in turn, granted the vassal chiefs the full measure of his military support. Yet these vassals had no sense of loyalty and were quite ready to revolt or transfer their allegiance to a stronger suzerain.[3] (See Plate 42, top.)

When Tezozomoc of Azcapotzalco saw his tribe develop to the point where it had to expand he found the southern Valley overpopulated, so that he had to challenge the power of Texcoco. His first move was to create disaffection in the vassal states, after which he could move against his rivals with good hope of military success. Yet so light was Tezozomoc's tenure of control that it was relatively easy for the conquered tribes to combine later and wreck his domination.

Alliances like that formed by Texcoco, Tenochtitlan and Tacuba were so very rare that much is made of this combination as an example of the excellence of Aztec statecraft. It would seem that the division of spoils, two parts each to the larger states, and one part to Tlacopan, was in force only for that campaign. Later Texcoco and Tenochtitlan undertook wars for their mutual advantage, but there was constant intrigue in the hope that one of the two could overcome the other and derive the full benefits of the booty taken. By the mid-fifteenth century both Tenochtitlan and Texcoco had grown to the point where they had to have additional supplies or else starve, so, because of this common necessity, the alliance endured fairly well.[4]

Despite their common background of language, thought, religion, custom and material culture, the Aztecs had no sense of unity. Tenochtitlan and Tlaltelolco, both of which are within the city limits of modern Mexico, existed side by side in complete independence for many years; not until 1473 did the Tenochcas make up their minds to conquer their neighbors. Each town and hamlet was sufficient unto itself, and its members felt no larger loyalty. In modern Teotihuacan this feeling still persists, and the members of one *barrio*, or ward, look upon those of the adjacent one as a congregation of the most horrible criminals. Not even the Spanish siege of Mexico brought unity to the Aztecs, and the Texcocans blithely joined the invaders to exterminate their former ally Tenochtitlan.

Although community was potentially hostile to community, individuals could move freely about the countryside. Trade in simple commodities was carried on extensively from the early times of the Middle Cultures. In the Aztec period the traveling merchants became a special class, and their security of body and property, preserved at first for the advantages which each town could derive from their wares, was guaranteed by the force of Aztec arms. Pilgrims going to worship at special shrines had free and unmolested passage; and a suggestion that such journeys were made in the distant past is given by the Middle Culture figurines of foreign origin. One site especially, Tetelpan, produced so great a variety of idols from such a wide area that it must have been an important religious center in Middle Culture times. However, neither trade nor religion broke down the sense of communal and political independence in Central Mexico. (See Plate 35; Fig. 2.)

Foreign relations centered around war, which, we have seen, was an important part of Aztec economy and religion. The same confusion of motives that we find in our modern culture affected the reasons for military action. We wage war for economic, territorial and political advantages and, while condemning the practice in our adversaries, justify our own participation by saying that we are fighting for freedom, to liberate someone, to extend civilization or to ensure peace. Soldiers on our own side are brave and attain glory, preserve our social virtues and sacrifice themselves for the public well-being. Those on the other side are aggressors, agents of evil and cowardly knaves. The Aztecs made war for defense, revenge and economic motives, which were inextricably confused with the need for the sacrificial victims requisite for proper adoration of their gods. Thus in warfare the great aim was to take captives, but behind this religious goal lurked the less holy urges of political and economic expediency.

The captive himself attained social status, since he went to a special warrior's heaven. A redoubtable Tlaxcalan chief, named Tlahuicol, was singled out for sacrifice to the sun and fought so successfully with his dummy weapons that he killed some of his adversaries and wounded a number of the others. He was pardoned and offered a chieftaincy in the Tenochcan army. Tlahuicol, however, rejected his pardon and gladly underwent sacrifice for the greater honor and glory in that death. This story illustrates the attitude of the individual warrior, which is not unlike that of the mediaeval knight or career soldier in our own culture.[5]

The Aztec reasons for fighting and their social and moral sanctions for war were not so very different from our own, except that we have many more, due to our superior rationalizations. The Aztec military technique, however, was definitely inferior, since it was not so completely developed a social tool as it is in our own culture. The basic organization of the army required the participation of every able-bodied man under the direction of the war chief. However, as Aztec society grew more intricate and greater numbers of warriors took the field, the military structure became more rigid.

The unit of organization was an aggregation of twenty men, several of which were combined into larger bodies of two to four hundred, roughly corresponding to our platoons and companies. Special detachments of from four to six men, who did scouting and raiding, operated much as do the squads of our own military system. The clan commander marshaled the larger bodies, much as a colonel handles his regiment. The clan troops were banded together in four divisions under the heads of the four municipal quarters, and the tribal war chiefs had the supreme command. In a very numerous army the troops from a given quarter, or *barrio*, were sometimes divided into brigades, composed of the forces from two or three clans.[6]

The high tribal officers, the war chief, the chiefs of the quarters and the clan chiefs commanded the larger bodies. The ordinary chiefs and members of the warrior orders, the Knights of the Eagle and the Tiger and of a third infrequently mentioned order, the Arrow, according to their particular ability, took over the lesser units. In other words, the executive officials of the tribe in peacetime became its military officers in time of war. There was no distinction made between the civil and military offices, since the tribe operated as an entity in both peace and war, and standing armies did not exist. (See Plate 34, bottom right.)

The soldiers were the able-bodied men of the tribe. The *telpuchcalli*, houses of youth, through which boys passed at the age of fifteen for formal instruction in the duties of manhood, taught them the usage of different weapons. Drill, in the sense of the accurate movements of modern troops, did not exist, but the great monthly ceremonies called for military demonstrations in which warriors showed their abilities and performed sham maneuvers. Each recruit followed an experienced warrior in battle, much as a mediaeval squire served an apprenticeship to a knight in full standing.

The chief offensive arms were wooden clubs, edged with sharp blades of obsidian, and the javelin, hurled by means of the *atl-atl*. Bows and arrows were used, but the heavier javelins were preferred for the close fighting of Aztec warfare. Slings and spears were weapons favored by some. For defensive armor shields of wickerwork covered with hide were most commonly in use, and some were elaborately painted or covered with feathers. The Aztecs also developed a body armor of quilted cotton, soaked in brine, which covered the whole body like an old-fashioned union suit. This was so effective a protection against clubs and missiles that the Spaniards rapidly adopted it, extolling it as cooler and lighter than steel armor.[7] Some warriors wore wooden helmets, which were elaborately carved to represent the insignia of the military orders. These had decorative rather than defensive values and added to the richness of costumes worn by the maturer warriors. A tribesman had the right to elaborate his dress in accordance with his prowess, and the great chiefs wore attached to their backs immense frames covered with feathers. Tribes, and even clans, wore special insignia, so that friend could be distinguished from foe and chief from common warrior. The term uniform could hardly be used, since the rich variety and indulgence in individual fancy produced a kaleidoscopic effect in the motley array of bright colors and strange forms.[8]

To supply these forces was a very considerable task. Each quarter of the town had its *tlacochcalco*, or house of darts, an arsenal where the military supplies were stored. This was situated near the chief temple, the lofty sides of which made it a natural strong point. At a call to arms the clan leaders could rapidly assemble their men and equip them at these rallying points, which were also centers of the religious and social life of the community.[9]

An offensive campaign was a more serious undertaking. Having no beasts of burden, the warriors had to carry their own food with them. Due to the governmental system, wherein each town was independent, the armies did not dare live off the country for fear of inciting revolt and also because most communities lacked the food to sustain a large body of men. Thus, prior to a war, negotiations had to be made whereby supplies could be concentrated and allies brought together at a point as near as possible to the zone of attack. Usually a single battle decided the issue, since the attacking force could not maintain itself in the field for more than a very few days. The calculations necessary to fight a war two or three hundred miles away in Oaxaca, say, were highly complex, and much of the Aztec force on such a campaign must have been composed of local tribesmen, stiffened with a *garde d'élite* of Tenochcas and Texcocans.

Owing to this difficulty in respect to transport, siege operations were virtually impossible, so that formal fortifications were rare. Some towns were built in very strategic locations, high on a mountainside or in the bend of a river, having access restricted to a narrow neck of land. Tenochtitlan, owing to its situation on the lake, was a natural fort. The causeways were penetrated by canals at intervals, so that removal of the portable bridges created natural barriers. The flat roof tops offered good points from which to harry the enemy in the street below, and the many temples were strong points difficult to reduce. (See Plate 37, top.)

Miles of defensive walls surrounded a site in Tlaxcala, where a ditch backed by a wall enclosed an area of several square miles. At Huexotla,* a fief of Texcoco, a wall at least fifteen feet high still exists and must have had a strong defensive value, although its ostensible purpose was to enclose the area about the main temple. Xochicalco† is situated on a high hill which was intensively terraced, and it was further strengthened by a wide ditch cut through the point of easiest access. Sometimes a site was chosen between two ravines which made impassable obstacles to an attacking force. However, while defensive *purposes* were often taken into account in building towns, strictly defensive *works*, in the nature of fortifications, were seldom undertaken.[10]

Open fighting, the difficulty of keeping up extended campaigns and the informal character of the military force were factors which stultified the development of tactics or strategy. In battle the howling mob which represented the collective

*Way-sho'-tla.   †Sho-chi-ca'l-co.

strength of one tribe tried to rout the yelling horde of their adversary, and the first to run lost the battle. Captives were taken, tribute imposed, the temple burned, and the defeated group was then left alone again.

To attain victory more easily surprise attacks, sometimes implemented by a little treachery, were instituted. However, the cumbrous process of getting an army onto the field of battle usually prevented this favored method of warfare. More often the Tenochcas and their allies would feint with a screen of warriors, who would be easily repulsed in a pretended rout. The main body would wait in a place of concealment until the pursuing enemy came into view, whereupon they would charge out and demolish them. Losses were chiefly felt in the number of captives taken, since these short hand-to-hand combats were not very damaging to the man power of either side. The capture of a chief or the recognition of a sign of evil portent was sufficient to demoralize an army and, despite their bravery and constant experience in warfare of this type, the Aztecs were little fitted to resist soldiers trained in European techniques.

There was rather more opportunity for strategy than for battle tactics. Considerable planning, as we have said, was necessary to move troops upon the field of battle. The Aztecs won campaigns in Oaxaca, Puebla, western Mexico and along the Vera Cruz coast, as far north as Tamaulipas.* Having to move step by step and to intimidate or win over town after town, they needed patience and knowledge of geographical and political conditions. One reason for the honor in which merchants were held was the information of this character which they could furnish from their travels.

*Ta-mow-le'e-pas.

The triple alliance was a typical example of Aztec strategy. Nezahualcoyotl wanted to restore the hegemony of Texcoco and destroy Tezozomoc's Tepanec power, the center of which was Azcapotzalco. The two towns were separated by the Lake of Mexico. To move troops overland would have required several days; to move them across the lake in canoes would have meant having a landing base on the western shore. Nezahualcoyotl, therefore, induced Tlacopan and Tenochtitlan, which were at the back door of Azcapotzalco and tributary to it as well, to declare war. Thus he had a base at which to land his canoes filled with troops, and while his allies engaged the enemy strongly in this quarter, the Texcocan chief had time to bring reinforcements around the lakes by the overland route to attack another point.

The town of Chiconauhtla offers another example of these simple strategic ideas. This settlement dominated the straits through which the northern lakes of Zumpango and Xaltocan empty into Lake Texcoco. The people here could destroy any force in canoes moving east against Texcoco or west against Azcapotzalco. Their forces also could make a flank attack on land armies skirting the lakes against either of those two objectives. Early in the thirteenth century Chiconauhtla became a fief of Texcoco and participated, as a sort of guardian of the western marches, in campaigns against rebellious western tribes and in the great war with Tezozomoc. Later it seems to have become part of the Tenochtitlan chain of vassal towns, and its chief had the honor of sharing a royal apartment in Montezuma's palace with the rulers of far more important city-states. To confirm this documentary evidence excavation of the site reveals, in the quantity and quality of the material culture surviving, evidence of participation in trade and booty far in excess of the apparent size and importance of the town.[11] (See map, end papers; Plates 41, top; 42, top; 43.)

The purely economic and military aspects of war are as crude, when judged by our modern technical standards, as the rest of the purely mechanical aspects of Aztec life. On the other hand, the ritualistic conception of war as the earthly re-enactment of the titanic struggle between opposing forces in nature has a quality almost sublime. The political and economic frictions that brought about conflict were welcomed by the warriors as an opportunity to vibrate to the deep rhythms of nature, rhythms which met in a celestial antiphony in the Sacred War which the Sun fights each day as he, by his own death and sacrifice, ensures the life of man.

The War of Flowers was undertaken to satisfy this yearning when no active campaign was in progress. In this incongruously named ceremonial combat the best warriors from several states met in a very real battle, so that feats of arms could be accomplished and captives taken to satisfy the hunger of the gods. One famous War of Flowers was repeated for several years, and the cream of the fighting men of Texcoco, Tenochtitlan and Tlacopan vied with the might of Cholula, Huexotcingo and Tlaxcala. If a warrior were captured he met the most glorious of deaths in direct sacrifice to the Sun. If he lived he gained renown. If he were slain, he was cremated, an honor reserved only for fighting men, and passed on to the special heaven where warriors dwell.[12]

Such warfare had no place in a conflict with Europeans, but, when reduced to fighting for their bare lives against the Spaniards, the Aztecs put up one of the most desperate defenses in history. It was the last sacrifice, in which Aztec civilization offered up its very existence in an effort to survive. Aztec culture achieved, with Stone Age tools, a civilization patterned to balance the life of man against the dimly perceived forces of the universe. Its downfall was inevitable when confronted with that inexorable European world of steel, objective reasoning and a religion adjusted to meet such totally different concepts as the demands of the powerful and the needs of the weak.

We cannot tell what Aztec civilization might have become. Like all the nations of the past, and of the present too, which have flourished and ultimately withered in death, the Aztecs nurtured within themselves the seeds of their own destruction. But before we turn from their remote splendor to the preoccupations of our modern life let us catch two last glimpses of Aztec civilization: one of the city of Tenochtitlan as the Spaniards first saw it, the other of the Aztecs in their ultimate war, profane and deadly on this final occasion.

CHAPTER XIII

GLIMPSE OF TENOCHTITLAN

*What the Spaniards saw when they entered this great
Aztec capital*

THE HISTORY of the Aztecs and their forebears is the most
complete record we have of the growth of any Indian civilization. Their conquest was the greatest feat in the European occupation of the American continent. The Aztecs
were at their zenith in 1519, when Cortes and his four hundred men first landed, and a description of Tenochtitlan,
taken from the contemporary records of the conquerors
themselves, will show us something of the external character
of Indian civilization in America.[1]

Bernal Diaz del Castillo, who left the most personal record
of the Spanish Conquest, tells how his comrade-in-arms on
first beholding Tenochtitlan, the ancient Mexico City, ex-
claimed, "It is like the enchantments they tell of in the legend
of Amadis! Are not the things we see a dream?"

This is lyric language from hard-bitten men-at-arms,
whose chief avocations, while engaged in converting the
heathen, lay in acquiring booty and enjoying the charms of
dusky Dulcineas. Yet in contrast to the drab towns and
tawny hills of Spain, Tenochtitlan must have appeared a
paradise, for its green gardens and white buildings were set
in the midst of blue lakes, ringed by lofty mountains. "Gaz-

ing on such wonderful sights," wrote Bernal Diaz, "we did not know what to say or whether what appeared before us was real, for on one side in the land there were great cities and in the lake ever so many more, and the lake itself was crowded with canoes, and in the causeway were many bridges at intervals, and in front of us stood the great City of Mexico, and we . . . we did not even number four hundred soldiers."[2]

Although socially and governmentally Tenochtitlan was distinctly an American Indian tribal town, outwardly it appeared the capital city of an empire. A bird's-eye view would have revealed an oval island connected with the mainland by three causeways which converged at the center of the city. These roads were cut by waterways over which removable bridges extended. The edges of the island were fringed by the green of the "floating gardens," while at the center the shiny white of the houses predominated, and the verdure was reduced to tiny green squares in the patio gardens. Thrust above the quadrate masses of the roof tops loomed the various clan temples, each set on its platform in the form of a truncated pyramid. The city had few streets or open spaces but was gridded with canals crossed by portable bridges. The two principal plazas were those of the Temple of Tlaltelolco and of the religious center of Tenochtitlan proper, open spaces which gave a welcome relief from the pyramids and official palaces clustered about them. There must have been a curiously living quality about this grouping, the temples seeming to ride like horsemen among the serrated ranks of the houses. (See Plate 37, top.)

Were a visitor to traverse Tenochtitlan from south to north, he would have been struck by the rich variety of sights.

Approaching along the causeway, the traveler of that time passed first between expanses of open water. Then gradually tiny islands of green appeared, made of masses of mud dredged up from the bottom of the shallow lake and held in place by wickerwork. White-clad farmers dexterously poled their tiny dugouts through the maze as they went about the cultivation of their gardens. These irregular islets merged gradually into a more orderly grouping where the accumulation of soil had become stabilized as the roots, striking downward, had established anchorage in the lake bottom and created solid ground. This artificially made land reduced the open water of the lake to mere canals. (See Plate 37, bottom.)

Save for the broad causeways, roads there were none; and along the canals the traveler saw, in increasing numbers, boatloads of produce headed toward the city. Here and there among the green of the crops and trees he caught glimpses of thatched roofs and wattled walls, the huts of the farmers. Then adobe walls of more substantial dwellings began to encroach on the gardens, and the waters of the lake shrank to a canal following the roadway. The adobe walls gave way to the fronts of more pretentious houses plastered white or washed with powdered pumice, a dull, rich red. Now the visitor could realize how the city expanded through the successive creation of artificial islands which bore first a crop, then a modest hut and finally became integral with the masonry of the city proper.

The causeway had now changed from a simple means of communication into a principal street with all its social complexity. Since canals took the place of roads, space for a saunter was so rare that the causeways were as much recreation grounds as arteries of traffic. Thus people out to see the sights, people on errands, people on their way to the myriad functions of religious import, swallowed up the long lines of trotting carriers who, bowed under their burdens, went to the city with produce and tribute or left with goods for barter. Not a wheel turned or a pack animal neighed; transport was on the backs of men or in the bottoms of boats.

Outside the city limits the monotony of antlike columns of laden folk had been but rarely relieved by the passage of a civil functionary, all pomp and feathers, or by a stern merchant with a handful of fighting men, followed by a chain of apprentices, showing the whites of their eyes as they peered from under the press of their tumplines. Now could be seen clan leaders, wearing rich mantles and sniffing flowers as they watched the milling crowd, and black-robed priests whose ears were shredded and whose hair was matted with the blood of self-inflicted penance. There was little sound, little hurry, save for the carriers trotting to reach relief from their burdens. There was an intense vitality, nonetheless, that of a multitude of units participating in complex action, knowing each its allotted part but never the substance of the whole. (See Plates 33–36.)

A glance into the doorway of a house gave welcome relief from the cold-blooded, almost insectlike quality of life outside. A shaded patio was flanked by buildings whose interiors were cool and spacious. Mats and straw cushions on the polished red of the cement floor welcomed the visitor to repose, while the rhythmic clap of hands and the scrape of stone on stone told that tortillas were being made and corn meal ground in a kitchen at the back. Seated in a corner, an elderly man was talking to two small boys, whose

serious faces showed that, already conscious of their participation in the tribal life, they heeded their uncle's precepts
as to conduct befitting boys and men. A fat little girl squatting in the doorway vainly tried to imitate with her stubby
fingers and toy implements the graceful movements of her
mother as she produced fine threads by the cunning manipu-
lation of her spindle. Lolling on a cushion, a young man
idly smoked a cigarette in a cane holder as he picked thought-
fully at the scarcely healed lobe of his ear, tattered by
penitential bloodletting with cactus spine and obsidian
blade.

A fiesta was going on in another house, and one heard the
rich vibration of wooden drums and the high squeal of reed
flutes. The patio was full of people, gay in the bright colors
of their holiday clothes, and the air was heavy with the cloy-
ing scent of lilies. The sharp smells of rich sauces cunningly
mixed from many peppers embroidered this odor, and occasionally a light breeze wafted the cool, mystic scent of incense. Somebody was celebrating his birthday, since in the
background one saw a painted figure adorned with amate
paper, representing the god who presided over that event. A
little apart from the feasters, who partook of their entertainment with dignified pleasure, was a group of old men whose
clownish gestures and burlesque solemnity could be easily
associated with the cups of pulque that a slave was industri-
ously filling for them. Not for nothing had these elders
passed through the rigid self-denial of young manhood; they
were permitted alcoholic indulgence in their old age whenever a feast came to pass. A last backward glance revealed
the musicians, garlanded with flowers, blowing their flutes
and conch shells, while one man beat the head of a cylin-

drical drum and another the wooden tongues in the side of the two-toned *teponaztli*.

Farther up the street the priests seemed to increase in number. More individuals wore the trappings of high office, such as nodding panaches of quetzal plumes and cloaks, the designs of which were worked in feathers like the personal insignia on their circular shields. Evidently the visitor was near the center of the town, and presently the causeway ended in a great open square, where the temples rose above the majestic planes of their pyramidal foundations. In the hard bright light of early afternoon, heat waves joined the smoke of incense in rendering indistinct and unearthly the outlines of the temples.

The short black shadows suggested unspeakable things. Was it imagination or reality, that sickening smell of a filthy butcher shop, that hung in the air in revolting contrast to the immaculate pavement of the temple courtyard? Imagination is too personal and egocentric a sensation for an Indian community, and the great block of the skull rack gave an answer only too firmly founded on fact. Thousands of skulls, threaded on poles, were piled up in orderly symmetry, and the black cavities of their orbits and nasal apertures suggested the marks on infernal dice. Undisturbed by this monument to human sacrifice, a few young men were practicing in a ball court near by. They thrust at a solid rubber ball with agile hips and elbows, in an effort to drive it through two rings set transversely to the walls in the length of the court.

A circular stone placed a short distance away was the scene of a most cruel game. Here, on certain ceremonial days, a tethered captive was forced to defend himself with a wooden club against the onslaught of an adversary whose weapon was set with razor-sharp obsidian blades. Usually he was killed in the most honorable of deaths, that of sacrificial victim to the Sun God, Tonatiuh, but sometimes he would resist so successfully that he gained a pardon. Other disk-shaped stones were placed about the plaza. One, thirteen feet in diameter, was set vertically on a special platform. Carved with a consummate mastery of design, it represented the symbolic history of the world. Another disk, set flat, was hollowed in the center, so that hearts wrung from war captives might be burned to nourish the great gods. This was carved on its surface and edge to commemorate the many conquests of War Chief Tizoc, who was shown dressed as a god, with his captives before him.

In another part of the plaza a sacrifice was to be made. Before a small temple dedicated to one of the myriad Aztec gods a group was gathered, some in the gay panoply of merchants and others wearing the sinister black of the priesthood. A tightly pinioned slave stood in their midst and looked unseeingly before him, resignation, not fear, on his face. The priests rushed him up the steep steps of the temple, followed by the merchants at a more leisurely pace. Two priests seized the slave by either arm, forcing him backward, while two others pulled his legs from under him until his body curved, belly upward, over the altar. A fifth priest plowed his flint knife in a long sweep from the breastbone to the base of the stomach and, reaching into the aperture, with a dexterous twist tore out the heart. This he burned, while it was still throbbing, in a carved stone vase, while the merchants, swinging long ladles of smoking incense, chanted their thanks for a safe and profitable excursion into the hot country. (See Plate 60.)

Paying only the most cursory attention to this pious little scene, knots of chiefs were converging on a large building at a corner of the plaza. The war chief, Montezuma, was planning an attack on a neighboring town, remiss in its tribute payment, so there must be a gathering of clan leaders to prepare for war. Adorned with helmets like the heads of jaguars, eagles and wolves, girt with armor of wadded cotton brocaded in many colors or embroidered with feathers, their faces set with nose and lip ornaments of jade and gold, these fierce-visaged chiefs passed proudly through the door, but in an anteroom to the council chamber they stripped off their ornaments. Then bareheaded and barefooted, with downcast eyes, they made their way to the throne, where sat the slim figure of Montezuma, simply dressed but for the gold crown and jade earrings of his exalted office. (See Plate 33.)

The austerity of the council chamber was not borne out by Montezuma's other apartments, which contained all the appurtenances of a sybaritic potentate. The war chief's two wives and his many concubines occupied magnificent quarters. Kitchens and storehouses were spread over another great space, for not only were there some three hundred guests served at each meal but also a thousand guards and attendants. In contrast to the profusion within, outside the kitchen door squatted patiently a threadbare group of countrymen from whose carrying bags swayed the mottled heads of the trussed turkeys which they had brought as offerings for the royal larder.

Other rooms in Montezuma's palace contained the tribal treasure, composed of the tribute wrung from many towns. Gold, jade, rich feather mantles, baskets of produce, were heaped in abundance. Clerks were listing the goods in picture writing to see that each subject town had fulfilled its quota or else were calculating the share that should be turned over to the various clan stewards. Another patio presented a more animated scene. Here acrobats were practicing their feats and poor, warped dwarfs were composing grosser contortions to win a chiefly smile. In another set of buildings was housed the zoo, where serpents undulated sluggishly and where, from behind wooden bars, peered the greedy, yellow eyes of jaguars and ocelots. In a side room a human arm projecting from a basket of raw meat showed how the bodies of some sacrificial victims were utilized.

The highway to Tlaltelolco extended north from this great plaza, which even today is the center of the city. This wide road, with a canal beside it, was filled with the same indecisive multitude that thronged the southern artery. The setting sun had brought people out on their roof tops. Some leaned over parapets to watch the crowd below, while idlers, squatting in a shaded bit of the street, took equal interest in the slow movements of the householders above them.

A path and a canal, debouching into the main avenue, led to a small square, in the center of which loomed a pyramid. From the patio of an adjacent building shrill cries arose and the dull clash of wooden instruments. Within, a number of boys were receiving instruction in the manual of arms. Each equipped with a small buckler and a flat wooden club, they learned the art of cut and parry under the scornful eye of a warrior. They dealt and received hard blows, but the clubs were not toothed with wedges of obsidian, the volcanic glass that made hand-to-hand combat so vicious in war. Another group was practicing with the *atl-atl*, or throwing stick. The marksman laid his spear along a narrow wooden trough with a hook at the farther end, the nearer end being grasped in the hand. By lengthening the arm in this way it was possible to give a greater propulsive force to the spear.

On the other side of the plaza the boys in the religious-training school presented a less animated scene. Their little legs and faces lacerated by maguey spines, their bodies thin from fasts and penance and their eyes dulled by the monotony of self-denial, these children were chanting strophes from a ritualistic chant. Their preceptor, who led the singing, showed by his own scarred and emaciated body that the propitiation of the gods was a relentless and never-ending task. Priest, chief, warrior or husband, every Aztec, from boyhood on, spent much of his life either in a kind of beseeching penance, to ensure his future, or in a state of grateful atonement for not having had a worst past. The Aztecs lived on intimate if uncomfortable terms with the supernatural powers.

Another aspect of this lack of individualism was to be seen in the *tecpan* or clan building. Here elders of the clan were arranging the affairs of the tribal unit, twenty of which made up the city-state of Tenochtitlan. One old man peered over picture maps as he adjusted a question of land tenure between two contesting families and made his final judgment on the basis of how much land each family could cultivate by its own efforts. Another elder distributed pottery vessels, given up as tribute by a town across the mountains, to some of the poorer members of the community. None of these people, litigants or applicants, bestowed more than occasional glances into the back courtyard, where an adulterer was being stoned to death by members of the affronted family. Urban existence contained too many interests and life was too cheap for them to view as an excitement the inevitable result of wrongdoing.

Each of the twenty tribal divisions regulated its own affairs. The great plaza where Montezuma had his palace and where all the gods were worshiped in many temples was for the use of all the clans together; and was the civic center for the sixty thousand households of Tenochtitlan. Yet in spite of the importance of this center of religion and government, the great plaza of Tlaltelolco near the northern edge of the islands was almost as striking. Once a Mexican tribe acknowledged the sway of another power it was supposed to furnish fighting men and tribute, but its government and economics were seldom modified.

Thus the recently conquered Tlaltelolco had a communal center as majestic as that of Tenochtitlan. It seemed more dramatic to Spanish eyes because its great temple to the War God, Huitzilopochtli, was thrust into prominence by the wide spread of the market place, while in Tenochtitlan the great buildings were so close together it was hard to gain an impression of their size.

The market place of Tlaltelolco consisted of a large area of polished pavement, bordered by arcades which sheltered many of the merchants. At one edge a basin opened out from the canal beside the northern causeway, where boats bringing goods and produce could find an anchorage. Each kind of product was concentrated in a special place. Thus one section was completely devoted to vegetables, and compactly squatting women sat watching their goods, arranged before them in symmetrical heaps on woven mats. In another section cotton mantles were being sold, some spread to show the full design and others neatly folded. Elsewhere was a row of vendors of implements and tools, such as obsidian blades, carved and burnished pottery, spindle whorls, deer-horn awls, bone bodkins and a few copper axes and needles. A brilliant mass of color characterized the booths of the feather salesmen. Some sold merely bunches of plumes, the lovely green of the quetzal, or trogon, and the multicolored plumage of parrots. At the other stands feather cloaks, mats and shields gave evidence of charming fancy in their design and patient toil in their execution. (See Plates 38–39.)

Jewelers displayed jade ornaments and gold worked into precious rings of filigree or massive beaten gorgets. It was the jade, however, that caught the envious eye and was pro-duced with furtive circumspection as a material of great price. Other merchants sold ornaments of shell, and the pinks, whites and subtle mottled browns of sea shells con-trasted with the rich dark sheen of tortoise carapaces. At one booth a rich warrior earnestly bargained with the pro-prietor for an exquisite pair of earplugs, cunningly inlaid with a mosaic of turquoise and mother-of-pearl.

The smiling whispers and admiring glances of the crowd at the jeweler's abruptly changed in the slave quarters to appraising stares. Some of the chattels wore wooden collars, and their brutish faces had a hopeless expression. These had sunk to servitude long ago as a result of crime or of capture in war. Others were thin and emaciated but did not wear the collar of bondage. They had met with misfortune and were selling themselves for the first time to ensure food and shelter.

A low hum rose from the market place; there was none of the strident shouting of the European fair. The bargaining for goods was carried on slowly, quietly, but, nonetheless, keenly. The Aztecs had no money, so that barter was the usual means of purchase. The cacao bean, however, had a standard value, and this, in equalizing exchanges, performed the nearest approach to the function of currency. Passing through the crowd were warriors who acted as police and, should a disagreement arise, haled disputants into a court where a tribal elder settled the question in his capacity as judge.

Beyond the market was a double line of walls which divided the market from the temple precinct of Tlaltelolco. Rectangular buildings, with patios in their centers, housed the priests and the various schools and councils of the central organization of the community. Farther on were grouped the principal shrines. In their midst the great temple to the War God shouldered its bulk into the sky. There was a skull rack here, like the one in Tenochtitlan, and another heap was made of the bones of the victims. Near the great pyramid stood a circular temple, the door of which was built to resemble the mouth of a serpent, the place of worship of the god Quetzalcoatl. The sacrificial block in front was black with the smoke of incense and the blood of victims. A pile of stone knives and axes gave a sinister indication of what rites were practiced there.

Pools fed by the pipes of an aqueduct leading from the mainland gave an impression of quiet peace. The reflections of the temples, distorted occasionally by the breeze, intensified the brooding mysticism of the sacred enclosure. In contrast to the austerity of the priests, young girls, their eyes virtuously downcast, slipped back and forth, carrying out the various errands of their training school within the enclosure. The great pyramid and the temple of the War God

PLATE 49

AZTEC ART

Porphyry mask, Teayo, Vera Cruz. This mask is an outstanding example of Aztec art, even though it was made outside of the borders of their domain. This carving and the Eagle Knight on Plate 40 are perhaps the finest secular sculptures from the Aztec period.

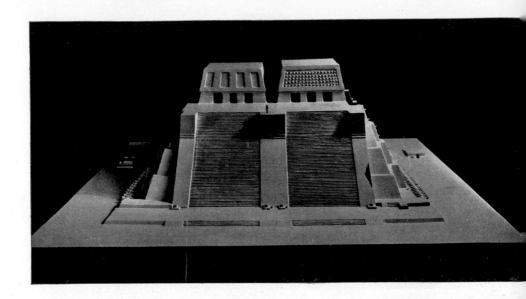

PLATE 50

AZTEC ARCHITECTURE

The temples were the most imposing aspect of Aztec architecture. Top: Model of the Temple of Tenayuca as it looked at the time of the Conquest. Bottom: The temple as it looked during excavation. The staircase focused the attention of the worshipers on the culmination of each ceremony, a human sacrifice. Compare also Plates 60 and 61.

PLATE 51

AZTEC ART

TOP: This modest shrine in honor of the War God is on the borders of the Aztec territory at Santiago Huatusco, Vera Cruz. This engraving of Dupaix, made a hundred years ago, shows that the temple has suffered little in the last hundred years, but few other buildings resisted the destruction of war and evangelism. BOTTOM: The Zocalo, Mexico City, looking northeast. This was the site of the great plaza of Tenochtitlan. The President's palace (*upper right*) rests on the foundations of Montezuma's palace. The great temple to the Gods of War and Rain stood just east of the cathedral. At the streetcar crossing in the foreground a large disk like the Calendar Stone (Plate 52) still lies buried. The present square is built on the remains of the Tenochcan city, twenty feet above the ancient level.

PLATE 52

AZTEC ART

TOP: The Calendar Stone, thirteen feet in diameter, represents the history of the world. It is arranged in concentric circles, at the center of which is the sun set within the sign Four Motion, the date of the present era. The dates of the preceding eras are given in the four arms of the Motion sign. The twenty day names encircle the central symbols, and they are enclosed by glyphs for turquoise and jade, signifying "precious" and the color of the heavens. Beyond this band radiate sun's rays and star symbols, while the outer border consists of two great fire snakes, symbolizing time. BOTTOM: The National Stone, a monolithic block in the Mexican National Museum, suggests how the Calendar Stone was probably set on a platform. Its symbolism represents the Sacred War, the eternal conflict between the contrasting and opposing forces of nature.

PLATE 53

AZTEC ART

Top: This feathered snake in the Mexican National Museum may well symbolize Quetzalcoatl, God of Learning and the Priesthood. This representation differs from the fire snake in that it lacks a raised crest over the head. Bottom: The enormous snake at the foot of the balustrade to the great temple in Mexico is a dramatic architectural ornament, frequently employed in Aztec temple building. Snakes were the major ornament at Tenayuca (Plate 50, above) and many other Aztec buildings, appearing also far to the east in Mexican Chichen Itza.

PLATE 54

AZTEC ART

TOP: Coatlicue, the Mother of the Gods, a highly important member of the pantheon. This representation, over eight feet high, displays her power in terms of such fearsome attributes as two snakeheads, a necklace of a skull, hands and hearts, a skirt of writhing snakes and claws on her feet. The bottom of the statue's feet is carved to represent the earth monster. BOTTOM: Wooden drum with two tongues (*teponaztli*) in the form of an ocelot. The smooth. simple outlines contrast with the macabre congestion of the presentation above.

PLATE 55
AZTEC ART

TOP: Another presentation of Coatlicue, the Mother of the Gods. An earth goddess, she is also associated with death, so that in this case her head is a human skull.
BOTTOM: *Left:* Small rock-crystal skull representing the Death God. This is a fine example of Aztec lapidary

work. *Right:* A box, symbolically carved, to hold human hearts. Note the glyph for jade, i.e., "precious," banding the sides of the container.

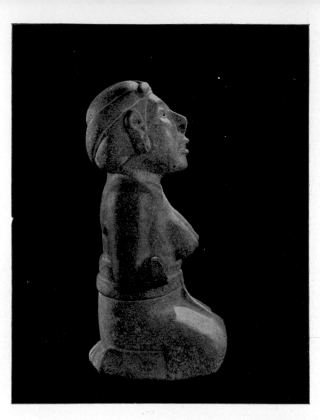

AZTEC ART

T<small>OP</small>: This Corn Goddess is envisage[d]
as a young girl. Her soft Indi[an]
beauty is brought out with the san[e]
sure simplicity which characterizes t[he]
warriors on Plates 40 and 49. B<small>OTTO</small>[M]:
A colossal head, nearly four feet hig[h,]
of Coyolxauhqui, sister of the W[ar]
God. She is shown dead. Simp[le]
handling of details enhances th[e]
monumental conception.

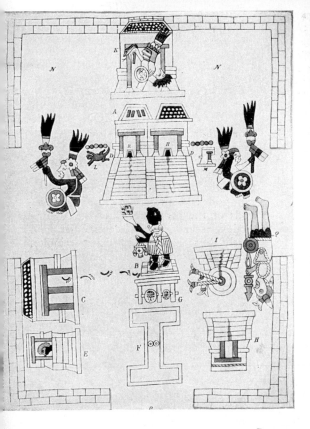

PLATE 57

AZTEC RELIGION

Top: Tezcatlipoca, Smoking Mirror, from fresco at Tizatlan. Bottom: *Left:* The Codex Florentino plan of Tenochtitlan (cf. Plate 37). A. The shrines of Huitzilopochtli and Tlaloc. B. Priest. C. Priests' quarters. D. Temple platform. E. Eagle warriors' quarters. F. Ball court. G. Skull rack. H. Temple of Xipe. I. Sacrificial stone. K. Old temple of Huitzilopochtli. L. Five Lizard (date) and Macuiixochitl, God of Flowers. M. Five House (date) and same god. N. Dancing places. Q. Image of Xipe. P. Doors into sacred enclosure. *Right:* Gold ornament representing the vertical universe; at top gods play ball, symbolizing the sky and the movement of the planets, next the sun disk, then a flint knife, representing the moon, and finally the earth monster.

PLATE 59
AZTEC RELIGION

TOP: *Left:* Tlaloc, God of Rain. *Right:* Quetzalcoatl, God of Learning, in guise of Ehecatl, God of Wind. BOTTOM: Page from *Tonalamatl* of Codex Borbonicus. The goddess Itzpapalotl, presiding over the fifteenth week, One House, is shown in the large division. The broken tree signifies Tamoanchan, a legendary homeland; the house below, with a man on top and the night sign in the door and the spider above, signifies the realm of darkness. The other symbols are offerings. The rectangular divisions refer to the days and their Gods. The day signs and numbers begin at the lower left with One House and end at top left with Thirteen Eagle. A Night God is drawn in each day square, beginning with Piltzintecuhtli and ending with Chalchihuitlicue (Table XVI, 194). The squares above the bottom row and to the right of the vertical row reveal the Gods of the Day Hours and their birds, beginning at the left with Xiuhtecuhtli and ending at the top with Ilamatecuhtli (Table XV).

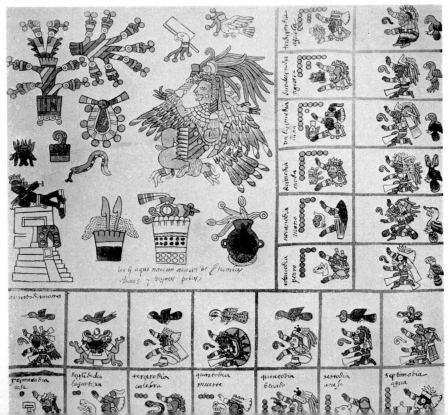

PLATE 60

AZTEC RELIGION

Top: *Left:* Priests and laymen sacrifice two victims in honor of the War God. *Right:* War captive on sacrificial stone defends himself against members of the warrior orders. Bottom: *Left:* Sacrificial knife with mosaic handle representing an Eagle Knight, in the British Museum. These pictures from the Codex Florentino reveal the technique of using a stone knife to make a deep enough incision to reach the heart and tear it out. *Right:* Sacrifice to the Sun.

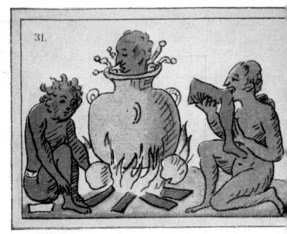

PLATE 61

AZTEC RITUAL

TOP: *Left:* Dressing a victim and equipping him with the proper headdress, shield and magical mirror to play the part of Tezcatlipoca. *Right:* Sacrifice of the victim after a year. Note the flutes discarded by him as he ascended the stair. MIDDLE: *Left:* Dressing a priest in the costume of Xipe, the Flayed God, who wears a human skin. *Right:* Musicians with rattle and skin-covered drum, *huehuetl.* BOTTOM: *Right:* Ceremonial cannibalism. The Codex Florentino artist had obviously never taken part in such a feast, fairly common before the Conquest.

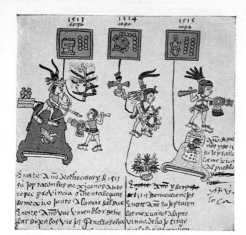

PLATE 62

AZTEC RECORDS

TOP: *Left:* Conquests of Montezuma II; see Plate 63 for method of reading (Telleriano-Remensis). MIDDLE: *Left:* The migration of the Aztec tribes. They leave an island by boat and reach a hill with a cave, where Huitzilopochtli lives. They divide into several migrant groups. The list here includes, from top to bottom, Matlatzincas, Tepanecas, Chichimecas, Malinalcas, Cuitlahuacas, Xochimilcas, Chalcas and Huexotzincas (Codex Boturini). *Right:* Meeting of Montezuma, Cortes, and Marina (Lienzo de Tlaxcala). BOTTOM: *Left:* Monthly Ceremony (Codex Bordonicus). *Right:* Tribute Roll (Codex Mendoza).

PLATE 63

AZTEC WRITING

A page from the Codex Telleriano-Remensis describes the period from 1424–39. The cartouches give the year names, indicating the succession of the four days with the thirteen numbers. The sequence may be readily followed: Ten Knife, Eleven House, Twelve Rabbit, Thirteen Reed, One Knife, Two House, etc. The death of Chimalpopoca (Smoking Shield) is recorded for the year Twelve Rabbit (1426), as is the accession of Itzcoatl (Snake of Knives). Each ruler is designated by his hieroglyph. The defeat of Maxtla (Breech Clout) is depicted as well as an eclipse of the sun shown by the disk obscured by a stone. The figures and descriptions were inserted after the Conquest by two priests (to judge from the handwriting), who made use of native informants. (Compare Plate 62, *top left.*)

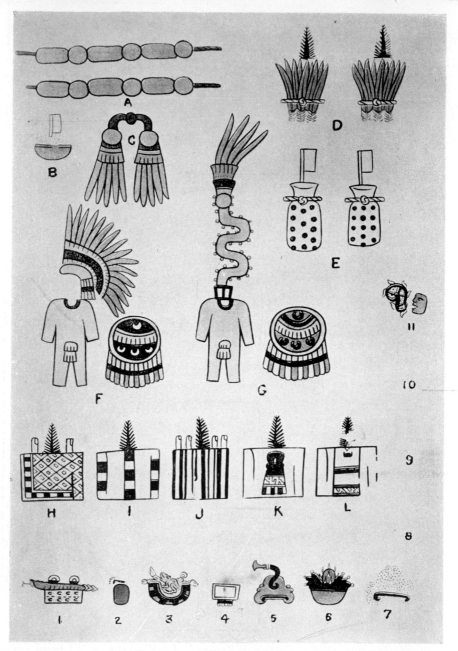

PLATE 64
AZTEC WRITING

A page from the Tribute Roll of Montezuma (after Spinden, 1928). The tributary towns are in the columns at bottom and right, designated by numbers. The goods comprised: (a) two strings of jade beads; (b) 20 gourd dishes of gold dust; (c) a royal headdress; (d) 800 bunches of feathers; (e) 40 bags of cochineal dye; (f–g) 2 warriors' costumes; (h) 402 cotton blankets of this pattern; (i) 400 blankets; (j) 404 blankets; (k) 400 blankets; (l) 400 blankets. Note the use of fingers for units, flags for twenties and treelike signs for four hundreds. The sign for eight thousand may be found on Plate 62 (*bottom right*) in the top left-hand corner, designating the number of containers of honey.

completely dominated the place. At regular intervals terraces broke the lines of the sloping sides and increased the impression of its size. A wide staircase of one hundred and fourteen narrow steps led up the western side, and so steep was this stair that not until one's head rose clear of the platform did the temple itself come into view.

The temple, in reality, comprised two shrines, built side by side, each having stone walls and soaring roofs of wood coated with plaster. Through the right-hand door one could clearly see the squat figure of Huitzilopochtli carved from the stone and covered with a paste in which were set jade, turquoise, gold and seed pearls. A girdle of gold snakes, picked out in precious stones, adorned his waist, and around his neck hung a string of gold masks covered with turquoise mosaic. By his side stood the statue of an attendant deity, equipped with a short lance and a gold shield, richly decorated with the customary mosaic.

In the adjoining shrine stood an image of Tezcatlipoca, one of the most prominent Aztec gods. His eye sockets were inlaid with mirrors of obsidian, the black depths of which reflected the red gleams of the afternoon light. This statue, too, was adorned with gold and precious stones. High in the wooden roof of this temple perched a small figure of Xipe, the God of Seedtime. Braziers of incense discharged greasy coils of smoke which deepened the gloom of the temples, whose walls were already black with the blood of many victims. In dim corners stood heaps of ritualistic paraphernalia, conch-shell trumpets, knives, banners and baskets of shapeless lumps of meat, surplus human hearts which, for some reason, had not yet been placed upon the braziers. The priests who glided through this murk seemed fitting satellites to the diabolic images to which they ministered. In front of the temples stood the great drum which was soon to throb across the lake as a nation suffered its death agony.

It was from this point that Montezuma showed Cortes his empire, and Bernal Diaz, who witnessed the scene, left us this unforgettable description:

"Then Montezuma took Cortes by the hand and told him to look at his great city and all the other cities that were standing in the water and the many other towns and the land around the lake. . . . So we stood looking about us, for that huge and cursed temple stood so high that from it one could see over everything very well, and we saw the three causeways which led into Mexico . . . and we saw the [aqueduct of] fresh water that comes from Chapultepec, which supplies the city, and we saw the bridges on the three causeways which were built at certain distances apart . . . and we beheld on the lake a great multitude of canoes, some coming with supplies of food, others returning loaded with cargoes of merchandise, and we saw that from every house of that great city and of all the other cities that were built in the water it was impossible to pass from house to house except by drawbridges, which were made of wood, or in canoes; and we saw in those cities Cues [temples] and oratories like towers and fortresses and all gleaming white, and it was a wonderful thing to behold!"[3]

CHAPTER XIV

THE DEATH THROES OF THE AZTEC NATION

A chapter in which are set forth the factors which brought about the success of the Spaniards and the downfall of the Aztecs

THE ROMANTIC CIRCUMSTANCES which attended the fall of the Aztec civilization have long captured the fancy of the European world. A whole nation submitting to a handful of desperate Spanish soldiers offers a dramatic situation, seldom paralleled in our annals. Yet given the unflinching generalship of a Cortes, the collapse of the Aztec tribes was inevitable. The psychological conditions inherent in this type of Indian culture could not withstand European military technique any more than could the varied civilizations which became colonies of Europe in every continent on the face of the globe.[1]

There are times in the histories of all peoples when the national will seems to disintegrate before intangible factors individually insignificant. All students of military affairs are familiar with these sudden routs affecting the high courage of victors as well as the grim fortitude of those who previously have unflinchingly endured successive defeats. The Aztecs' war against the Spanish Conquistadors is an elusive example of the paralysis of the national morale, followed by a defense carried on with that courage found in forsaken men, in this case abandoned by their very gods. We have seen, in the bitter year of 1940, the same pattern repeated when France collapsed and England found a new strength in despair.

An examination of the Mexican social structure in relation to the psychological state of the Aztec mind shows that the Spaniards arrived at a time very favorable for conquest. Comparison of the Aztec military technique with the European discipline and armament of the day reveals an exceptional opportunity for the triumph of European tactics. To explain the familiar tale of the Conquest from the Indian point of view may throw into sharper relief this conflict between two systems of civilization.

Aztec war was highly ceremonial and fought in a spirit very different from the realistic calculation of European strife. The *technical* equipment of the Indians did not meet the requirements of a conflict waged in terms of European military *practice*. Moreover, Cortes arrived at the end of the summer, when the tribes of Mexico were too busy harvesting the crops essential for their survival to think seriously of military affairs. A final factor dooming the Aztecs to inevitable defeat was the political structure of Indian Mexico, which provided no way of converting military success to the establishment of a powerfully consolidated state.

The Aztec theocracy did not lend itself to governing or absorbing conquered peoples, although in time a social mechanism might have been developed. While the Aztecs received tribute from over a wide territory, there were constant revolts and betrayals. Probably this same process went on among the other tribal groups in Mexico, so that the political organization of the region as a whole was far from that of an empire. In reality a multitude of independent city-states seethed with intrigue and war and were further disunited by differences in language, dialect, physical type and geographic economy. An invader, with a strongly disciplined force small enough to live off the country and thus to stay in the field, could have an astonishing success, particularly if he had a taste for intrigue. Cortes, as events proved, was the ideal man for such a purpose, and he was further favored by the psychological reaction of the Aztecs to his arrival.

The years before the Spanish Conquest had, to the Aztecs, been full of portents suggestive of future evil. There seems to have been in the air that same sense of paralysis that the French knew to their cost in 1939 and 1940. Montezuma, the war chief of the Aztecs and an amateur of witchcraft, had had an experience calculated completely to shake his nerve. He and Nezahualpilli, the chief of Texcoco, had fallen to arguing about the respective merits of their soothsayers, since the Texcocan held that strangers were going to rule the land of Anahuac. So convinced was Nezahualpilli of the correctness of his interpretation that he wagered his kingdom against three turkey cocks, the result to be decided by a ritualistic ball game with Montezuma. The latter won the first two games, but Nezahualpilli took the last three in a row. The defeat must have been disheartening to Montezuma, not only because he had so much to fear from the future, but also because his own experts had been held so cheap. (See Fig. 3.)

In close succession followed a series of phenomena, each bearing its message of woe to come. A column of fire was seen every midnight throughout the year; two temples were destroyed, one by a sudden fire, the other by lightning unaccompanied by thunder. A comet was seen by day, and sudden waves came up on the Lake of Texcoco. A sixth sign was a woman's voice crying, "My children, we are lost." Monsters appeared and were brought before the chief, only to disappear as soon as he had seen them. Most sinister of all

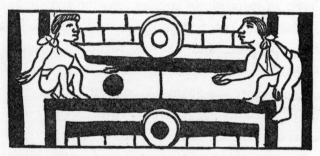

Fig. 3. The years before the Spanish Conquest had been full of evil omens for the Aztecs. To determine whether the dire predictions of Nezahualpilli, chief of Texcoco, were correct, Montezuma played and lost a ritualistic game of "basketball" with him as depicted above. *Codex Florentino*

was a bird brought in by some hunters. This bird had a mirror in its head, revealing the heavens, and when Montezuma peered at it a second time a host of armed men was disclosed. When the chief brought his soothsayers to witness this augury and to explain its significance, the bird flew away. Distorted as these occurrences seem to us, they must have had a most upsetting effect on the population of the Valley of Mexico.[2] (See Figs. 4, 28A–B.)

Consequently the emotional condition of the people was peculiarly receptive to the rumors, drifting in from the southeast, which told of four-legged monsters with human bodies issuing from their backs. As these strange beings moved up the coast Montezuma's spies and ambassadors began to bring back more precise reports as to their nature, and even presents and messages for their chief. (See Fig. 5.)

FIG. 4. Montezuma views the magical bird in the head of which was a mirror, showing first the heavens, then hosts of armed men, foretelling, according to tradition, the Spanish Conquest. *Codex Florentino*

The strangers were human, for they were vulnerable, receiving wounds and dying from assaults upon them. They had new and strange weapons, noisy and lethal, for cannon, muskets, crossbows and steel swords were unknown to the Aztecs. Also novel and dreadful adjuncts of war were the horses and the savage mastiffs of the Spaniards. In battle the strangers were invincible, operating in a manner completely

FIG. 5. The Spaniards land in 1519 at the site of Vera Cruz. Their ship and equipment are carefully shown. At the right, Marina, Cortes' interpreter, is exercising her diplomacy on a native. *Codex Florentino*

FIG. 6. Aztec sorcerers, sent from the highland, offer bewitched food to Cortes and his staff, who disdain the viands. *Codex Florentino*

foreign to Indian principles of war. The simple Indian methods of mass attack were of little avail against the maneuvering of a well-drilled force, for the native tactics could only bring the merest fraction of their fighting force in direct contact with the enemy.

The Spaniards also resisted witchcraft on the occasion when Montezuma seriously applied it. However, sorcery, according to native standards, was at best a two-edged weapon, so that it is doubtful if this failure had any other than a confirmatory bearing on the Indian attitude of mind toward the supernatural quality of the Spaniards. The problem that beset Montezuma was not that the invaders were themselves gods, but that they were the symbols, the vicars on earth, as it were, of vast unearthly forces bent on establishing a new social order. As such the Spaniards required the most gingerly handling.[3] (See Fig. 6.)

When the Spaniards were approaching the capital a political problem entered to complicate the spiritual one. The

city-states, or pueblos, between the Valley of Mexico and
the coast were independent communities and, even if tributary to the Valley powers, were often reluctantly so. Therefore, many of these tribes, like the Totonacs, welcomed the
invaders as the spearhead for an open revolt. Others, like the
completely independent and warlike Tlaxcalans, put the
power of Cortes to a practical test in open battle and, when
the Spaniards won, became the most loyal of Cortes' sup-
porters. Cholula, a large town loosely allied to the Aztecs,
met the Spaniards as friends, plotting to overcome them by
treachery, a good Indian political maneuver instigated, perhaps, by Montezuma. The Spaniards, suspecting such a move,
counteracted its efficacy by a judiciously executed massacre,
thus, if not gaining a friendly community, at least creating a
noncombatant one. (See Figs. 7–9.)

Montezuma and his more cautious counselors watched this

FIG. 7. Cortes and his
army, on passing the
great volcanoes southeast
of Mexico City, ask the
way. Note the smoke
issuing from the crater of
Popocatepetl. *Codex Florentino*

Fig. 8. Montezuma, upset by the magical premonitions of disaster and by the failure of his sorcerers, does not know whether to flee or hide in a cave. *Codex Florentino*

slow ascent from the coast with apprehensive interest. He has been condemned by many commentators as an appeaser and has been made the scapegoat of this great debacle of Indian civilization. Yet consider his position. While the leading man in his community, he was not an authoritarian monarch. For mass action he had to rely on the group decision of the clans comprising his tribe, as well as on the very doubtful allegiances of the vassal states, whose immediate needs transcended any sacrifice of a far-reaching political nature. Thus not only the demands of the harvest season but also the fear of damage to the communal property made communities loath for war. Montezuma had no method of enforcing a long-range diplomatic policy, such as is so characteristic of European and oriental political history. Nor must the extraordinary gifts of Cortes and his Indian mistress Marina be underrated. The pair played on Indian psychology as master pianists would execute a duet on the piano.

His hands tied by both practical and psychological con-
siderations, Montezuma received Cortes and the Spaniards
without having struck a positive blow. Then ensued a new
chapter in the story. Cortes promptly seized Montezuma as
a hostage, and the latter's power to influence his tribesmen
disintegrated. A mass revulsion against the invaders slowly
began to crystallize, but it was confined to the city itself,
without extending to the neighboring towns. People kept
themselves within their houses; the market closed, yet no
overt act was made. Cortes was allowed to leave for the coast
to subjugate his new commander Narvaez, without open hos-
tilities on the part of the Aztecs. (See Figs. 10–13.)

The storm broke during Cortes' absence. Some inhabitants

FIG. 9. Cortes meets high dignitaries from Tlaxcala, the pueblo
most loyal to the conquerors. Marina interprets while supplies of
corn, tortillas, turkeys, etc., are accumulated. *Lienzo de Tlaxcala*

FIG. 10. The Spanish forces reach Tenochtitlan, the modern Mexico City, and Montezuma and his nobles come to greet Cortes. *Codex Florentino*

FIG. 11. Marina's value to Cortes cannot be underestimated. Here she is ordering an Aztec to perform some duty. To judge from the speech scrolls, he complies with ill grace. *Codex Florentino*

FIG. 12. A great aid to the Spanish military success was the use of cavalry. Here we see mounted crossbowmen, whose weapons were no less deadly than the firearms of the day. *Codex Florentino*

FIG. 13. Cortes seizes Montezuma as a hostage. The Aztec chief tries to calm his rebellious subjects who treat him with the contempt due a traitor. *Codex Florentino*

of Tenochtitlan had assembled to celebrate the feast of the god Huitzilopochtli. Alvarado, a tough soldier, lacking all Cortes' gifts of intrigue, scented trouble in this gathering, the actual innocence of which he had no way of knowing. Following the Spanish technique at Cholula, he fell upon the celebrants and killed them all. The city rose like one man and drove the garrison to cover. Actuated by the single motive of revenge against the invaders, the Aztecs were ready to destroy the Spanish garrison. However, the structural weakness of the Indian government became bitterly evident when the chiefs permitted Cortes and his reinforce-

Fig. 14. Following a series of outrages committed by the invaders, the citizens rise in arms against the Spanish. The Spaniards and their Tlaxcalan allies are besieged in the palace of Axayacatl. In this scene a field piece is shown in action, while the horsemen are held in reserve for a sortie. *Lienzo de Tlaxcala*

ments from the army of Narvaez to join the beleaguered
troops of Alvarado. The ceremonial aspect of war in Indian
Mexico did not envisage the splitting of an adversary's army
and the separate destruction of its weakened parts, a rudimentary law of European military tactics.

Yet once the Spaniards were united in the city they ceased
to be a military problem and became the emotional focus of
the Indians' wrath and fear. They had to shut themselves up
in the palace of Axayacatl to resist the force of this uprising
in which the whole tribe participated. The Aztecs, having
immobilized their enemies, visited their hate and rage in a
manner unparalleled in the annals of Indian campaigns.
Every citizen joined in hurling missiles at the besieged in-

Fig. 15. Here the Spanish are dislodging the Aztecs from a temple,
where the Indians had gathered to enfilade them. *Lienzo de Tlaxcala*

ve q;que qubxac alt.

FIG. 16. Wooden tanks were built by Cortes to protect his men when Aztecs took up positions on the housetops out of reach of the sallies of Spanish cavalry. This spirited picture reveals the tanks separated by a canal into which a horse had fallen. The Aztecs on the roofs impede its rescue. *Lienzo de Tlaxcala*

vaders, and masses of warriors blocked every sally the Spaniards made from their refuge. (See Figs. 14–15.)

The Spaniards could not maneuver in the narrow foot-paths along the canals, and the portable fortresses they constructed of wood, the first tanks used in the New World, were useless against enemies on housetops and in canoes.[4] (See Fig. 16.) The Spaniards lost heavily, and the unfortunate Montezuma met his death either at the hands of his own people, whom he was trying to calm, or, as two excellent authorities have it, at those of the Spaniards.[5] After having passed a week shut up in the palace Cortes decided to withdraw from Tenochtitlan. Just before dawn his forces made

their way through the hushed streets out along the causeway
to Tacuba.

A woman getting water from a canal, saw them and raised
the alarm. The whole male population surged forth along
the roofs and through the streets. Some seized canoes and at-
tacked the flanks of the marching column. The Aztecs tore
up the bridges, and many Spaniards, laden down with gold,
sank ignominiously beneath the waters or, while trying to
keep afloat, were clubbed to death by warriors in boats.
Alvarado, ever the precipitous man of action, confronted
by a wide gap in the causeway, plunged his lance into the lake
bottom and in full armor vaulted over to the other side.[6]
The panic increased, and order was not restored until the
Spaniards reached Tacuba. Cortes sat under a giant cypress
and wept as he took toll of his losses. Three quarters of the
Spanish army had been lost in this rout and in the preceding
siege. (See Fig. 18.)

The Spaniards found a temporary sanctuary on the hill
of Los Remedios. Their adversaries, instead of following up

FIG. 17. A handful of the
Spaniards reach the main-
land. The Aztecs, instead of
following up their advan-
tages, plunder the bodies of
the killed and drowned. Be
it remembered, however, the
Spanish carried off the entire
Aztec treasure. *Codex Florentino*

FIG. 18. Supplies run low and Cortes secretly tries to reach the mainland along a causeway. His retreat is discovered and the Aztecs, massing their forces in canoes, wreak havoc on the Spanish forces. Tearing up the bridges, the Aztecs further hindered the retreat and all but destroyed the invading army. *Lienzo de Tlaxcala*

their advantage, plundered the dead and tried to recover the booty stolen by the Spaniards from the Aztec treasury. They lost a precious opportunity to destroy the remnants of the Spanish army by not carrying their attack to its logical conclusion. (See Fig. 17.)

However, the Indians did make some effort toward concerted action later. The Texcocans, formerly the principal allies of the Aztecs, gathered their forces together and tried to intercept the Spaniards as they made their way cross country to the homeland of their allies, the Tlaxcalans. At Otumba battle was joined. The Indians in their battle formation could not overcome the mobility and tactical sense of the Spaniards. Wounded as every man was, and exhausted from lack of food and sleep, they kept their discipline; and a desperate charge by the cavalry reached the chiefs, who fell before the Spanish swords. Once their leaders were slain, the scant Indian discipline dissolved, and the tribesmen took flight. The Spaniards made their way to Tlaxcala to recuperate and to await reinforcements.

Montezuma was succeeded by his brother Cuitlahuac, and he, dying of the fever after four months, was replaced as war chief by their nephew, the heroic Cuauhtemoc. This strong and courageous leader was unable to overcome the mutual distrust of the Indian communities for each other. When the Aztecs might have joined together with other tribes to overwhelm the Spaniards by sheer weight of numbers, they did nothing.

In the meantime Cortes, having rested his army, began to consolidate his position. He made two series of campaigns, one eastward to the sea and the other in a south and westerly direction in the present state of Morelos. Utilizing Indian allies both as carriers and as a screen to conceal his more serious tactical movements, he subjugated town after town.

chalchicueyeca

Fig. 19. Due to the hesitancy of the Aztecs, Cortes was able to reach Tlaxcala and refit his army. Here we see military supplies being brought from the coast. In the left center a minor disaster, involving the drowning of several Indian allies, is depicted. *Lienzo de Tlaxcala*

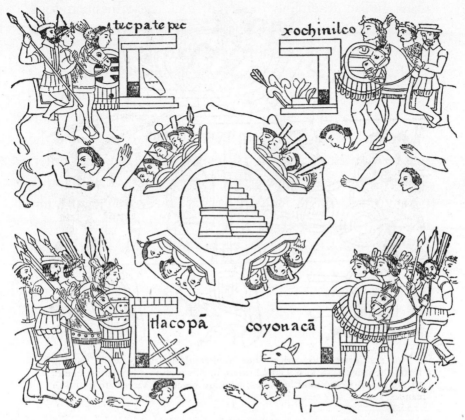

FIG. 20. Cortes' plan to retake Tenochtitlan involved isolating the island city from the mainland. Tenochtitlan is shown in the center of the picture, surrounded by the lake on which float the war canoes of its defenders. The Spanish forces devote themselves to reducing the mainland towns. *Lienzo de Tlaxcala*

In each case the Indian war convention of a single decisive mêlée proved worthless against the versatility of the Spanish attack. Cortes soon pacified the eastern country sufficiently to try to regain Tenochtitlan. (See Fig. 19.)

Typical Indian perfidy, from our point of view today, but common sense to the people of that era, virtually accomplished the downfall of Mexico. The Texcocans, closest allies of the Aztecs, and for that reason perhaps the most jealous

FIG. 21. Cortes built brigantines to defend his flanks while moving along the causeways into Tenochtitlan. In this picture a brigantine comes to the aid of Cortes and his allies, who are beset by Aztecs afoot and in canoes. *Lienzo de Tlaxcala*

of their success, resented the part Montezuma had taken in forcing the election of a war chief. When the Aztecs had had a strong chance of maintaining their supremacy after Cortes' retreat from Mexico the Texcocans valiantly took the field at Otumba. Now they switched to the Spanish side, seeing a chance of assuming a dominant position in Valley of Mexico affairs. Their defection gave the Spaniards a base on the Lake of Mexico and a means of mopping up whatever tribes remained unsubjugated in the previous campaign.

Having quieted the countryside, Cortes put into effect his plan of siege. He launched a fleet of small galleys armed with cannon, which had been constructed in Tlaxcala and brought piecemeal across the mountains, to be assembled on the lake. These ships were to sweep the lake clear of canoes and protect the Spanish flanks as they moved in across the three causeways to the island city, Tenochtitlan. Cortes divided his forces in three parts to move along these approaches and close in on the capital. (See Figs. 20, 22.)

The galleys soon cleared the lake of any hostile fleets of canoes, and the Spaniards began to invest the city. The Aztecs, fighting for their lives, stubbornly defended their position. Every night they sallied forth to destroy the bridges the Spaniards had made across the canals during the day. In fighting of this kind the Spaniards could not manipulate

FIG. 22. The Spanish flotilla puts to sea. These galleys, equipped with oars and a sail and armed with a cannon in the bow, could play havoc with the Aztec war canoes. *Codex Florentino*

their troops, and neither side had any great advantage. The
Aztecs, however, still persisted in trying to take prisoners
to sacrifice to their War God instead of exterminating their
enemies whenever the occasion offered. To offset this gain
the thousands of Indian allies, who flocked to the Spanish
side to participate in the expected victory, jammed the causeways and hampered rather than helped the besiegers. (See
Fig. 21.)

FIG. 23. Time and again the brigantines relieved situations like this
where armed tribesmen in canoes sailed up to attack the Spanish rear.
Codex Florentino

FIG. 24. The Spanish military problem was to raze enough of the city to permit the use of cavalry. The drawing at the right shows the gunboats taking part in an offensive with this end in view. *Codex Florentino*

Cortes decided to change his manner of campaign, and his solution, while reasonable to us, must have been little short of miraculous to the tribesmen. He sent the Indian allies forward to tear down all the houses they could find and fill the canals with the debris. When counterattacked, the allies retired, leaving room for the Spaniards on horse and foot to deal with the Aztecs. Each day the Spanish forces gained more room to maneuver and thus could count on recovering more ground on the morrow. The Aztecs, animated by a rare unity, fought desperately but without avail. (See Figs. 23–24.)

Toward the end of the siege an event occurred which indicated to the now-desperate Aztecs hope of eventual release in a common rising against the invaders. The people from the islands at the south of the lake, the Xochimilcas and

their neighbor tribesmen, filtered through the Spanish galleys by night and told the Aztecs that, as neighbors, they
would make common cause against the whites. Overjoyed,
Cuauhtemoc and his chiefs loaded them with ornaments, fine
mantles and cacao beans, precious for the favorite drink of
the Aztecs, chocolate. When night closed in again on the
beleaguered city the Aztecs were startled by a great com-
motion. The new allies were trying to drag off the Aztec
women and children as slaves. It is pleasant to record that
this knavery received its just reward, and the Xochimilcas
were all either slaughtered or disposed of in sacrifice.[7]

Only when its members were too weak to resist and could

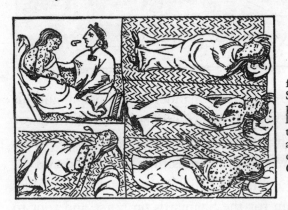

Fig. 25. Pestilence was a
formidable ally on the
Spanish side. Colds, smallpox, measles, and the
like, were unknown to
the Indians who, lacking
any sort of immunity,
died by the thousands.
Codex Florentino

Fig. 26. A factor in
the downfall of the
Aztecs was their cus-
tom of taking captives
for sacrifice rather
than to kill in direct
battle. The heads of
the sacrificed victims,
both men and horses,
were displayed in
front of the temples.
Codex Florentino

y epolínhǭ mexiica

FIG. 27. Cuauhtemoc, who conducted the defense of Tenochtitlan, is received with all the honors of war by Cortes and his consort, Marina. In the upper right Cortes may be seen greeting Cuauhtemoc's wife and family. The legend translated reads: "With this event, the Mexicans were finished." *Lienzo de Tlaxcala*

no longer deal wounding blows did the garrison yield. Cuauhtemoc and his family took to the lake in a canoe, as did many others. He was picked up by one of the Spanish galleys and brought before Cortes, where his dignity and chiefly demeanor received the respectful attention of the Spanish general staff. The request for treasure brought the answer that there was none: it lay under the lake with the Spaniards who were slain the preceding winter in their disastrous flight from the city. Cuauhtemoc then underwent

FIGS. 28A–28B. The story of the Conquest of Mexico
in native characters. In the cartouches are to be seen the
symbols One Reed and Two Knife, the Aztec names for
the years 1519 and 1520. Under One Reed is a Spaniard
below whose horse's feet are the shield, club and
arrows symbolic of war. At the right the bearded Cortes

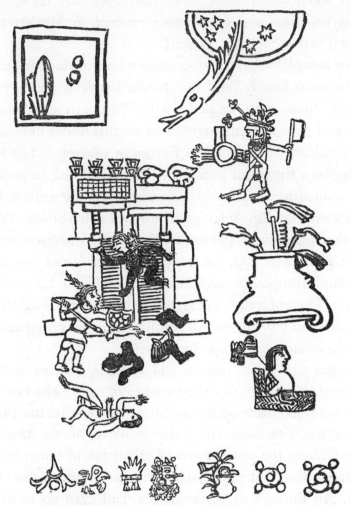

sits in the temple of Tenochtitlan, represented by the
cactus. An Indian with the glyph of Montezuma offers
a tribute of gold beads. Under Two Knife we find
Alvarado massacring the Indians at the great temple and
at upper right a comet in the sky. *Codex Vaticanus A*

prison and torture, to be murdered years later on Cortes' march to Honduras. He is now revered in Mexico as a national hero. (See Figs. 25-27.)

The downfall of the Aztecs cannot be explained in terms of European history, and the standard reasons give a false picture. Montezuma, singled out by European authors as a weak and vacillating monarch, was a tribal leader devoid of the constitutional rights of a European sovereign. His empire is also a European creation, since it consisted, in reality, of communities sufficiently intimidated to pay tribute but in no wise bound to Aztec governmental conventions. Warriors the Aztecs were, but not soldiers in the European sense. Given, as we have said, the requisite leadership and organization, any European expeditionary force could have taken Mexico. The tragically courageous resistance at Tenochtitlan was not a military defense so much as a heroic group action by individuals fighting for their lives.

Hunger and thirst, plagues and wounds, had literally so weakened the Aztecs that they could not resist. The horrors of the last stand made by these desperate people are too awful to describe. For long after, the memory of the tragedy lingered about the place, a sort of exhalation of spiritual uncleanliness like that of a haunted house or the scene of a crime. All through the Colonial era, and even up to now, the northern district of Mexico has found favor neither as a residential quarter nor as a business center. Today there are railroad yards and slums where the Aztec civilization bled to death. The ghosts of its heroic defenders still haunt the place.

CHAPTER XV

THE AZTECS AFTER THEIR CONQUEST

The history of the Aztecs after the Conquest and suggestions for a tour through their domain

AZTEC civilization died, but the Aztecs still live. Remove the pure-blooded Indian from Mexico, and you lose two fifths of the population; take out those with Indian blood in their veins, and a bare twentieth of the population will remain. The face of Mexico is an Indian face. Yet travel in Mexico and read its history, and you will see, as if in strata, the impress of the colonial period, the republic, the empire of Maximilian, the dictatorship of Diaz and the modern social thinking of the Revolution. The Indian civilization you do not see, except for its descendants, who are everywhere, who are the Mexican people. Though their outward aspect and their material and social culture are European, the stamp of the Aztec character is on their minds, just as the masonry of broken Aztec temples is built into the walls of their churches.[1]

The original purpose of the Crown and the Church was to convert the Indian population into Spanish citizens with full civic rights. For two generations the authorities almost succeeded in their intent; but finally the individualism so emphasized in European culture broke through their legislative controls, and the white conquerors reduced the Indians to slavery. Now, after four hundred years, it seems that the present Republican government might achieve by means of their Indian education program the humane purpose formulated under the colonial system.

After 1520, when the Conquest was established, the Spaniards began the process of converting a matured Indian culture into a European one. The conquerors were granted lands and in return were supposed to exploit the new territory for the economic advantage of Spain. The Church had in its custody the education of the Indians and their spiritual and corporal welfare. The different monastic orders undertook the control of the Indians in specified localities. Their first steps were to eradicate the local idolatry and to learn the language and customs of their new charges, the better to accomplish conversion.[2]

The friars, especially selected for the task, showed great understanding. They immediately replaced one theological structure with another. The Indians tore down their temples to build churches and monasteries in their place. The use of statues and paintings in Catholic ritual answered so well the requirements of Aztec worship that the friars had great trouble in preventing adoration of the images themselves. (See Plate 26, middle.)

The studies that the friars made of the Indian customs were admirable, with the Franciscans and Dominicans showing exceptional abilities.[3] The children of Indian tribal leaders were educated in schools to spread the gospel. Under this Spanish control there was no recognition of the old communal land tenure, so the Aztecs were frozen into possession of the lands that they occupied by tribal sanction. The chiefs who had held the usage of the official lands found themselves the owners of extensive estates by which their descendants could profit. The Spaniards married into chiefly families, which they believed hereditary, according to their own cultural pattern. In some cases chiefs, like those of Tlaxcala, received coats of arms and patents of nobility from the king for their service in the Spanish cause. Out of 190 coats of arms presented for services during the Conquest of Middle and South America, at least twenty were granted to Indians. In consequence there took place a modest renascence of Indian culture. Indian authors like Ixtlilxochitl and Chimalpahin set forth, in Spanish or Nahuatl, the annals of their forebears as proof of their descent from great Indian nobles and of their right to Spanish honors as well.[4] (See Plate 44.)

The old culture died slowly. In the Indian towns the records were kept in both Spanish and the old Aztec pictographic system to avoid dispute. Dress maintained its old form, except that the friars insisted on trousering the Indians. The rich agriculture was a great boon to the conquerors, who modified it little except for the addition of fruit trees and wheat. Household utensils, like pottery, revealed an engaging fusion of Indian and Spanish ideas, and glazing delighted the Indians, who applied the flux to purely aboriginal forms. Some enchanting little sculptures in clay reveal the old gods and goddesses masquerading as saints in a very thin disguise.

The Indians were used to building temples, and it seemed to them perfectly fitting that they should labor long hours in great numbers to rear structures honoring the new gods. The conversion was so popular that the churches were too small to hold the worshipers, and several conventual temples, like Acolman, Actopan and Tlalmanalco, had chapels which opened on a large court to accommodate converts who gathered literally in the tens of thousands. Indian craftsmen found steel tools a superb improvement on their stone hammers and chisels. After the original plateresque architecture shifted into baroque, they reveled in shaping the blocks into ornate shapes, for it was as easy as cutting cheese in comparison to the labor of their aboriginal days.[5]

This period of fusion lasted for almost a century. In the meantime the original Conquistadors and their descendants, together with later immigrants to the new colony, had encroached more and more on the natives. The development of the mining industries absorbed thousands of Indians, lured to work for a pittance under noisome conditions which brought sickness and even death. The exercise of the *encomienda*, an arrangement whereby a man had the right to a native's labor in return for his care and the assurance of his religious instruction, led to abuse of the privilege, and the luckless Indians were reduced to serfdom. European diseases, like smallpox, measles and tuberculosis, wiped out great sections of the population, which had no hereditary resistance to such maladies. The Crown and the Church, through its Council of the Indies, sent questionnaires and enacted ameliorative legislation on the basis of the information received, but such laws were more honored in the breach than in the observance. Many of the whites who went to New Spain wanted to get rich and enjoy an easy old age in the homeland. Others who had settled in the country enjoyed an almost feudal existence, no part of the profits and comforts of which they wished to yield, either for the betterment of the Indians or for the enrichment of the Crown. When the British destroyed the Armada in 1588 and weakened Spanish sea power, the communication between the mother country and the colonies became increasingly difficult. Control was loosened, and laws for the benefit of the Indians were ignored. They became, indeed, an inferior majority, laboring as peons without hope of legal or social justice.[6]

Most of the Indians lost their land and labored on haciendas or in the mines. Some communities like Tlaxcala, having performed notable service to the Crown during the Conquest, kept their land although they had lost social status. Other groups, like the lake peoples of Xochimilco and Chalco, occupied territory which the Spaniards considered unsuitable for their own purposes. A fourth group lived relatively unmolested in primitive little villages tucked away in the mountains. These refugees had taken to the hills not only because of the white conquerors but also to avoid the rising Indian powers in the centuries before the Conquest. The several-score languages and dialects spoken in Mexico are preserved in these tiny villages where inhabitants are only lightly veneered with Christianity.

What remains of Indian culture today is largely the blend of early indigenous practices with the teachings of the friars in the sixteenth century. Yet the physical type and the languages have resisted absorption for four centuries. In Mexico there is hardly a group which remains as completely Indian as some of the North American tribes, but they, after all, have for the most part been conquered and put on reservations only in the last three generations. The groups who had earlier contact with the whites were exterminated many years ago.[7]

The Mexican Indians have endured and have done the work of Mexico for four centuries. They have seen the whites struggle for the right to consume the fruits of their labor. They probably do not realize that the unmixed group of the ruling class gets smaller each generation, having in the last century dropped from thirteen per cent to seven per cent of the population. Individuals, like Juarez the Liberator, and Diaz, the greatest of Mexican dictators, shouldered their way from the anonymous Indian mass to lead the country and modernize its culture. The men of the Revolution had Indian blood in their veins, and one of them, former President Lazaro Cardenas, has made superhuman efforts to drag the Indians out of bondage into participation in the active and political life of the country.

The crafts of Mexico are the product of Indian hands. Humble artisans have handed down from generation to generation the love of the old days, the traditions of form and pattern. This background, like that of the social make-up of the people, was illumined in the Mexican Renascence, when during the Revolution, Mexican painters like Orozco, Rivera and Goitia, and foreigners like Charlot, became conscious of Mexico's native American background. It is beside the point that Mexico's art is technically derivative from Europe. Socially and emotionally it is the only really national art which lives in the world today.[8]

The visitor to Mexico is strongly conscious of the Indian. Sometimes he is appalled by the apathy of the people who have been oppressed for so many years, whose nations and whose temples have been leveled to make the foundations of a new society. Yet in these days, when our American world has greater meaning for us, we can think more deeply of those earlier colonists from another continent who, like ourselves, built a new world.

Mexico, the most American of American nations, opens a thrilling perspective down the corridors of time. One can read widely and yet completely miss the sense of a still-living past which affects the visitor to this extraordinary country. To take a car and drive through the rich valleys, hemmed in by their mountain ramparts, is to absorb the full flavor of our Indian past. A fortnight so spent will enable a visitor to survey much of the Aztec domain.[9]

The first day one should visit the Museum, just to realize the bulk and quantity of the infinitesimal part of Indian workmanship housed there. A block away, near the Cathedral, yawns an excavation which reveals a corner of the Great Temple's stair. The street behind the Cathedral, running east and west, produced myriads of ceremonial objects, cast out from the temple by the outraged conquerors. The *Zocalo*, the great Plaza de la Constitucion, covers the main square of Tenochtitlan. Its twenty feet of foundation are made of the temples torn down for the greater glory of God, and heaven knows what incomparable masterpieces of Aztec art are buried there. The Presidential Palace on the west rests on the ancient halls of Montezuma. A few blocks north the murals of the Ministry of Public Education show the tragedy of the Indian and his liberation, painted in the full tide of Rivera's genius.[10] (See Plate 51, bottom.)

After lunch in the neighborhood the visitor may well drive west past the Palace of Bellas Artes, built just beyond the ancient shore of Tenochtitlan in the former lake bottom. The hill and park of Chapultepec merit a visit, for the cypresses, hoary with Spanish moss, date from Montezuma's time. Here the Tenochcas made their first settlement, the elder Montezuma built the aqueduct for his city and the younger had a relief carved in his honor. Crowning the hill stands the palace of the Austrian Maximilian, emperor of all the Mexicans during our Civil War, and at this place a few years previously a handful of Mexican military-school cadets stood off a brigade of United States Regulars in our one unhappy conflict with our southern neighbor.

Turning south, one may visit the little palace of the chief of Mixcoac and go on through the Villa Obregon (San Angel) to see the remains of the Lower Middle Culture peoples buried under the lava of Copilco. Then turning west and south, one may pass through Tizapan, where the Tenochcas spent the unhappy years of their captivity, and drive out over the Pedregal to Cuicuilco. Here the oval temple of the Upper Middle peoples emerges from the surrounding lava waste, a dismal and uncanny background, appropriate to this earliest monument of Mexican religion. Then the visitor can return to Mexico via Tlalpam and Coyoacan, on a road built over the same causeway which Cortes followed into Tenochtitlan. (See Plate 18, bottom.)

The second day, equipped with lunch or self-control, the visitor might drive out the Calle de Tacuba, which follows the old western causeway to ancient Tlacopan. Here Cortes made his dismal retreat, and two blocks are named for Alvarado's famous leap. The cypress beneath which Cortes wept is worth a glance, and the church in the main plaza of Azcapotzalco, capital of Toltec and Tepanec chiefs, squats heavily on the remains of a once-lofty platform. The votive temple of Los Remedios on the hills behind was built where Cortes re-formed his shattered army and has a wonder-working statue of the Virgin, patroness of the Conquistadores.

Descending the hill, the visitor can pass through Tlalne-pantla, where the church is built from the ruins of temples, and go on to Tenayuca. Here the Mexican archaeologists have dissected, as with a surgeon's knife, the six temples that epitomize the history of that town from its Chichimec foundation until its conquest in 1520. On the hills to the east, at the foot of which runs a Spanish aqueduct, are strung the Middle Culture sites of El Arbolillo, Ticoman and Zacatenco. (See Plates 1, 50.)

It would be worth while to visit, on returning, the Villa de Guadalupe, built in honor of the apparition of the Virgin to Juan Diego. Her portrait, miraculously painted, is preserved in the church; and in December the Indians come from miles around to honor their special patroness, just as before the Conquest they made pilgrimages to this very spot to do honor to Tonantzin, the Aztec Goddess of Motherhood. Returning by way of the ancient northern causeway, the visitors should turn right at Peralvillo and pass by the grubby railroad yards and slums which cover Tlaltelolco and its famous market place and the site of the Aztec Cuauhtemoc's last stand against the Spaniards.

On the third day the tourist should visit Teotihuacan, re-traversing the northern causeway and passing through Guadalupe. The road skirts the salt Lake of Texcoco and crosses, on a causeway of Spanish construction, the straits between it and the now-drained Xaltocan. The strategic site of Chiconauhtla at its northern terminus offers little to see, but farther on it is well to turn right and visit the great Acolman Indian School, or Convent, "convento," as the Spaniards called any establishment where the friars educated the Indians. In the distance loom the pyramids of Teotihuacan; a short drive through Indian villages brings the motorist to this site, the most imposing in Mexico. The ruins are a tribute to the cultural interests of the present government, which has expended much time and money in interpreting and uncovering the remains. There is a good museum where one can see the craftsmanship of the builders of this magnificent sacred city, which still retains much of the grandeur of its ancient days. (See Plates 21–24.)

There is a good restaurant at Teotihuacan, and after lunch the visitor should go back as far as Tepexpan and take the abominable road to Texcoco, except in the rainy season, when the town can be reached only by the main road from a point south of Mexico City. On the way one should visit the remains of Nezahualcoyotl's palace, where magnificent cypresses border a garden, and in their shade one can evoke memories of the life of the poet king. Some rough miles farther on Texcoco reflects none of its former grandeur. It is an old, sad town, dim and ruined. A few mounds at the eastern entrance are gloomy reminders of its ancient splendors. One passes Huexotla and its great wall as one returns to Mexico by the main road, and hard by at the agricultural school in the hacienda of Chapingo are some of the best of Rivera's frescos, symbolizing the growth and fertility of the Mexican earth and translating Aztec ideas into modern painting.

An alternative procedure would be to give a fourth day to the Texcoco region. Leaving Mexico by the eastern road, pass south along the desolate salt marshes of Lake Texcoco and turn east at Los Reyes on the main road to Texcoco. At Coatlinchan a tip will command the services of an Indian to take one to see the massive Toltec monument to the Goddess of the Waters, which lies unfinished in a gulley, a long half-hour's walk from the town. Returning to the car, go to Chapingo and Huexotla, and at Texcoco turn off to see the rock-cut baths of Nezahualcoyotl, built into the hill behind Texcotcingo. The countryside is dotted with little towns, and the Indian and Colonial periods are very close to the surface.

The fourth day (or fifth, if a day each is given to Teotihuacan and Texcoco) could commence a profitable two-day tour to Cuernavaca. The motorist will have an unforgettable experience if he takes the back road via Xochimilco, Tulyahualco and Chalco, where direct descendants of the ancient tribesmen occupy their old lakelands and till them as did their ancestors. Still speaking Nahuatl, they pole their canoes through the network of canals surrounding their *chinampas*, or garden plots. Leaving the lakes, one climbs high into the mountains, approaching the great volcanoes of Popocatépetl (Smoking Mountain) and Ixtaccíhuatl (White Lady) by the nearest route. Tlalmanalco is the first stop, and here a fine open chapel combines pure elements of Indian and European sculpture in a church built from the stones of a destroyed temple. The road ascends past the shrine of Amecameca, through Ozumba, and drops into a new world, the hot Valley of Morelos, home of the Tlahuicas. The motorist goes past sugar haciendas burned during the revolution, through Yolotepec, seat of a Tlahuica tribe and home of the feared revolutionary leader Zapata, and ascends again to reach Cuernavaca for lunch.

Here the Conquest is starkly represented by the huge fortified church and Cortes' palace, now the seat of the state government, where Rivera has painted an exciting fresco of the conquest and subjugation of the once-powerful Tlahuicas. At the railroad station is a cluster of temples, one of which is extraordinarily well preserved and represents the dramatic values of Aztec architecture. Later one can drive in half an hour to the Nahuatl-speaking village of Tepoztlan, whose people blend the material and spiritual cultures of Indian Mexico, colonial Spain and the modern republic. The great convent towers over the shattered sculptures from the ancient temples, but, high in the mountains and easily accessible to those sound in wind and limb, the temple of the Tepozteco stands battered but unsubdued. Returning to Cuernavaca, a few mounds on the right of the road at Tlaltenango are a furtive monument to the Upper Middle Culture people whose remains at Gualupita were studied in a brickyard near the Hotel Selva. (See Plate 28, bottom.)

After passing the night in one of the many good hotels in this charming resort of Cuernavaca, one can drive down the Taxco road and turn at Alpuyeca to visit the hill city of Xochicalco. The main temple has a superb carved façade which would suggest a Maya origin were it not for the fire snakes, dates and ritualistic symbolism of Mixteca-Puebla Culture. Probably of eleventh-century origin, this may have been a main outpost of those people whose culture originated Aztec civilization. The site is almost untouched, and the uncovered mounds and terraces undoubtedly contain sculptures and pottery that will illumine many dark places in Indian history. Taxco can be fitted in for lunch and Mexico City reached by nightfall over a fine road across the mountains. The traveler will realize how the mountain chains sealed off one group of people from another, so that language, art and culture could develop along special lines without outside influence. Coming down from the heights, the panorama of the southern Valley is laid out below one: the lakes, the valley floor and, looming up in the center, the Hill of the Star, where each fifty-two years the Aztecs received the promise of continued life.

On the sixth day (seventh in the alternative schedule) the rugged traveler who can maintain this schedule might take a dramatic two-day trip to Puebla. Driving down the southern shore of Texcoco, "where the sedge is withered from the lake and no birds sing," he crosses the mountain chain to the southeast, close under the snow-covered shoulders of the great volcanoes. As he emerges from the pine forests on the other side, the rich Valley of Puebla opens before him. At San Cristobal a mound crowning a big hill on the left was the chief offertory of a group of Middle Culture mounds at the base, but they are not worth the time available, so that the motorist pushes on to Texmelucan, where he turns left on the road to Tlaxcala. Here the Indian population is prosperous because Spain recognized the services of its most effective allies and did not let them be despoiled. The town itself is old and charming, little affected by change since the eighteenth century. The oldest church in Mexico, where the first Indian baptism took place, is on an eminence near the center of the town. Across the river at Tizatlan there is a little temple whose painted altars, their colors still preserved, depict the great god Tezcatlipoca and some of the symbolism of the ancient religion. Near by a former open chapel, delightfully naïve, is screened by an atrocious nineteenth-century church. There are also the dubious remains of an early sixteenth-century house, said to be the residence, after the Conquest, of Xicotencatl, who led the armies of Tlaxcala. Near by can be seen the spot where Cortes built his brigantines to be transported, piecemeal, to the lakes of the Valley. (See Plate 57, top.)

Returning to Texmelucan for lunch, one regains the Puebla road and stops at the once-important city-state Huexotcingo. The earliest civilization is obliterated by a marvelous old Franciscan convent, where simple, honest construction reflects the virtues of these holy men who accomplished the conversion of the Indians. The measure of their success can be gauged by the huge court, or *atrio*, where the Indians congregated in thousands to hear Mass.

Back to the road, in less than an hour Cholula looms on the horizon. Hundreds of little churches, whose colored tiles shimmer in the sun, bear witness to a dense population which once had a temple in each place where a church is now. One can see why people from this region made their way to the Valley to get living space. Even today every field is cultivated. The people themselves are very Indian, and the strange sounds of Nahuatl often break in on the smooth syllables of Spanish. The big temple of Cholula is incredible. It seems like the counterpart of Babel, to which the friars compared it. On top the church rests proudly, and on a terrace below are the remains of rooms and the altar enclosing human burials, all carefully excavated by government archaeologists. Within the big mound run more than a mile of tunnels, which the archaeologists hollowed from the adobe bricks to follow the walls and stairs of the Toltec ceremonial precinct of earlier times. Deep inside frescoed representations of the Butterfly God are awe-inspiring in the dim lantern light. (See Plate 26, middle.)

Passing on to Puebla itself, one finds a large provincial town, whose dull respectability is leavened by the burst of inventive creativeness reflected in the ornate church architecture. Examination of Puebla and its museum can be made during the morning of the next day, after which the return to Mexico City is accomplished leisurely.

Another variation is to drive past Puebla to Tepeaca, the old Segura de la Frontera of the Conquest, and thence through a desolate waste to Tehuacan. Here one may turn up over the hills to Orizaba and down into the moist, tropical regions of Cordoba, through populous Indian territory. Or one may leave one's car and take the train to Oaxaca, if the road has not yet been completed.

Oaxaca is a charming provincial capital, unchanged since colonial days. The lofty hill which dominates the city is completely transformed by the terraces, temples and tombs which constitute the great Zapotec site of Monte Alban. Another valley, another culture, another language, make this region into one more Indian world. The ruins of Mitla are exquisite great buildings, and their intricate wall carvings attest the skill of their Mixtec architects. The regional museum in Oaxaca houses, besides collections drawn from Mitla and other parts of the state, the superb jewel collection found in Tomb 7 at Monte Alban. Indian life is near the surface at Oaxaca, and at the market one can hear not only the Zapotec and Mixtec of the rival groups who contested the hegemony of the valley, but the language of other mountain traders who bring their own obscure tongues to this modern babel. (See Plates 8–9, 11.)

A trip easily accomplished from Mexico City leads over the mountains to Toluca, the capital of the state of Mexico, where an enlightened governor constructed a state museum, showing the varied handiwork of the Matlatzincas, the Indian group who held this valley. Beyond Toluca the ruins of Calixtlahuaca boast a round temple to the Wind among the structures reared in honor of their gods. The more venturesome motorist who has no fear of bad roads should drive down past Metepec to Tenancingo, and from there go by car, by horse or on foot to Malinalco. These rock-cut temples are really thrilling, both because of the fine carving and for the strangely remote effect they produce on the visitor. In this mountain niche one can look far down the valley and back to the temples which, hewn from the rock, were cognate to their gods, envisaged in the manifold variety of nature.

If our visitor has not yet been overwhelmed by these skeletons of a once-lively civilization he can fly to Yucatan. Chichen Itza, Uxmal, Labnah, are great white ceremonial centers that thrust themselves from the enveloping bush. Half hidden in thatched villages, growing their corn in little clearings, the modern Mayas carry on their ancient life, but their religion has lost much, and a simple Catholicism tinged with magic provides a slender bond with the supernatural. A visit to Yucatan will enhance the conception of the variety of the Mexican world, where once men of many tongues and many tribes wrought out their destinies. (See Plates 6–7, 12.)

The civilization of the Indian may not offer a direct inspiration to us modern individualists, yet we have profited from their labor in our food plants and the wealth produced by our neighbor republics to the south. In this world, torn with hate and war, adrift without an anchor or a compass with which to chart our course, we may well consider their example. The Indians worked together for their common good, and no sacrifice was too great for their corporate well-being. Man's strength lay in the physical and spiritual welfare of the tribe, and the individual was honored only inasmuch as he contributed to that communal good. The Indian civilization may have been powerless to resist the culture of the Western world, but it did not consume itself, as we are doing, in the expression of military power.

The American countries today share the ideal of the republic and individual freedom. We share also an older tradition left us by our Indian forebears, that of mutual service for the benefit of man. With our continents spread before us, we have boundless opportunity to create on earth a wider life for everyone, an American civilization where old and new contributions to human welfare may be fused and amalgamated for the benefit of all.

NOTES

CHAPTER I

The recent dates of authorities cited indicate how rapidly ideas on the genesis of Indian culture are changing. New finds, new conclusions, new datings, appear each year. The summary in Chapter I is frankly interpretative, and no one will be more ready than the author to change his views as fresh evidence appears. The four works listed here: Swanton Essays; Maya and Their Neighbors; Wissler, American Indian, and Means, Ancient Civilizations, give a broad background for New World archaeology. Their detailed references are listed under their appropriate footnote number. The full titles of the four background volumes are:

Essays in Historical Anthropology of North America. Published in honor of John R. Swanton (Smithsonian Miscellaneous Collections, Vol. 100, Washington, 1940).

The Maya and Their Neighbors, New York, 1940.

Means, Philip, Ancient Civilizations of the Andes, New York, 1931.

Wissler, Clark, The American Indian, New York, 3rd ed., 1938.

[1]Howells, Origins, 1940. Nelson, Antiquity of Man, 1933. MacCurdy, ed., Early Man, 1937. Howard, Evidence of Early Man, 1935.

[2]Wissler, American Indian, 1938.

[3]Howells, Origins, 1940. Hooton, Racial Types, 1933. Dixon, Racial History of Man, 1923. Hrdlicka, Origin and Antiquity of American Indian, 1923.

[4]Nelson, Antiquity of Man, 1933. Roberts, Pre-Pottery Horizon, 1940. Howard, Evidence of Early Man, 1935. Bird, Antiquity and Migrations, 1938.

[5]Wissler, American Indian, 1938. Swanton Essays, 1940. Kroeber, Cultural and Natural Areas, 1939.

[6]Gladwin, Snaketown, II, 1937. Sayles, Survey of Texas, 1935.

[7]Kroeber, Cultural and Natural Areas, 1939.

[8]Sauer, American Agricultural Origins, 1936. Yanovski, Food Plants, 1936. Mangelsdorf and Reeves, Origin of Maize, 1938.

[9]Wissler, American Indian, 1938.

[10]Linton, Crops, Soils and Culture, 1940.

[11]Roberts, Survey of Southwestern Archaeology, 1935. Kidder, Intro-

duction to Southwestern Archaeology, 1924. Gladwin and Others, Snake-town, I and II, 1937.

[12]Spinden, Ancient Civilizations, 1928. Means, Ancient Civilizations, 1931. Vaillant, Early Cultures, 1935.

[13]Means, Ancient Civilizations, 1931.

[14]Spinden, Ancient Civilizations, 1928. Spinden, Maya Art, 1913.

[15]Linton, Crops, Soil and Culture, 1940. Vaillant, Patterns in Culture, 1940.

[16]Spinden, Ancient Civilizations, 1928. Vaillant, Early Cultures, 1935.

[17]Vaillant, Patterns in Culture, 1940.

[18]Spinden, Ancient Civilizations, 1928.

[19]Gann and Thompson, History of the Maya, 1931. The Maya and Their Neighbors, 1940. Thompson, Civilization of the Mayas, 1932.

[20]Morley, Introduction to Maya Hieroglyphs, 1915. Spinden, Reduction of Mayan Dates, 1924. Teeple, Maya Astronomy, 1931. Thompson, Maya Chronology, 1935. Andrews, Chronology and Astronomy, 1940.

[21]Donnelly, Atlantis, 1882. Le Plongeon, Queen Moo, 1896. Church-ward, Lost Continent of Mu, 1926.

[22]Vaillant, Chronology and Stratigraphy, 1935. Gann, Mounds in Northern Honduras, 1900. Tozzer, Maya and Toltec Figures, 1930. Ban-croft, Native Races, 1883. Butler, Alta Vera Paz, 1940.

[23]Stirling, Great Stone Faces, 1940; Initial Series from Vera Cruz, 1940; Oldest Dated Work, 1939. Weiant, Manuscript, 1939. Vaillant, Bearded Mystery, 1931; Pre-Columbian Jade, 1932. Ricketson and Ricketson, Uaxactun, 1937. Caso, Exploraciones, 1931–32, 1934–35, 1936–37. Holmes, Nephrite Statue, 1907.

[24]Batres, Exploraciones en Monte Alban, 1902. Caso, Exploraciones, 1934–35, 1936–37. Dauterman, Pottery Yard Stick, 1938.

[25]Vaillant, Correlation, 1938.

CHAPTER II

There are no really popular accounts of the Middle Cultures. Dr Spinden's excellent Ancient Civilization of Mexico and Central America sketches a broad outline; the author's Early Cultures sums up the results of the most recent excavations. The Middle Cultures are at that stage where technical studies have made great progress, but the subject matter has not passed into the hands of social and historical thinkers for intellectual rather than technical appraisal.

[1]POPULAR: Vaillant, Threshold of Civilization, 1929; Beginnings of a History, 1930. Beyer, Antiguedades del Pedregal, 1917.

TECHNICAL: Cummings, Ruins of Cuicuilco, 1923; Cuicuilco, 1923; Cuicuilco, 1926; Cuicuilco, 1933. Gamio, Excavaciones del Pedregal, 1920. Kroeber, Archaic Culture Horizons, 1925. Vaillant, Zacatenco, 1930; Ticoman, 1931; El Arbolillo, 1935; Early Cultures, 1935. Vaillant and Vaillant, Gualupita, 1934.

[2]Vaillant, Early Cultures, 1935.

[3]Vaillant, Early Cultures, 1935.

[4]Vaillant, Prehistoric Cotton, 1939.

[5]Vaillant, El Arbolillo, 1935.

[6]Vaillant, El Arbolillo, 1935.

[7]Cummings, Cuicuilco, 1933. Noguera, Teotihuacan, 1935. Vaillant, Ticoman, 1931. Vaillant and Vaillant, Gualupita, 1934.

[8]Linné, Teotihuacan, 1934, pp. 162–67.

[9]Vaillant and Vaillant, Gualupita, 1934.

[10]Vaillant and Vaillant, Gualupita, 1934.   Stirling, Stone Faces, 1940.

[11]Cummings, Cuicuilco, 1923a, 1923b, 1926, 1933.

[12]Cummings, Cuicuilco, 1933. Mena and Hyde, Antiguedad del Hombre, 1922. Nuttall, Aztecs and Their Predecessors, 1926.

[13]Kidder, Introduction, 1924, pp. 16–35; Pottery, I, 1931. Vaillant, El Arbolillo, 1935, pp. 160–67.

[14]Vaillant, Early Cultures, 1935.

CHAPTER III

The so-called Toltec question is covered by an enormous speculative literature and a relatively small number of reports on excavations scientifically carried out. The extensive work of the Swedish archaeologist Linné has appeared in part only, and much of the modern Mexican work and the results of the writer's excavations have not yet reached print. The interpretation given here explains a number of features, but further work will correct and expand many of these opinions.

[1]Brinton, Essays, 1890, pp. 83–100.

[2]Ixtlilxochitl, Relaciones, 1891; this sixteenth-century writer is underestimated. He was a descendant of the old Texcocan lineage and had access to many of the ancient records.

[3]Anales de Cuauhtitlan, 1885; Historia Tolteca-Chichimeca, 1937, and Muñoz Camargo, 1892, describe these later lineages. The great writer on customs and religion, Father Bernadino Sahagun, was confused by this double usage. History was difficult for him, while ethnology was an open book.

[4]Ixtlilxochitl, Relaciones, 1891; Historia Chichimeca, 1892. Bancroft, Native Races, 1883, Vol. 5. This historian is a veritable mine of information, but he worked from written records without the archaeological check accessible to modern students. Krickeberg, Alten Kulturen Mittel-Amerikas, 1937, an excellent summary of current and past interpretation of history. Beyer, in Gamio, Teotihuacan, 1922. Vaillant, Correlation, 1938, an effort to tie in historical with archaeological information in the Valley of Mexico.

[5]Caso, Conocimiento del Tonalpohualli, 1937.

[6]Sahagun, Historia General, 1938, Vol. 1, Book 1, p. 8; Vol. 2, Book 8, Chap. 5; Vol. 3, Book 10, Chap. 29, paragraph 1, 12. Anales de Cuauhtitlan, 1885. Ixtlilxochitl, Relaciones, 1891.

[7]Ixtlilxochitl, Relaciones, 1891. Anales de Cuauhtitlan, 1885. Bancroft, Native Races, Vol. 5, 1883.

[8]Linné, Teotihuacan, 1934, the best English work on Teotihuacan. Gamio, ed., Teotihuacan, 1922, the three-volume Mexican study on the archaeology, history and sociology of modern and ancient Teotihuacan. Charnay, Ancient Cities, 1888, an early account of the ruins and some excavations. Seler, Teotihuacan-Kultur, 1915, the standard scholarly work on this culture, now outdated by Gamio and Linné.

[9]Noguera, Antecedentes de la Cultura Teotihuacana, 1935, the single exhaustive study on this epoch.

[10]Linné, Teotihuacan, 1934.

[11]Linné, Teotihuacan, 1934.

[12]Chavero, Monolito de Coatlinchan, 1903.

[13]Linné, Teotihuacan, 1934; Expedition to Mexico, 1936.

[14]These Cholula excavations are still incomplete and reports on them unpublished.

[15]Morris, Charlot and Morris, Temple of the Warriors, 1928.

[16]Nuttall, Teotihuacan, unpublished; cf. Noguera, Conclusiones, 1937.

[17]Seler, Teotihuacan-Kultur, 1915. Tozzer, Santiago Ahuitzotla, 1921, a complete study of a building. Vaillant, Correlation, 1938.

CHAPTER IV

This era is just emerging from darkness and confusion. Recent definition of the Mazapan culture reinforces Dr Tozzer's work at Coyotlatelco by giving archaeological checks on the annals.

The writer's suggested identification of ceremonial dumps helps to clarify the confusion in the annals. The author believes the new finds corroborate Orozco y Berra's correlation of tribal rulers, but the late Dr Lehmann's exhaustive research does not agree. New data, worked out from newly discovered documents by Wigberto Jimenez Moreno, will clarify the picture when published fully.

[1]Joyce, Mexican Archaeology, 1914, gives a straightforward interpretation. Anales de Cuauhtitlan, 1885. Relacion de Genealogia and Origen de los Mexicanos are abridgments of the Anales de Cuauhtitlan. Lehmann, Geschichte von Colhuacan und Mexico, 1939, is a careful, analytical translation of the Annals of Cuauhtitlan. Orozco y Berra, Ojeada de Cronologia, 1878, is a useful critique. Kirchhoff, Pueblos, 1940, is important for interpretation of annals. Vaillant, Correlation, 1938, gives a résumé of the basis of this chapter.

[2]Ixtlilxochitl, Historia Chichimeca, 1892. Mapa Quinatzin, Mapa Tlotzin, Codex Xolotl; important picture manuscripts for this period.

[3]Codex Ramirez, Historia de los Mexicanos, in Radin, Sources, 1920. Codex Boturini, Codex of 1576; picture manuscripts.

[4]Bancroft, Native Races, Vol. 5, 1883, Chaps. V–VII cites early authorities. Orozco y Berra, Historia Antigua, 1880, cites early authorities and picture writings. Radin, Sources, 1920, an invaluable series of translations of early Mexican records.

[5]Vaillant, Correlation, 1938. Linné, Teotihuacan, 1934; Mazapan Grave, 1938.

[6]Vaillant, Chronology and Stratigraphy, 1935. Butler, Alta Vera Paz, 1940.

[7]Tozzer, Santiago Ahuitzotla, 1921. Boas, Album, 1911–12. Noguera, in Tenayuca, 1935.

[8]Boas, Album, 1911–12, Pls. 1–10. Gamio, Texto, 1921. Brenner, Influence of Technique in Culhuacan, 1931.

[9]Vaillant, Correlation, 1938; History and Stratigraphy, 1937.

[10]Marquina, Reygadas Vertiz and Noguera, in Tenayuca, 1935.

[11]Noguera, Altar de los Craneos, 1937; Conclusiones, 1937.

[12]Preuss and Mengin, Historia Tolteca-Chichimeca, 1937. Lehmann, Geschichte von Colhuacan und Mexiko, 1937. Muñoz Camargo, Historia, 1892. Sahagun, Historia General, 1938, Vol. 3, Book 10, Chapter XXIX. Bancroft, Native Races, Vol. 5, Chapters XI–XIII.

[13]Ekholm, Results, 1939; Archaeology, 1940.

CHAPTER V

The picture is much clearer for Aztec times; the archaeology is better known, and the historical records are more in accord. The cyclical constructions and destructions of the Aztecs are especially helpful. A confusing point is the foundation date of Tenochtitlan, for which the author provides a theory.

[1]EXHAUSTIVE ACCOUNTS OF AZTEC HISTORY: Bancroft, Native Races, 1883, Vol. 5; Orozco y Berra, Historia Antigua, 1880.

POPULAR ENGLISH DIGESTS: Thompson, Mexico before Cortes, 1933; Joyce, Mexican Archaeology, 1914. Radin, Sources, 1922, gives translations and reproductions of important native sources, as well as a superb critical analysis.

OTHER SOURCES: Torquemada, Monarquia, 1723; Clavigero, History of Mexico, 1783.

PICTURE WRITINGS: the codices of 1560, 1590, Boturini, Mendoza, Siguenza, Telleriano-Remensis, Vaticanus A, Tepechpan.

DIGESTS OF PICTURE WRITINGS IN SPANISH AND NAHUATL: Anales de Cuauhtitlan, 1885; Chimalpahin, Anales, 1889; Codex Ramirez, 1878; Tezozomoc's Cronica, 1878; Histoire Mexicaine, 1891; Historia de los Mexicanos, 1886; Ixtlilxochitl, Historia Chichimeca, 1892; Duran, Historia de las Indias, 1867, 1880.

Tenayuca, 1935, is the great work of the Department of Monuments of the Mexican Ministry of Public Education, which blends archaeology and history in a masterly exposition of the Aztec past.

[2]Codex Boturini.

[3]Historia de los Mexicanos.

[4]Anales de Cuauhtitlan, 1885, p. 49, Year 8 Rabbit. Palacios, Fundacion de Mexico, 1925, résumé of historical evidence for founding of Mexico. Codex of 1590 shows Acamapichtli being crowned by the chief of Tlaltelolco in the presence of the Tenochca clan council; cf. Vaillant, Correlation, 1938, p. 563.

[5]Sahagun, Historia General, 1938, Vol. 3, Book 10, Chap. XXIX, pp. 137–38.

[6]Bancroft, Native Races, 1883, Vol. 5, quotes early authorities on pp. 414–15.

[7]Bancroft, Native Races, 1883, Vol. 5, p. 434; Tezozomoc, Chapter LIV. Duran, Historia de las Indians, I, 1867, Chapter XXXII.

[8]Tezozomoc, Cronica, 1878, Chapters XLI–XLII.

[9]Tezozomoc, Cronica, 1872, Chapter LI. Duran, Historia de las Indias, I, 1867, Chapter XXXVI.

[10]Ixtlilxochitl, Historia Chichimeca, 1892.

[11]Bancroft, Native Races, 1883, p. 449, quotes Torquemada, Clavigero and Ixtlilxochitl.

[12]Saville, Tizoc, 1929.

[13]Bancroft, Native Races, 1883, pp. 439–40, quotes Ixtlilxochitl, Duran, Torquemada and Codex Telleriano-Remensis.

[14]Bancroft, Native Races, 1883, p. 471, quotes Tezozomoc, Torquemada and Duran.

[15]Bancroft, Native Races, 1883, p. 507, quotes Ixtlilxochitl.

[16]Diaz del Castillo, True History, 1908–16. Cortes, Letters, 1908.

CHAPTER VI

The customs of the Aztecs were a source of great interest to the conquerors and their palliative companions, the friars. The system of controlling the conquered depended on knowledge of the native methods of life. Consequently there is a full literature based on contemporary reports sent back to Spain by her civil and ecclesiastical administrators in the new colony.

[1]EXCELLENT POPULAR ACCOUNTS: Thompson, Mexico before Cortes, 1933; Biart, The Aztecs, 1883; Joyce, Mexican Archaeology, 1914; Prescott, Conquest of Mexico, 1922.

EXHAUSTIVE ENGLISH STUDIES: Bandelier, Social Organization, 1880; Bancroft, Native Races, 1883, Vols. 2 and 5.

MEXICAN STUDY: Orozco y Berra, Historia Antigua, 1880.

BEST CONTEMPORARY ACCOUNTS: Sahagun, Historia General, 1938; Pomar, Relacion, 1891; Zurita, Breve Relacion, 1891; Motolinia, Historia, 1914; Torquemada, Monarquia, 1723; Clavigero, History of Mexico, 1787.

PICTURE WRITINGS: Codex Mendoza, Codex Florentino (illustrations for Sahagun's Historia General).

The transition from the tribal council to the domination of the chiefs is shown by the presence of individual members in the early times and their disappearance after the foundation of the lineage; cf. Vaillant, Correlation, 1938, pp. 563–64; Bandelier, Social Organization, 1880, pp. 576–88; Mapa de Siguenza, Codex of 1590; Histoire Mexicaine; Codex Mendoza, and Codex Telleriano-Remensis.

[2]Codex Mendoza; Sahagun, Historia General, 1938, Vol. 2, Book 6.

[3]Bandelier, Social Organization, 1880, cites early authorities.

[4]Bandelier, Social Organization, 1880; Bancroft, Native Races, 1883, Vol. 2.

[5]Codex Mendoza.

⁶Bandelier, Social Organization, 1880; cf. Waterman, Bandelier's Contribution, 1917, for a critique of Bandelier.

⁷Sahagun, Historia General, 1938, Vol. 1, Book 3, Appendix; Vol. 2, Books 6, 9; Vol. 3, Book 10; see also Codex Florentino and Codex Mendoza.

⁸Bancroft, Native Races, 1883, Vol. 2; Bandelier, Social Organization, 1880.

⁹Ceballos Novelo, Instituciones, 1935. Kohler, Derecho de los Aztecas, 1924. Moreno, Organizacion de los Aztecas, 1931.

CHAPTER VII

This aspect of life is fully covered in the contemporary literature of the Conquest.

[1]POPULAR AUTHORS: Thompson, Mexico before Cortes, 1931; Joyce, Mexican Archaeology, 1914; Biart, The Aztecs, 1883.

EXHAUSTIVE ENGLISH STUDIES: Bandelier, Tenure of Lands, 1878; Bancroft, Native Races, 1883.

EXHAUSTIVE MEXICAN STUDY: Orozco y Berra, Historia Antigua, 1880.

CONTEMPORARY ACCOUNTS: Sahagun, Historia General, 1938; Torquemada, Monarquia, 1723; Clavigero, History of Mexico, 1787.

PICTURE WRITINGS: Codex Florentino (illustrations for Sahagun's Historia General), Codex Mendoza, Tribute Roll of Montezuma.

[2]Bandelier, Tenure of Lands, 1878.

[3]Mapa Tlotzin. Cortes, Letters, 1908, p. 221, referring to Valley of Puebla, "Such is the multitude of people who live in these parts that there is not a palm of land which is not cultivated . . . many places they suffer for want of bread."

[4]Nuttall, Mexican Gardens, 1925.

[5]Bandelier, Tenure of Land, 1878.

[6]Tribute Roll of Montezuma, Codex Mendoza, Tribute Roll.

[7]Articles on Shell and Commerce in Hodge, Handbook, 1907. Lumholtz, Unknown Mexico, 1902, plumbate ware in Tepic. Lothrop, Coclé, 1937, gold in Yucatan.

[8]Diaz del Castillo, True History, 1908–16, Chapter XCII. McBryde, Solola, 1933.

[9]Blom, Commerce of the Maya, 1932.

[10]Nuttall, Chalchihuitl, 1901. Diaz del Castillo, True History, 1908–16, Chapter CXXVIII.

[11]Saville, Goldsmith's Art, 1920. Sahagun, Historia General, 1938, Vol. 5, pp. 193–219.

[12]Sahagun, Historia General, 1938, Vol. 3, Book 11. Emmart, Badianus Manuscript, 1940. Sauer, Agricultural Origins, 1936. Hernandez, Historia Plantarum, 1790. Spinden, Ancient Civilizations, 1928.

[13]Alcocer, Comidas, 1938.

[14]Bancroft, Native Races, 1883, Vol. 2, pp. 160–74, 553–74; cites authorities.

[15]Vaillant, Twilight of Aztecs, 1938.

[16]Anonymous Conqueror, 1917, narrative.

[17]Motolinia, Historia, 1914, Book 1, Chapter XII; Bandelier's translation in Art of War, 1877, p. 104.

[18]Bernal Diaz, True History, 1908–16, Chapter XCII, p. 72.

[19]Bancroft, Native Races, 1883, Vol. 2, pp. 553–74; cites authorities on temple architecture. Tenayuca, 1935. Marquina, Estudio Arquitectonico, 1928.

[20]Codex Mendoza, Codex Florentino. Seler, Altmexikanischer Schmuck, 1904. Peñafiel, Indumentaria Antigua, 1903.

CHAPTER VIII

There are abundant data on crafts and craftsmanship to be drawn from the contemporary authorities and from museum collections. Examples of the textile art, however, are conspicuously lacking, since few fabrics have survived natural disintegration or have survived from collections made by the Conquistadors. Pictures in the manuscripts do give the impression, nonetheless, that this art was on a par with the others.

[1]POPULAR ENGLISH DIGESTS are found in Thompson, Mexico before Cortes, 1935; Joyce, Mexican Archaeology, 1922, Maya and Mexican Art, 1927; Spinden, Ancient Civilizations, 1928; Vaillant, Artists and Craftsmen, 1935.

SERIOUS SPECIAL STUDIES: Saville, Goldsmith's Art, 1920; Turquoise Mosaic Art, 1922; Woodcarver's Art, 1925.

[2]Saville, Onyx Jar, 1900. Holmes, Handbook, 1919. Nuttall, Penitential Rite, 1904.

[3]Holmes, Masterpieces of Aboriginal Art, 1914–19.

[4]Mason, Mirrors, 1927.

[5]Saville, Onyx Jar, 1900. Holmes, Handbook, 1919.

[6]Sahagun, Historia General, 1938. Peñafiel, Indumentaria Antigua, 1903. Codex Mendoza, Codex Magliabecchiano, Tribute Roll of Montezuma.

[7]Nuttall, Feather Work, 1895; Standard or Headdress, 1888. Seler, Feather Ornaments, 1904. Sahagun, Historia General, 1938. Codex Florentino.

[8]Saville, Turquoise Mosaic Art, 1922.

[9]Holmes, Archaeological Studies, 1895. Saville, Cruciform Structures, 1909.

[10]Saville, Woodcarver's Art, 1925.

[11]Saville, Goldsmith's Art, 1920. Sahagun, Historia General, 1938, Vol. 5, orfebreria.

[12]Caso, Monte Alban, 1932; Reading the Riddle, 1932.

[13]Lothrop, Coclé, 1937.

[14]Noguera, Decorative Aspects of Pottery, 1930; Caracteristicas de la Ceramica, 1930; in Tenayuca, 1935. Boas, Album, 1911–12. Brenner, Influence of Technique, 1931. Vaillant, History and Stratigraphy, 1937; Correlation, 1938, Figs. 3 and 4.

[15]Boas, Album, 1911–12, Pls. 1–10.

[16]Boas, Album, 1911–12, Pls. 11–24.

[17]Boas, Album, 1911–12, Pls. 25–31.
[18]Noguera, in Tenayuca, 1935, Pls. 58; Ceramica del Templo Mayor, 1934.
[19]Vaillant, History and Stratigraphy, 1937. Noguera, in Tenayuca, 1935.
[20]Vaillant, Correlation, 1938, Figs. 2 and 5-x.
[21]Noguera, Ladrillo como Material, 1928; Tizatlan, 1927.

CHAPTER IX

The study of Middle American art is in its infancy. We are only just realizing, in this and other American fields, the great contribution which the Indian has made. There are few publications dedicated especially to this purpose. I am including under footnote 1 a few books which cover the field of American Indian Art.

[1]NORTH AMERICA: Douglas and d'Harnoncourt, Indian Art, 1941. Vaillant, Indian Arts, 1939.

MIDDLE AMERICA: Caso, Thirteen Masterpieces, 1938. Cahill, American Sources, 1933. Castro Leal, Twenty Centuries of Mexican Art, 1940. Holmes, Masterpieces, 1914–19. Marquina, Estudio Arquitectonico, 1928. Escultura Mexicana Antigua, 1934. Spinden, Maya Art, 1913. Totten, Maya Architecture, 1926. Vaillant, Artists and Craftsmen, 1935.

SOUTH AMERICA: Lehmann and Doering, Kunstgeschichte des Peru, 1924. Nordenskiöld, Archéologie de L'Amazon, 1930.

[2]Marquina, Estudio Arquitectonico, 1928. Tenayuca, 1935. Holmes, Archaeological Studies, 1895–97. Vaillant, Artists and Craftsmen, 1935.
[3]Cummings, Cuicuilco, 1933.
[4]Gamio, Teotihuacan, 1922.
[5]Noguera, Altar de los Craneos, 1937.
[6]Tenayuca, 1935. Saville, Tepoztlan, 1896. Seler, Tepoztlan, 1904. Larsen, Malinalco, 1938. Marquina, Estudio Arquitectonico, 1928. Pollock, Round Temples, 1936.
[7]Pollock, Round Temples, 1936.
[8]Gallop, Ancient Monuments, 1938. Larsen, Malinalco, 1938.
[9]Vaillant, Artists and Craftsmen, 1935.
[10]Vaillant, Artists and Craftsmen, 1935.
[11]Spinden, Ancient Civilizations, 1928.
[12]Caso, El Teocalli, 1927.
[13]Saville, Tizoc, 1929.
[14]Caso, Reading the Riddle, 1932. Compare the Mixtec Codices Cospi, Vaticanus B, Borgia, with the Aztec Codices Telleriano-Remensis and Borbonicus.
[15]Goldsmith's Art, 1920; Turquoise Mosaic Art, 1922; Woodcarver's Art, 1925.
[16]Caso, Tizatlan, 1927. Vaillant, Artists and Craftsmen, 1935.
[17]PRE-CONQUEST MANUSCRIPTS: Codex Borbonicus, Codex Bocurini, Tonalamatl Aubin.

POST-CONQUEST MANUSCRIPTS: Codex Telleriano-Remensis, Codex Vaticanus A, Codex of 1576, Codex of 1590, Manuscrit Mexicaine.

Post-Conquest drawings to Spanish order: Codex Mendoza, Codex Florentino, Lienzo de Tlaxcala.

[18]Castañeda, Pequeños Percutores, 1933.

[19]Codex Borbonicus.

[20]Orozco y Berra, Historia Antigua, 1880. Spinden, Ancient Civilizations, 1928. For oratory, Sahagun, Historia General, 1938, Vol. II, Book 6. Brinton, Ancient Nahuatl Poetry, 1887.

CHAPTER X

Aztec religion is a fascinating and confusing subject. Ritualism ran wild, and the early Spanish observers, trained in rigorous Christian theology, found the subject interesting but baffling. Sahagun is far and away the best contemporary source. He checked his data in three different localities and spent many years in the process. The late Eduard Seler was the great modern authority, bringing a philosophical background to aid a meticulous interest in ritual. Spence, the best English writer, was his disciple, as was the infinitely learned Hermann Beyer. Alfonso Caso, the distinguished Mexican scholar, has combined brilliantly the meticulousness of the German school with the long-continued Mexican tradition, passed on by many sympathetic and learned minds. Among modern American students J. Eric Thompson is outstanding.

[1]Popular English accounts: Thompson, Mexico before Cortes, 1933. Spinden, Ancient Civilizations, 1928. Caso, Aztec Religion, 1937.

More detailed studies: Bancroft, Native Races, 1883, Vol. III. Spence, Gods of Mexico, 1923, standard text. Mrs Bandelier's translation of Sahagun, Historia General, Books 1–4, 1932.

Foreign language: Beuchat, Manuel d'Archeologie Americaine, 1912. Caso, El Teocalli, 1927. Paso y Troncoso, Descripcion del Codice Pictorico, 1898. Seler, Gesammelte Abhandlungen, 1902–23; Commentaries on Codices Borgia, 1904–09, Fejervary-Mayer, 1901–02, Vaticanus B, 1902, and Tonalamatl Aubin, 1900–01.

[2]Caso, El Teocalli, 1927. Spence, Gods of Mexico, 1923. Official version of Calendar Stone.

[3]At Teotihuacan, Azcapotzalco, Culhuacan.

[4]Spence, Gods of Mexico, 1923.

[5]Spence, Gods of Mexico, 1923.

[6]Spence, Gods of Mexico, 1923.

[7]For definitions of gods: Caso, Aztec Religion, 1927; Spence, Gods of Mexico, 1923; Seler, Commentaries.

[8]Bandelier, Archaeological Tour, 1884.

[9]For further definitions: Caso, Religion Azteca, 1938; El Teocalli, 1928. Spence, Gods of Mexico, 1923. Seler, Commentaries.

CHAPTER XI

The religious organization of the Aztecs is relatively clear. The ritual and the identification of deities is much more perplexing, as a certain amount of interpretation is involved. The working of the calendar has puzzled many a distinguished scholar, but its main principles are known. So elaborate a system of worship must have led to considerable local variation, so the student need not too greatly despair over the lack of agreement among authorities. The methods of pictographic writing are well known.

[1]POPULAR ACCOUNTS: Thompson, Mexico before Cortes, 1933; Joyce, Mexican Archaeology, 1922; Spinden, Ancient Civilizations, 1928.

MORE DETAILED STUDIES: *for the priesthood:* Bandelier, Social Organization, 1880; *for ritual:* Spence, Gods of Mexico, 1923; Seler, Commentaries, 1900–09; Bancroft, Native Races, 1883, Vols. 1, 3; Del Paso y Troncoso, Codice Pictorico, 1898; Beuchat, Manuel, 1911; Robelo, Diccionario de Mitologia, 1905; *for calendar:* Caso, Correlacion, 1939; De Jonghe, Le Calendrier Mexicaine, 1906; Orozco y Berra, Historia Antigua, 1880; Palacios, Fundacion de Mexico-Tenochtitlan, 1925; Seler, in Bulletin 28, 1904; Gesammelte Abhandlungen, 1902–23; Spence, Gods of Mexico, 1923; Spinden, Indian Manuscripts, 1933; Diffusion of Maya Astronomy, 1940; *for writing:* Aubin, Memoires sur la Peinture, 1885; Orozco y Berra, Historia Antigua, 1880; Peñafiel, Nombres Geograficos, 1885; Nomenclatura Geografica, 1895.

CONTEMPORARY: Sahagun, Historia General, 1938; Codex Florentino; Torquemada, Monarquia, 1923.

[2]Bandelier, Social Organization, 1880; cites early authorities.

[3]Thompson, Mexico before Cortes, 1933; Beuchat, Manuel, 1911; De Jonghe, Calendrier Mexicaine, 1906; Spence, Gods of Mexico, 1923; Spinden, Indian Manuscripts, 1933; Diffusion of Maya Astronomy, 1940; Caso, Correlacion, 1940; Morley, Introduction to Maya Hieroglyphs, 1915; Orozco y Berra, Historia Antigua, 1880; Seler, in Bulletin 28, 1904; Commentaries on Codex Vaticanus B, Fejervary–Mayer, Borgia, and Tonalamatl of Aubin Collection, 1900–09.

[4]Seler, Commentaries on Tonalamatl Aubin, Codex Fejervary–Mayer, Codex Vaticanus B; Paso y Troncoso, Codice Pictorica (Borbonicus).

[5]AZTEC RECORDS: Tonalamatl Aubin, Codex Borbonicus, Codex Florentino, Codex Telleriano-Remensis, Vaticanus A.

MIXTECA-PUEBLA RECORDS: Vaticanus B, Borgia, Bologna (Cospi).

[6]Caso, Correlacion, 1940; Duran, Historia de las Indias, II, 1880; Sahagun, Historia General, 1938; Codex Borbonicus; Beuchat, Manuel, 1911.

[7]De Jonghe, Calendrier Mexicaine, 1906. Codex Mariano Jimenez. Sahagun, Historia General, 1938. Fewkes, Central American Ceremony, p. 285, 1893.

[8]Seler, Venus Period, 1904.

[9]Bancroft, Native Races, 1883, Vol. 3, pp. 393–96; cites authorities.

[10]Duran, Historia, II, 1880, pp. 155–60.

[11]Linton, Pawnee Sacrifice, 1926. Wissler and Spinden, Pawnee Sacrifice, 1916.

[12]Bancroft, Native Races, 1883, Vol. 3, pp. 387–88.

[13]Sahagun, Historia General, 1938; Codex Florentino.

[14]Bancroft, Native Races, 1883, Vol. 3, pp. 422–25. Blom, Maya Ball

Game, 1932. Duran, Historia de las Indias, II, 1880, Vol. 2, Chapter CI. Oviedo, Historia General, 1851, Vol. I, p. 165.

[15]Caso, Patolli, 1927.

[16]Clavigero, Historia Antigua, 1787, Book 7, Section 46. Larsen, Volador, 1937.

[17]Bancroft, Native Races, 1883, Vols. 2 and 3. Nuttall, Penitential Rite, 1904.

[18]Codex Borbonicus for monthly ceremonies.

Telleriano-Remensis and copy Vaticanus A record this sacrifice in year 8 Reed (1487).

Bancroft, Native Races, 1883, Vol. 2, pp. 585–86; cites authors.

[19]Orozco y Berra, Historia Antigua, 1880; Spinden, Ancient Civilizations, 1928; Peñafiel, Nomenclatura, 1897; Nombres Geograficos, 1885; Codex Mendoza; Tribute Roll of Montezuma.

[20]Memorial de Tepetlaostoc.

[21]Chimalpahin, Anales, 1889, Introduction, pp. vii–viii.

[22]TEXCOCAN STYLE: Mapa Tlotzin, Mapa Quinatzin, Codex Xolotl, Mapa de Siguenza.

TENOCHCAN STYLE: Codices Boturini, 1576, 1590, Telleriano-Remensis, Vaticanus A, Historia Mexicaine, Mapa de Tepechpan.

[23]Sahagun, Historia General, 1938, Vol. 3, Book 10, Chapter XXIX, pp. 137–38, paragraph 12.

[24]Codex Mendoza, Tribute Roll of Montezuma.

[25]Codex Chalchihuitzin Vasquez, in Vaillant, Aztec Twilight, 1939. Boban, Documents, 1891. Tlaquiltenango Manuscript, in American Museum of Natural History.

[26]Tozzer, Value of Manuscripts, 1912. Boban, Documents, 1891.

CHAPTER XII

The post-Conquest native historians approached Aztec history from an annalistic point of view. Only occasionally did economic and political ideas enter in. Bancroft's and Orozco y Berra's recapitulations of the early history give fullest materials for a detailed scrutiny of Aztec foreign affairs and war. Bandelier's technical study of their method of warfare is the best general outline of Aztecan procedure in this field.

[1]Bancroft, Native Races, 1883. Orozco y Berra, Historia de la Conquista, 1880. Bandelier, Art of War, 1877.

OLDER AUTHORITIES: Duran, Historia, 1867, 1880; Ixtlilxochitl, Relaciones, 1891, Historia, 1892; Tezozomoc, Cronica, 1878; Torquemada, Monarquia, 1723; Clavigero, History of Mexico, 1787.

[2]Mapa Tlotzin.

[3]Ixtlilxochitl, Historia Chichimeca, 1892.

[4]Commentary of Hamy in Codex Telleriano-Remensis. Aragon, Expansion del Imperio Mexicano, 1931.

[5]Bancroft, Native Races, Vol. 5; cites versions of various authorities.

[6]Bandelier, Art of War, 1877.

[7]Diaz del Castillo, True History, 1908, Vol. 1, Chapter IX, p. 43; Chapter XX, p. 74; Chapter XXIII, p. 85.

[8]Codex Mendoza.
[9]Bandelier, Art of War, 1877.
[10]Bandelier, Art of War, 1877.
[11]Vaillant, Correlation, 1938, footnote 81. Codex Mendoza.
[12]Bancroft, Native Races, 1883, Vol. 2, pp. 603–23.

CHAPTER XIII

This chapter was adapted from Natural History, Vol. 33, No. 1, pp. 17–30, January–February, 1933. It is based on contemporary accounts of Tenochtitlan and on various later archaeological studies on the topography of Tenochtitlan, the ancient Mexico City.

[1]CONTEMPORARY ACCOUNTS: Cortes, Letters, 1908; Diaz del Castillo, True History, 1908–16; Anonymous Conqueror, 1917; Mendieta, Historia Eclesiastica, 1870; Motolinia, Historia de las Indias, 1914; Sahagun, Historia General, 1938, Vol. 4, Book 12; Codex Florentino.

LATER STUDIES: Prescott, Conquest of Mexico, 1922; Maudslay, Great Temple Enclosures, 1912; Peñafiel, Destruccion del Templo Mayor, 1910; Alcocer, Mexico-Tenochtitlan, 1935; Maps reproduced in Maudslay's edition of Bernal Diaz del Castillo, True History, 1908–16, Vol. 3: Plan on Maguey Paper, Map of 1524, Map of Alonso de Santa Cruz, 1560.

[2]Diaz del Castillo, True History, 1908–16, Vol. 2, Chapter LXXXVIII.
[3]Diaz del Castillo, True History, 1908–16, Vol. 2, Chapter XCII.

CHAPTER XIV

Prescott has unforgettably told the story of the Conquest of Mexico. This chapter seeks to stress the Indian side of the Conquest, as told by Sahagun, Duran and others and as illustrated in the Codex Florentino and the Lienzo de Tlaxcala. The latter was prepared as a memorial to show the services Tlaxcalan warriors rendered the cause of Spain. This chapter is adapted from Natural History, Vol. 39, No. 3, pp. 185–95, March, 1937.

[1]Prescott, Conquest of Mexico, 1922. Orozco y Berra, Historia Antigua, 1880. Cortes, Letters, 1908. Diaz del Castillo, True History, 1908–16. Anonymous Conqueror, 1917. Duran, Historia, 1867, 1880. Ixtlilxochitl, Horribles Crueldades, 1829. Sahagun, Historia General, 1938, Vol. 4, Book 12. Codex Florentino. Lienzo de Tlaxcala.

[2]Sahagun, Historia General, 1938, Vol. 4, Book 12, Chapter I. Codex Florentino.

[3]Sahagun, Historia General, 1938, Vol. 4, Book 12, Chapter VIII.
[4]Lienzo de Tlaxcala, Pl. 17.
[5]Sahagun, Historia General, 1938, Vol. 4, Book 12, Chapter XXIII. Duran, Historia, II, 1880, Chapter LXXVI, p. 50.

[6]Diaz del Castillo, True History, 1908–16, Vol. 2, Chapter CXXVIII, p. 247, says no!! Bancroft, Conquest, Vol. 1, p. 480, says yes!! on authority.

[7]Sahagun, Historia General, 1938, Vol. 4, Book 12, Chapter XXXIII.

CHAPTER XV

This chapter is the merest résumé of what the visitor to Mexico may see of the Indian past. Very properly one may insert here, as footnote 1, the twelve English books on Mexico, which, in the writer's judgment, are best suited to prepare the visitor for what he may see.

[1]Henry Bamford Parkes, History of Mexico, Houghton Mifflin Co., Boston, 1938. A history devoted chiefly to colonial and republican Mexico.

Herbert Joseph Spinden, Ancient Civilization of Mexico and Middle America, American Museum of Natural History, Handbook Series, No. 3, New York, 1928. A masterpiece of exposition, short and simple, incredibly packed with knowledge, a sine qua non for the understanding of Indian civilization.

Charles Flandrau, Viva Mexico, D. Appleton & Company, New York, 1908. An enchanting series of impressions of Mexico under Diaz.

Bernal Diaz del Castillo, The True History of the Conquest of New Spain, Hackluyt Society, Series 2, Vols. 23–25, 30, 40, London, 1908–16. This old warrior, a soldier under Cortes, gives the most personal account of the Conquest.

William Hickling Prescott, The Conquest of Mexico, Henry Holt and Co., New York, 1922. Not only a brilliant account of the Conquest as seen through Spanish eyes, but one of the masterpieces of American literature.

J. Eric Thompson, Mexico before Cortes, Scribners, New York, 1933. An intimately alive picture of the Aztec civilization.

George C. Vaillant, Artists and Craftsmen in Ancient Central America, American Museum of Natural History Guide Leaflet Series 88 and 103, 1935. A survey of Middle American art, fully illustrated, for a very low price.

Anita Brenner, Idols behind Altars, Payson and Clarke, Ltd., New York, 1929. A superb picture of the Mexican artistic renaissance of 1918 and the essential continuity of Indian life.

Ernest Gruening, Mexico and Its Heritage, the Century Co., New York, 1928. A carefully documented study of the conflicts inherent in modern Mexican economic and social life.

C. S. Braden, Religious Aspects of the Conquest of Mexico, Duke University Press, Durham, N.C., 1930. The theory of the evangelization of the Mexican Indian, showing the humanitarian theories behind the consolidation of the Spanish Conquest.

Madame Calderon de la Barca, Life in Mexico, E. P. Dutton and Co., New York, 1931. The Scottish wife of the Spanish ambassador to Mexico in 1828 writes a most entertaining account of contemporary habits and customs. A classic.

Stuart Chase, Mexico, A Study of Two Americas, Macmillan Co., New York, 1931. A succinct, slightly *simpliste* account of contemporary Mexico with special emphasis on the virtues of unmechanized life.

[2]Braden, Religious Aspects, 1930. Ricard, Conquête Spirituelle, 1933.

[3]The amount of writing by the different monastic orders is interesting as a reflection of direct interest in Indian affairs: Franciscan, 68; Jesuit, 19; Dominican, 18; Augustinian, 3; parish priests, 18; civilians, 6; cf. Clavigero, History, 1787, and Ricard, Conquête Spirituelle: Spanish Friars, 61; Indians and Mestizos, 61; Spanish Civilians, 6; Foreign Friars, 7.

[4]Indian authors and approximate dates of composition: Tezozomoc, before 1561; Anales de Cuauhtitlan, 1570; Duran, 1581; Ixtlilxochitl, 1600; Chimalpahin, 1613.

Post-Conquest picture writings and closing dates: Codex Telleriano-Remensis and Vaticanus A, 1563; Codex of 1576, 1607; Codex of 1590, 1590; Histoire Mexicaine, 1521.

[5]——, Tres Siglos de Arquitectura Colonial, 1933, p. 27. Garcia Granados y MacGregor, Huexotcingo, 1934.

[6]Nuttall, Official Reports, 1926. Del Paso y Troncoso, Papeles de Nueva España, 1905–06.

[7]Redfield, Tepoztlan, 1930. Parsons, Mitla, 1936.

[8]Brenner, Idols behind Altars, 1929. Chase, Mexico, 1931.

[9]The perfect guide for Mexico has yet to be written. Terry, Guide, 1927, the most full, approaching Baedeker. Brenner, Your Mexican Holiday, 1932, good for the traveler. Marett, Archaeological Tours, 1934, good for a person interested in archaeology, since many ruins are not on beaten path. ——, Tres Siglos de Arquitectura Colonial, 1933, brief illustrated guide. ——, Monumentos Arqueológicos, 1933, brief illustrated guide.

[10]The index will provide references to descriptions of the sites given in the text.

BIBLIOGRAPHY

ALCOCER, I
1935 Apuntes sobre la Antigua Mexico-Tenochtitlan (Instituto Panamericano de Geografia e Historia, Tacubaya).
1938 Comidas de los Mexicanos, in Sahagun, Historia General, Vol. 3,
pp. 365–74.

DE ALVA IXTLILXOCHITL, F.
See Ixtlilxochitl, F. de Alva.

ANALES DE CUAUHTITLAN (CODEX CHIMALPOPOCA)
1885 Anales del Museo Nacional de Mexico, Tomo 3, Appendix,
Mexico.
See also Lehmann, Die Geschichte von Colhuacan und Mexico,
1938.

ANDREWS, E. WYLLYS
1940 Chronology and Astronomy in the Maya Area (in The Maya
and Their Neighbors, pp. 150–61, New York).

ANONYMOUS CONQUEROR
1917 Narrative of Some Things of New Spain and the Great City of
Temestitan, Mexico. Translated into English by Marshall H.
Saville (Documents and Narratives Concerning the Discovery
and Conquest of Latin America, No. 1, The Cortes Society,
New York).

ANTIGUEDADES MEXICANAS
1892 Antiguedades Mexicanas. Publicadas por la Junta Colombino de
Mexico en el Cuarto Centenario de Descubrimiento de
America. Mexico.

ARAGON, JAVIER O.
1931 Expansion Territorial del Imperio Mexicano (Anales del Museo
Nacional de Arqueología, Historia y Etnografía, 4a Época,
Tomo 7, pp. 5–64, Mexico).

AUBIN, J. M. A.

1885 Mémoires sur la Peinture Didactique (Mission Scientifique au Mexique et dans l'Amérique Centrale: Recherches Historiques et Archéologiques. Pre.nière Partie—Histoire. Paris).

1893 Histoire de la Nation Mexicaine (Reproduction du Codex de 1576, Paris). *See also* Codex of 1576.

BANCROFT, HUBERT HOWE.

1883a The Conquest of Mexico (3 vols., New York).

1883b The Native Races (5 vols., San Francisco).

BANDELIER, ADOLPH F.

1877 On the Art of War and Mode of Warfare of the Ancient Mexicans (Tenth Annual Report of the Peabody Museum of American Archaeology and Ethnology, Vol. 2, pp. 95–161, Cambridge).

1878 On the Distribution and Tenure of Lands, and the Customs with Respect to Inheritance, among the Ancient Mexicans (Eleventh Annual Report of the Peabody Museum of American Archaeology and Ethnology, Vol. 2, pp. 385–448, Cambridge).

1880 On the Social Organization and Mode of Government of the Ancient Mexicans (Twelfth Annual Report of the Peabody Museum of American Archaeology and Ethnology, Vol. 2, pp. 557–699, Cambridge).

1884 Report of an Archaeological Tour in Mexico in 1881 (Papers, Archaeological Institute of America, American Series, Vol. 2, Boston).

BATRES, LEOPOLDO

1902a Explorations in Escalerillas Street, Mexico City. Mexico.

1902b Exploraciones de Monte Albán, México. México.

1904 Exploraciones en Huexotla, Texcoco, y El Gavilán, México. México.

BEALS, RALPH L.

1932 The Comparative Ethnology of Northern Mexico before 1750 (Ibero-Americana: 2, University of California, Berkeley).

BENNETT, WENDELL C., AND ZINGG, R. M.

1935 The Tarahumara. Chicago.

BEUCHAT, HENRI

1912 Manuel d'Archéologie Américaine. Paris.

BEYER, HERMANN

1921 Sobre Antiguedades del Pedregal de San Angel (Memorias de la Sociedad Cientifica "Antonio Alzate," Tomo 37, pp. 1–16, Mexico).

BIART, LUCIEN

1913 The Aztecs. Translated by J. L. Garner. Chicago.

BIBLIOTECA MEXICANA

1878 Cronica Mexicana escrita por D. Hernando Alvarado Tezozomoc
. . . anotada por el Sr. Lic. D. Manuel Orozco y Berra, y
precedida del Codice Ramirez, Manuscrito del Siglo XVI intit-
ulado: Relacion del Origen de los Indios que habitan esta
Nueva España segun sus Historias, y de un Examen de Ambas
Obras al cual va anexo un estudio de Cronologia Mexicana
por el mismo Sr. Orozco y Berra, Biblioteca Mexicana, José
M. Vigil, editor, Mexico).

BIRD, JUNIUS

1938 Antiquity and Migrations of the Early Inhabitants of Patagonia
(Geographical Review, Vol. 28, pp. 250–75, New York).

BLOM, FRANS

1932a Commerce, Trade and Monetary Units of the Maya (Middle
American Research Series, pub. no. 4, pp. 531–56, Tulane
University, New Orleans).

1932b The Maya Ball-Game *Pok-ta-pok* (called *tlachtli* by the Aztecs)
(Middle American Research Series, pub. no. 4, pp. 485–530,
Tulane University, New Orleans).

BOAS, FRANZ

1911–12 Album de Colecciones Arqueológicas (Publicaciones de la
Escuela Internacional de Arqueología y Etnología Americanas, México). *See* Gamio, Text, 1921.

BOBAN, EUGENE

1891 Documents pour servir a l'Histoire du Mexique. Catalogue
Raisonné de la Collection de M. E. Eugène Goupil (2 vols. of
text and atlas, Paris).

BRADEN, C. S.

1930 Religious Aspects of the Conquest of Mexico (Duke University
Press, Durham).

BRAND, DONALD

1932 *See* Sauer and Brand.

BRENNER, ANITA

1929 Idols behind Altars. New York.

1931 The Influence of Technique on the Decorative Style in the
Domestic Pottery of Culhuacan (Columbia University Contributions to Anthropology, Vol. 13, New York).

1932 Your Mexican Holiday. New York and London.

BRINTON, DANIEL G.

1887 Ancient Nahuatl Poetry. Philadelphia.

1890a Rig Veda Americanus. Philadelphia.

1890b Essays of an Americanist. Philadelphia.

BULLETIN 28

1904 Mexican and Central American Antiquities, Calendar Systems and History, Papers by Seler and others (Bureau of American Ethnology, Bulletin 28, Washington).

BUTLER, MARY

1940 A Pottery Sequence from the Alta Verapaz, Guatemala (in The Maya and Their Neighbors, pp. 250–67, New York).

CAHILL, HOLGER

1933 American Sources of Modern Art (The Museum of Modern Art, New York).

CALDERON DE LA BARCA, MADAME

1931 Life in Mexico. New York.

CASO, ALFONSO

1924–27 Un Antiguo Juego Mexicano: El Patolli (El Mexico Antiguo, Vol. 2, pp. 203–11, Mexico).

1927a Las Ruinas de Tizatlan, Tlaxcala (Revista Mexicana de Estudios Historicos, Vol. 1, pp. 139–72, Mexico).

1927b El Teocalli de la Guerra Sagrada. México.

1928 Las Estelas Zapotecas. México.

1932a Monte Albán, Richest Archaeological Find in America (The National Geographic Magazine, Vol. 62, pp. 487–512, Washington).

1932b Reading the Riddle of Ancient Jewels (Natural History, Vol. 32, pp. 464–80, New York).

1932c Las Exploraciones en Monte Albán, Temporada 1931–32 (Instituto Panamericano de Geografía e Historia, pub. no. 7, México).

1935 Las Exploraciones en Monte Albán, Temporada 1934–35 (Instituto Panamericano de Geografía e Historia, pub. no. 19, México).

1937a The Religion of the Aztecs. Mexico.

1937b Tenian los Teotihuacanos Conocimiento del Tonalpohualli? (El Mexico Antiguo, Vol. 4, Nos. 3–4, pp. 131–43, Mexico).

1938a Exploraciones en Oaxaca. Quinta y Sexta Temporadas 1936–37 (Instituto Panamericano de Geografía e Historia, pub. no. 34, Tacubaya).

1938b Thirteen Masterpieces of Mexican Archaeology. Mexico.

1939 La Correlacion de los Años Azteca y Cristiano (Revista Mexicana de Estudios Antropologicos, Vol. 3, No. 1, pp. 11–45, Mexico).

CASO, ALFONSO, WITH RUBIN DE LA BORBOLLA, D. F.

1936 Exploraciones en Mitla, Temporada 1934–35 (Instituto Panamericano de Geografía e Historia, pub. no. 21, México).

CASTAÑEDA, D., AND MENDOZA, V. T.
1933   Los Pequeños Percutores de las Civilizaciones Precortesianas
        (Anales del Museo Nacional de Arqueología, Historia y
        Etnografía, 4a Epoca, Tomo 8, pp. 449–576, Mexico).

CASTRO LEAD, ANTONIO, AND OTHERS
1940   Twenty Centuries of Mexican Art. Mexico.

CATHERWOOD, FREDERICK
1844   Views of Ancient Monuments in Central America, Chiapas and
        Yucatan. London.

CEBALLOS NOVELO, R. J.
1935   Las Instituciones Aztecas. Mexico.

CHARLOT, JEAN
1931   See Morris, Charlot and Morris.

CHARNAY, DÉSIRÉ
1887   The Ancient Cities of the New World. Translated by J. G. and
        H. S. Conant. New York.

CHARNAY, DÉSIRÉ, AND VIOLLET-LE-DUC, E. E.
1863   Cités et Ruines Américaines (1 vol. text and atlas of plates,
        Paris).

CHASE, STUART
1931   Mexico, A Study of Two Americas. New York.

CHAVERO, A.
1887   Historia Antigua y de la Conquista (Vol. 1 of V. Riva Palacio,
        México a través de los Siglos, Mexico and Barcelona).
1904   El Monolito de Coatlinchan (Anales del Museo Nacional de
        México, 2a Epoca, Tomo 1, pp. 281–305, Mexico).

CHIMALPAHIN
1889   Anales de Chimalpahin Quauhtlehuanitzin, Sixième et Septième
        Relations, publiées et traduite par Remi Siméon (Bibliothèque
        Linguistique Américaine, tome 12, Paris).

CHURCHWARD, JAMES
1926   Lost Continent of Mu. London.

CLAVIGERO, FRANCESCO SAVERIO
1787   The History of Mexico. Translated by Charles Cullen (2 vols.,
        London).

CODICES
        See also Lienzo, Mapa, Tonalamatl and Tribute Roll of Mon-
        tezuma.

CODEX OF 1576
        A Post-Columbian Codex in the Goupil Collection, National
        Library, Paris.
        See Aubin, Histoire, 1893.

Codex Mexicanus of 1590
    See Boban, Documents, 1891, Pls. 23–24.

Codex Bologna
    See Codex Cospi.

Codex Borbonicus
    1899 A Pre-Columbian Codex Preserved in the Library of the Cham-
            ber of Deputies, Paris.
            See Paso y Troncoso, Codice Pictorico, 1898, and Vaillant, ed.,
            Sacred Almanac, 1940.

Codex Borgia
    1898 A Pre-Columbian Codex Preserved in the Ethnographical
            Museum of the Vatican, Rome. Published by le Duc de
            Loubat, Rome.
            See also Kingsborough, Antiquities of Mexico, 1830, Vol. 3, Pt. 1,
            pp. 1–76; and Seler, Commentary, 1904–08.

Codex Boturini (Tira del Museo)
            See Garcia Cubas, Atlas, 1858; Radin, Sources, 1920, pp. 11–12,
            33–35, Pls. 1 and 2; Orozco y Berra, Historia Antigua, 1880,
            Vol. 3, Chap. 4; Kingsborough, Antiquities of Mexico, 1830,
            Vol. 1, Pt. 3, pp. 1–23.

Codex Chalchihuitzin Vasquez
            See Vaillant, Twilight, 1939.

Codex Chimalpopoca
            See Anales de Cuauhtitlan.

Codex Cospi (Bologna)
    1898 A Pre-Columbian Codex in the Library of the University of
            Bologna. Published by le Duc de Loubat, Rome.
            Kingsborough, Antiquities of Mexico 1830, Vol. 2, Pt. 3, pp.
            1–24.

Codex Fejervary-Mayer
    1901 An Old Mexican Picture Manuscript in the Liverpool Free Pub-
            lic Museum. Published by le Duc de Loubat, Paris.
            See Seler, Commentary, 1902.

Codex Florentino
    1905 Illustrations for Sahagun's Historia de las Cosas de Nueva
            España. Published by Francisco del Paso y Troncoso, Vol. 5,
            Madrid.

Codex Kingsborough
    1912 *See* Memorial de los Indios de Tepetlaostoc.

Codex Magliabecchiano, XIII-3
    1904 Manuscrit Mexicain Post-Colombien de la Bibliothèque Na-
            tionale de Florence. Reproduit au Frais du Duc de Loubat.
            Rome.
            See Nuttall, The Book of Life, 1903.

CODEX MARIANO JIMENEZ
n. d. Codice Mariano Jimenez. Edited by Nicolas Léon, Mexico.

CODEX MENDOCINO
See Codex Mendoza.

CODEX MENDOZA (MENDOCINO)
1938 Codex Mendoza. Edited and translated by James Cooper Clark
(3 vols., London).
See also Museo Nacional de Arqueología, Historia y Etnografía, Mexico, 1925; Kingsborough, Antiquities of Mexico,
1830, Vol. 1, London.

CODEX NUTTALL (CODEX ZOUCHE)
1902 Ancient Mexican Codex belonging to Lord Zouche of Hary-
worth. Introduction by Zelia Nuttall (Peabody Museum of
American Archaeology and Ethnology, Cambridge).

CODEX RAMIREZ
See Historia de los Mexicanos por sus Pinturas.

CODEX TELLERIANO-REMENSIS
1899 A Post-Columbian Codex published by le Duc de Loubat, Paris.
Commentary by E. T. Hamy.

CODEX VATICANUS 3738 (VATICANUS A) (Rios) (Copy of Codex Telleriano-Remensis).
1900 A Post-Columbian Codex Preserved in the Library of the Vati-
can, Rome. Published by le Duc de Loubat, Rome.
See Kingsborough, Antiquities of Mexico, 1830, Vol. 2, Pt. 1,
pp. 1–149.

CODEX VATICANUS 3773 (VATICANUS B)
1896 A Pre-Columbian Codex Preserved in the Library of the Vati-
can, Rome. Published by le Duc de Loubat, Rome.
See also Kingsborough, Antiquities of Mexico, 1830, Vol 3,
Pt. 4, pp. 1–96; Seler, Commentary, 1903.

CODEX VIENNA
See Codex Vindobonensis.

CODEX VINDOBONENSIS (VIENNA)
1929 Codex Vindobonensis Mexic. I. Facsimile. Text by Walter
Lehmann and Ottokar Smital. Vienna.
See Kingsborough, Antiquities of Mexico, 1830, Vol. 2, Pt. 4,
pp. 1–66.

CODEX XOLOTL
See Boban, Documents, 1891, Pls. 1–10; Radin, Sources, 1920, pp.
17–18, 41–45.

CODEX ZOUCHE
See Codex Nuttall.

CORTES, HERNANDO

1908 Letters of Cortes. Translated and Edited by F. A. MacNutt (2 vols., New York and London).

CUMMINGS, BYRON C.

1923a Ruins of Cuicuilco May Revolutionize Our History of Ancient America (The National Geographic Magazine, Vol. 44, pp. 203–20, Washington).

1923b Cuicuilco, The Oldest Temple Discovered in North America (Art and Archaeology, Vol. 16, nos. 1–2, pp. 51–58, Washington).

1926 Cuicuilco and the Archaic Culture of Mexico (The Scientific Monthly, Vol. 34, no. 8, pp. 289–304, Lancaster).

1933 Cuicuilco and the Archaic Culture of Mexico (University of Arizona Bulletin, Vol. 4, no. 8, Social Science Bulletin, No. 4, pp. 1–56, Tucson).

DAUTERMAN, C. C.

1938 The Pottery Yard Stick at Monte Alban (The Scientific Monthly, Vol. 46, pp. 157–65, Lancaster).

DÍAZ DEL CASTILLO, BERNAL

1908–16 The True History of the Conquest of New Spain. Translated by A. P. Maudslay (Hakluyt Society, 5 vols., London).

DIXON, R. B.

1923 The Racial History of Man. New York.

DONNELLY, I.

1882 Atlantis, the Antedeluvian World, New York

DOUGLAS, FREDERIC C., AND D'HARNONCOURT, RENÉ.

1941 Indian Art of the United States (The Museum of Modern Art, New York).

DUPAIX, GUILLELMO

1834 Antiquités Mexicaines (2 vols. and atlas, Paris).

DURÁN, D.

1867, 1880 Historia de las Indias de Nueva-España (XVI Century) (2 vols. and atlas, Mexico).

EKHOLM, GORDON F.

1939 Results of an Archaeological Survey of Sonora and Northern Sinaloa (Revista Mexicana de Estudios Antropologicos, Vol. 3, no. 1, pp. 7–10, Mexico).

1940a The Archaeology of Northern and Western Mexico (in The Maya and Their Neighbors, pp. 320–30, New York).

1940b Prehistoric "Lacquer" from Sinaloa (Revista Mexicana de Estudios Antropologicos, Vol. 4, nos. 1–2, pp. 10–15, Mexico).

EMMART, EMILY W.

1940 The Badianus Manuscript. An Aztec Herbal of 1552. Baltimore.

1934 Escultura Mexicana Antigua. Mexico.

1936 Essays in Anthropology presented to Alfred Louis Kroeber. Berkeley. (*See* Lowie.)

1940 Essays in Historical Anthropology of North America. Published in honor of John R. Swanton (Smithsonian Miscellaneous Collections, Vol. 100, Washington).

FEWKES, J. WALTER

1893 A Central American Ceremony Which Suggests the Snake Dance of the Tusayan Villagers (American Anthropologist, o.s., Vol. 6, pp. 285–306, Washington).

FLANDRAU, C. M.

1908 Viva Mexico. New York.

GALLOP, R.

1938 Ancient Monuments of Mexico (The Geographical Magazine, Vol. 7, pp. 321–38, London).

GAMIO, MANUEL

1910 Los Monumentos Arqueológicos de las Inmediaciones de Chalchihuites (Anales del Museo Nacional de Arqueología, Historia, y Etnología, 3a. Epoca, Tomo 2, pp. 469–92, México).

1920 Las Excavaciones del Pedregal de San Angel y la Cultura Arcaica del Valle de México (American Anthropologist, n.s., Vol. 22, pp. 127–43, Lancaster).

1921 Album de Colecciones Arqueológicas, Texto (Publicaciones, Escuela Internacional de Arqueología y Etnología Americanas, México).
See Boas, 1911–12.

1924 The Sequence of Cultures in Mexico (American Anthropologist, n.s., Vol. 26, pp. 307–22, Menasha).

GAMIO, MANUEL, AND OTHERS

1922 La Poblacion del Valle de Teotihuacan (Secretaría de Agricultura y Fomento, Direccion de Antropología, 3 vols., México).

GANN, THOMAS

1900 Mounds in Northern Honduras (19th Annual Report, Bureau of American Ethnology, Pt. 2, pp. 655–92, Washington).

GANN, THOMAS, AND THOMPSON, J. ERIC

1931 The History of the Maya. New York.

GARCIA CUBAS, A.
1858 Atlas Geográfico y Estadístico de los Estados Unidos de Mexico. Mexico.

GARCIA GRANADOS, R., AND MacGREGOR, L.
1934 Huejotzingo. La Ciudad y el Convento Franciscano. Mexico.

GARCIA ICAZBALCETA, J.
1886–92 Nueva Coleccion de Documentos para la Historia de Mexico (5 vols., Mexico).

GLADWIN, HAROLD S.
1937 Excavations at Snaketown: Comparisons and Theories (Medallion Papers, Gila Pueblo, No. 26, Globe).

GLADWIN, HAROLD S., GLADWIN, NORA, HAURY, EMIL, AND SAYLES, E. B.
1937 Excavations at Snaketown: Material Culture (Medallion Papers, Gila Pueblo, No. 25, Globe).

GORDON, G. B. (editor)
1925 Examples of Maya Pottery in the Museum and Other Collections (The University Museum, University of Pennsylvania, Philadelphia).

See Mason, Maya Pottery, 1928.

GRUENING, ERNEST
1928 Mexico and Its Heritage. New York.

D'HARNONCOURT, RENÉ
1941 *See* Douglas and d'Harnoncourt.

HAURY, EMIL W.
1937 *See* Gladwin, Gladwin, Haury and Sayles.

HEGER, FRANZ
1908 Der Altamerikanische Federschmuch in den Sammlungen der anthropologisch-ethnographischen Abteilung des k. k. naturhistorischen Hofmuseums in Wien (Festschrift herausgegeben anläszlich d. Tagung d. XVI Internationalen Amerikanisten-Kongresses in Wien, September 1908, vom Organisationskomitee, Wien).

HERNANDEZ, F.
1790 De Historia Novae Hispaniae Plantarum. Madrid.

HISTOIRE DU MECHIQUE
See de Jonghe, ed., Histoire, 1905.

HISTOIRE MEXICAINE
See Boban, Documents, 1891, Pls. 59–64.

HISTORIA de los MEXICANOS por sus PINTURAS (CODEX RAMIREZ)
1886   Anales del Museo Nacional, la Epoca, Tomo 2, pp. 83–106, Mexico.
   See also Phillips, Notes, 1883; Radin, Sources, 1920, pp. 57–66; Garcia Icazbalceta Nueva Coleccion, 1886–92, Vol. 3; Biblioteca Mexicana, 1878, Codex Ramirez.

HISTORIA TOLTECA-CHICHIMECA
1937, 1939   *See* Preuss and Mengin.

HODGE, F. W.
1907   Handbook of the American Indian (Bureau of American Ethnology, Bulletin 30, 2 vols., Washington).

HOLMES, WILLIAM H.
1895–97 Archaeological Studies among the Ancient Cities of Mexico (Field Columbian Museum, Anthropological Series, Vol. 1, no. 1, Chicago).
1907   On a Nephrite Statuette from San Andres Tuxtla, Vera Cruz, Mexico (American Anthropologist, n.s., Vol. 9, pp. 691–701, Lancaster).
1914–19 Masterpieces of Aboriginal American Art (Art and Archaeology, Vol. 1, pp. 1–12, 91–102, 242–55; Vol. 3, pp. 70–85; Vol. 4, pp. 267–78; Vol. 5, pp. 38–49; Vol. 8, pp. 348–60, Washington).
1919   Handbook of Aboriginal American Antiquities. Pt. 1. Introductory. The Lithic Industries (Bulletin 60, Bureau of American Ethnology, Washington).

HOOTON, ERNEST A.
1933   Racial Types in America and Their Relations to Old World Types (in Jenness, ed., American Aborigines, pp. 131–63).

HOWARD, EDGAR B.
1935   Evidence of Early Man in North America (Museum Journal, University Museum, University of Pennsylvania, Vol. 24, nos. 2–3, pp. 61–175, Philadelphia).

HOWELLS, WILLIAM W.
1940   Origins of American Indian Race Types (in The Maya and Their Neighbors, pp. 3–9, New York).

HRDLIČKA, ALEŠ
1903   The Region of the Ancient "Chichimecs," with Notes on the Tepecanos and the Ruin of La Quemada, Mexico (American Anthropologist, n.s., Vol. 5, pp. 385–440, Lancaster).
1923   Origin and Antiquity of the American Indian (Annual Report of the Smithsonian Institution for 1923, pp. 481–94, Washington).

310 Bibliography

HUMBOLDT, A.
1810 Vues des Cordillères et Monuments des Peuples Indigènes de l'Amérique. Paris.

HYDE, G.
1922 *See* Mena and Hyde.

IXTLILXOCHITL, FERNANDO DE ALVA
1829 Horribles Crueldades de los Conquistadores de Mexico. Mexico.
1891–92 Obras Históricas (XVI Century); Relaciones, Vol. 1; Historia Chichimeca, Vol. 2. Mexico.

JENNESS, D. (editor)
1933 The American Aborigines. Their Origin and Antiquity. Toronto.

JOHNSON, FREDERICK
1940 *See* Mason and Johnson.

DE JONGHE, E.
1906 Le Calendrier Mexicain (Journal de la Société des Américanistes de Paris, n.s., Vol. 3, pp. 197–227, Paris).

DE JONGHE, E. (editor)
1905 Histoire du Méchique, Manuscrit Français inédit du XVIᵉ Siècle (Journal de la Société des Americanistes de Paris, n.s., Tome 2, pp. 1–41, Paris).

JOYCE, THOMAS A.
1914, 1920 Mexican Archaeology. London.
1916 Central American and West Indian Archaeology. London.
1927 Maya and Mexican Art. London.

KIDDER, A. V.
1924 An Introduction to the Study of Southwestern Archaeology with a Preliminary Account of the Excavations at Pecos (Papers of the Phillips Academy, Andover, Southwestern Expedition, No. 1, New Haven).
1931 The Pottery of Pecos, Vol. 1, The Dull-Paint Wares (Papers of the Phillips Academy, Andover, Southwestern Expedition, No. 5, New Haven).

KINGSBOROUGH, EDWARD KING, LORD
1830–48 Antiquities of Mexico (9 vols., London).

KIRCHHOFF, PAUL
1940 Los Pueblos de la Historia Tolteca-Chichimeca: sus Migraciones y Parentesco (Revista Mexicana de Estudios Antropológicos, Vol. 4, nos. 1–2, pp. 77–104, México).

KOHLER, J.
1924 El Derecho de los Aztecas (Spanish Translation. Edicion de la Revista Juridica de la Escuela Libre de Derecho, México).

KRICKEBERG, W.
  1918-22, 1925 Die Totonaken (Baessler Archiv, Vol. 7, pp. 1-55; Vol. 9, pp. 1-75, Berlin. Spanish Translation, Mexico, 1933).
  1937 Berichte über Neue Forschungen zur Geschichte der Alten Kulturen Mittel-Amerikas (Die Welt als Geschichte, 3 Jahrgang, pp. 194-230, Stuttgart).

KROEBER, ALFRED L.
  1925 Archaic Culture Horizons in the Valley of Mexico (University of California Publications in American Archaeology and Ethnology, Vol. 17, pp. 373-408, Berkeley).
  1939 Cultural and Natural Areas of Native North America (University of California, Publications in American Archaeology and Ethnology, Vol. 38, Berkeley).

LARSEN, H.
  1937 Notes on the Volador and Its Associated Ceremonies and Superstitions (Ethnos, Vol. 2, no. 4, pp. 179-92, Stockholm).
  1938 The Monolithic Rock Temple of Malinalco, Mexico (Ethnos, Vol. 3, nos. 2-3, pp. 59-63, Stockholm).

LEHMANN, WALTER
  1909 Methods and Results in Mexican Research (Translated by Seymour de Ricci from Archiv für Anthropologie, Vol. 6, pp. 113-68, Paris).
  1920 Zentral-Amerika (2 vols., Berlin).
  1933 Aus den Pyramidenstädten in Alt-Mexiko. Berlin.
  1938 Die Geschichte der Königreiche von Colhuacan und Mexico (Quellenwerke zur Alten Geschichte Amerikas, Ibero-Amerikanischen Institut, Berlin). See also Anales de Cuauhtitlan.

LEHMANN, W., AND DOERING, H.
  1924 Kunstgeschichte des Alten Peru. Berlin.

LEÓN, NICOLÁS
  1904 Los Tarascos. Pt. 1. México. (Reprinted from Boletin del Museo Nacional de México, 2a Epoca, Vol. 1, August, 1903 through June, 1904, México).
  1903, 1906 Los Tarascos. Pts. 2 and 3 (Anales del Museo Nacional de México, 2a Epoca, Vol. 1, pp. 392-502, 592, México; and Vol. 3, pp. 298-479, México).
  See also Codex Mariano Jimenez.

LEON Y GAMA, ANTONIO
  1832 Descripcion Historica y Cronologica de las Dos Piedras que se Hallaron en al Año 1790 en la Plaza Principal de Mexico. Mexico.

LE PLONGEON, AUGUSTUS
  1896 Queen Moo and the Egyptian Sphinx. New York.

LIENZO DE TLAXCALA

1892 Lienzo de Tlaxcala (in Antiguedades Mexicanas, Junta Colombino, Pls. 66–175, Mexico).

LINNÉ, S.

1924 Archaeological Researches at Teotihuacan, Mexico (The Ethnographical Museum of Sweden, New Series, pub. no. 1, Stockholm).

1937 The Expedition to Mexico, 1934–35 (Ethnos, Vol. 1, no. 2, pp. 39–48, Stockholm).

1938 A Mazapan Grave at Teotihuacan Mexico (Ethnos, Vol. 3, no. 6, pp. 167–78, Stockholm).

1939 Zapotecan Antiquities and the Paulsen Collection in the Ethnographical Museum of Sweden (Publications, Ethnographical Museum of Sweden, n.s., Vol. 4, Stockholm).

LINTON, RALPH

1924 The Significance of Certain Traits in North American Maize Culture (American Anthropologist, n.s., Vol. 26, pp. 345–49, Menasha).

1926 The Origin of the Skidi Pawnee Sacrifice to the Morning Star (American Anthropologist, n.s., Vol. 28, pp. 457–66, Menasha).

1940 Crops, Soils and Culture in America (in The Maya and Their Neighbors, pp. 32–40, New York).

LOTHROP, SAMUEL K.

1924 Tulum (Carnegie Institution of Washington, pub. no. 335, Washington).

1927 Pottery Types and Their Sequence in El Salvador (Indian Notes and Monographs Museum of the American Indian, Heye Foundation, Vol. 1, no. 4, pp. 165–220, New York).

1933 Atitlan. An Archaeological Study of Ancient Remains on the Borders of Lake Atitlan, Guatemala (Carnegie Institution of Washington, pub. no. 444, Washington).

1936 Zacualpa. A Study of Ancient Quiché Artifacts (Carnegie Institution of Washington, pub. no. 472, Washington).

1937 Coclé. An Archaeological Study of Central Panama (Pt. 1, Memoirs, Peabody Museum of American Archaeology and Ethnology, Harvard University, Vol. 7, Cambridge).

LOWIE, ROBERT L. (editor)

1936 Essays in Anthropology presented to Alfred Louis Krober, Berkeley.

LUMHOLTZ, C.

1902 Unknown Mexico (2 vols., New York).

MACCURDY, G. G. (editor)

1937 Early Man. Philadelphia and New York.

MANGELSDORF, P. C., AND REEVES, R. G.

1938 The Origin of Maize (Proceedings of the National Academy of Sciences, Vol. 24, pp. 303–12, Lancaster).

1939 Origin of Indian Corn and Its Relatives (Texas Agricultural Experiment Station, Bulletin 574, College Station, Texas).

MAPA QUINATZIN

1885 See Aubin, Memoires.

MAPA DE SIGUENZA

See Radin, Sources, 1920, pp. 12–13; Kingsborough, Antiquities of Mexico, 1830, Vol. 4; Orozco y Berra, Historia Antigua, 1880, Vol. 3, pp. 131–53; Garcia Cubas, Atlas, 1858.

MAPA DE TEPECHPAN

1887 See Anales del Museo Nacional (Tomo 3, la Epoca, Entrega 2, p. 368, Mexico).

MAPA TLOTZIN

1885 See Aubin, Memoires.

MARETT, R. H. K.

1934 Archaeological Tours from Mexico City. London and Mexico.

MARQUINA, IGNACIO

1928 Estudio Arquitectónico Comparativo de los Monumentos Arqueológicos de México (Secretaría de Educación Pública, México).

MASON, J. ALDEN

1927 Mirrors of Ancient America (The Museum Journal, Museum of the University of Pennsylvania, Vol. 18, no. 2, pp. 201–09, Philadelphia).

1935 The Place of Texas in Pre-Columbian Relationships between the United States and Mexico (Bulletin of the Texas Archaeological and Palaeontological Society, Vol. 7, pp. 29–46, Abilene).

1937a Further Remarks on the Pre-Columbian Relationships between the United States and Mexico (Bulletin of the Texas Archaeological and Palaeontological Society, Vol. 9, pp. 120–29, Abilene).

1937b Late Archaeological Sites in Durango, Mexico, from Chalchihuites to Zape (Twenty-fifth Anniversary Studies, Philadelphia Anthropological Society, Vol. 1, pp. 127–46, Philadelphia).

MASON, J. ALDEN (editor)

1928 Examples of Maya Pottery in the Museum and Other Collections (The University Museum, University of Pennsylvania, Philadelphia).

Mason, J. A., and Johnson, F.
1940 The Native Languages of Middle America and the Linguistic Map of Central America (in The Maya and Their Neighbors, pp. 52–114, New York).

Maudslay, A. P.
1889–1902 Archaeology (Biologia Centrali Americana, 4 vols. plates. 1 vol. text, London).
1912 A Note on the Position and Extent of the Great Temple Enclosure of Tenochtitlan. London.
———
1940 The Maya and Their Neighbors. Dedicated to Alfred M. Tozzer. New York.

McBride, G. McC.
1923 The Land Systems of Mexico (Research Series, American Geographical Society, No. 12, New York).

McBryde, Webster
1933 Sololá, a Guatemalan Town and Cakchiquel Market-Center. A Preliminary Report (Middle American Research Series, pub. no. 5, pp. 43–152, Tulane University, New Orleans).

Means, Philip Ainsworth
1931 Ancient Civilizations of the Andes. New York and London.

Memorial de los Indios de Tepetlaostoc
1912 (Codex Kingsborough.) (Editor, F. Paso y Troncoso, Madrid).

Mena, R., and Hyde, G.
1922 Antigüedad del Hombre en el Valle de México. Nueva Orientación Arqueológica e Histórica (Conferencias dadas en el Museo Nacional de Arqueología, Historia y Etnología, la noche del 27 diciembre de 1921. México).

De Mendieta, Fray Geronimo
1870 Historia Eclesiástica Indiana (XVI Century). México.

Mendoza, V. T.
1933 *See* Castañeda and Mendoza.

Mengin, E.
1937, 1938 *See* Preuss and Mengin.
1939 Unos Anales Historicos de la Nacion Mexicana; Pt. 1 (Baessler Archiv, Vol. 22, Berlin).

Merwin, R. E., and Vaillant, G. C.
1932 The Ruins of Holmul, Guatemala (Memoirs, Peabody Museum of American Archaeology and Ethnology, Harvard University, Vol. 3, no. 2, Cambridge).
———
1933 Monumentos Arqueologicos de Mexico. Departamento de Monumentos, Secretaria de Educacion Publica. Mexico.

MORENO, M.
1931 La Organización Política y Social de los Aztecas. Universidad Nacional de México Autónoma. Sección Editorial. México.

MORLEY, SYLVANUS G.
1915 An Introduction to the Study of Maya Hieroglyphs (Bureau of American Ethnology, Bulletin 57, Washington).
1920 The Inscriptions at Copan (Carnegie Institution of Washington, pub. no. 219, Washington).

MORRIS, ANN A.
1931 *See* Morris, Charlot and Morris.

MORRIS, EARL H., CHARLOT, JEAN, AND MORRIS, ANN A.
1931 The Temple of the Warriors at Chichen Itza, Yucatan (Carnegie Institution of Washington, pub. no. 406, Washington).

MOTOLINÍA (DE BENAVENTE, T.)
1914 Historia de los Índios de la Nueva España (XVI Century). Barcelona.

MUÑOZ CAMARGO, D.
1892 Historia de Tlaxcala (XVI Century). México.

MURDOCK, G. P.
1934 Our Primitive Contemporaries. New York.

NELSON, N. C.
1933 The Antiquity of Man in America in the Light of Archaeology (in Jenness, ed., The American Aborigines, pp. 87–130).

NOGUERA, EDUARDO
1927 Ruinas de Tizatlan, Tlaxcala (Publicaciones de la Secretaria de Educacion Publica, Mexico).
1928 El Ladrillo como Material de Construccion entre los Pueblos Nahuas (Revista Mexicana de Estudios Historicos, Tomo 2, pp. 64–68, Mexico).
1930a Decorative Aspects of Certain Types of Mexican Pottery (Proceedings, XXIII International Congress of Americanists, New York, 1928, pp. 85–92, New York).
1930b Algunas Características de la Cerámica de México (Journal de la Société des Américanistes de Paris n.s., Vol 22, pp. 249–310, Paris).
1934 Estudio de la Cerámica Encontrada donde Estaba el Templo Mayor de México (Anales del Museo Nacional de Arqueología, Historia y Etnografía, 5a. Epoca, Tomo 1, pp. 267–81, México).
1935 Antecedentes y Relaciones de la Cultura Teotihuacana (El México Antiguo, Vol. 3, nos. 5–8, pp. 1–81, México).
1937a El Altar de Los Cráneos Esculpidos de Cholula. México.
1937b Conclusiones Principales Obtenidas por el Estudio de la Cerámica Arqueológica en Cholula (Mimeograph, México).

NORDENSKIÖLD, ERLAND
   1930 L'Archéologie du Bassin de l'Amazone (Ars Americana, I, Paris).

NUTTALL, ZELIA
   1888 Standard or Head-Dress? (Papers, Peabody Museum of American Archaeology and Ethnology, Harvard University, Vol. 1, no. 1, Cambridge).
   1901 Chalchihuitl in Ancient Mexico (American Anthropologist, n.s., Vol. 3, pp. 227–37, New York).
   1903 The Book of Life of the Ancient Mexicans. Pt. 1, Introduction and Facsimile. Berkeley.
   1904 A Penitential Rite of the Ancient Mexicans (Papers, Peabody Museum of American Archaeology and Ethnology, Harvard University, Vol. 1, no. 7, Cambridge).
   1910 The Island of Sacrificios (American Anthropologist, n.s., Vol. 12, pp. 257–95, Lancaster).
   1925 Gardens of Ancient Mexico (The Smithsonian Institution, Annual Report, 1923, pp. 453–64, Washington).
   1926 Official Reports (on Mexican towns) sent by Castañeda to Philip II in 1580, translated and edited (Papers, Peabody Museum of American Archaeology and Ethnology, Harvard University, Vol. 11, no. 2, Cambridge).
   1926 The Aztecs and Their Predecessors in the Valley of Mexico (Proceedings, American Philosophical Society, Vol. 65, pp. 242–55, Philadelphia).

ORIGEN DE LOS MEXICANOS
   1886–92 See Garcia Icazbalceta, Nueva Coleccion, Vol. 3, pp. 281–308.

OROZCO Y BERRA, MANUEL
   1864 Geografía de las Lenguas y Carta Etnográfica de México. México.
   1878 Ojeada de Cronologia Mexicana, in Biblioteca Mexicana, pp. 151–222.
   1880 Historia Antigua y de la Conquista de México (4 vols. and atlas, México).
   1887 El Tonalamatl (Anales del Museo Nacional, la Epoca, Vol. 4, pp. 30–44, Mexico).

PALACIOS, ENRIQUE JUAN
   1925 La Fundacion de Mexico-Tenochtitlan (Anales del Museo Nacional de Arqueología, Historia y Etnografía, 5a Epoca, Tomo 1, No. 3, pp. 230–54, México).

PARKES, HENRY B.
   1938 A History of Mexico. Boston.

PARSONS, ELSIE C.
   1936 Mitla, Town of Souls. Chicago.

DEL PASO Y TRONCOSO, F.
1898 Descripcion Historia y Exposicion del Codice Pictorico de los Antiguas Nauas que se conserva en la Biblioteca de la Camara de Diputados de Paris. (Commentary on Codex Borbonicus) Florence.

DEL PASO Y TRONCOSO, F. (editor)
1905 *See* Codex Florentino.
1912 *See* Memorial de los Indios de Tepetlaostoc.

PAYÓN, J. GARCÍA
1936 Zona Arqueológica de Tecaxic-Calixtlahuaca, Pt. 1 (Departamento de Monumentos, México).

PEÑAFIEL, ANTONIO
1885 Nombres Geográficos de México (Secrataria de Fomento, Mexico).
1890 Monumentos del Arte Mexicano Antiguo (1 vol., text; 2 vols., plates; Berlin).
1897 Nomenclatura Geografica de Mexico (1 vol. and atlas, Mexico).
1903 Indumentaria Antigua (Secretaria de Fomento, Mexico).
1910 Destruccion del Templo Mayor de Mexico Antiguo. Mexico.

PHILLIPS, H.
1883 Notes upon the Codex Ramirez, with a translation of the same (Proceedings, American Philosophical Society, Vol. 21, pp. 616–51, Philadelphia).

POLLOCK, H. E. D.
1936 Round Structures of Aboriginal Middle America (Carnegie Institution of Washington, pub. no. 471, Washington).

POMAR, JUAN BAUTISTA
1891 Relación de Tezcoco (Garcia Icazbalceta, Nueva Colección de Documentos para la Historia de México, vol. 3, pp. 1–69, Mexico).

PRESCOTT, WILLIAM H.
1843 The Conquest of Mexico (3 vols., New York).
1922 The Conquest of Mexico (edited by T. A. Joyce and illustrated by Keith Henderson, 2 vols., New York).

PREUSS, K. T., AND MENGIN, E.
1937 Die Mexikanische Bilderhandschrift Historia Tolteca-Chichimeca. Pt. 1 (Baessler Archiv, Beiheft 9, Berlin).
1938 Die Mexikanische Bilderhandschrift Historia Tolteca-Chichimeca. Pt. 2 (Baessler Archiv, Vol. 21, Berlin).

RADIN, PAUL
1920 The Sources and Authenticity of the History of the Ancient Mexicans (University of California Publications in American Archaeology and Ethnology, Vol. 17, no. 1, Berkeley).

REDFIELD, ROBERT
1930 Tepoztlan. Chicago.

RELACION DE GENEALOGIA Y LINAGE DE LOS SEÑORES QUE HAN SEÑOREADO
ESTE TIERRA DE LA NUEVA ESPAÑA
    See Garcia Icazbalceta, Nueva Coleccion, 1886–92, Vol. 3, pp.
    263–81.

RICARD, R.
1933 La "Conquête Spirituelle" de Mexico (Université de Paris, Tra-
    vaux et Memoires de L'Institut d'Ethnologie, Vol. 20, Paris).

RIVA PALACIO, VICENTE (editor)
1887–89 México a Través de los Siglos (5 vols., México and Barce-
    lona).

ROBELO, CECILIO A.
1911 Diccionario de la Mitología Nahuatl. México.

ROBERTS, FRANK H. H., JR.
1935 A Survey of Southwestern Archaeology (American Anthropol-
    ogist, n.s., Vol. 37, pp. 1–35, Menasha).
1940 Developments in the Problem of the North American Paleo-
    Indian (in Essays in Historical Anthropology in North Amer-
    ica, pp. 51–116, Washington).

RUBIN DE BORBOLLA, D.
1936 *See* Caso with Rubin de Borbolla.

DE SAHAGUN, BERNARDINO
1829 Historia General de las Cosas de Nueva España (3 vols.,
    Mexico).
1905 Codex Florentino: Illustrations for Sahagun's Historia General
    de las Cosas de Nueva España. Edited by Francisco del Paso
    y Troncoso, Vol. 5, Madrid.
1932 Historia General de las Cosas de Nueva España. Books 1–4 trans-
    lated by Fanny Bandelier. Nashville.
1938 Historia General de las Cosas de Nueva España (5 vols.,
    Mexico).

SAUER, CARL ORTWIN
1932 The Road to Cibola (Ibero-Americana: 3, Berkeley).
1936 American Agricultural Origins: A Consideration of Nature and
    Culture (Essays in Anthropology in Honor of Alfred Louis
    Kroeber, pp. 279–97, Berkeley).

SAUER, CARL, AND BRAND, DONALD
1932 Aztatlan, Prehistoric Mexican Frontier on the Pacific Coast
    (Ibero-Americana: 1, Berkeley).

SAVILLE, MARSHALL H.

1896 The Temple of Tepoztlan, Mexico (Bulletin, American Museum of Natural History, Vol. 8, pp. 221–26, New York).

1899 Exploration of Zapotecan Tombs in Southern Mexico (American Anthropologist, n.s., Vol. 1, pp. 350–62, New York).

1900a A Shell Gorget from the Huasteca, Mexico (Bulletin, American Museum of Natural History, Vol. 13, pp. 99–103, New York).

1900b An Onyx Jar from Mexico in Process of Manufacture (Bulletin, American Museum of Natural History, Vol. 13, art. 11, pp. 105–07, New York).

1901 Mexican Codices, a List of Recent Reproductions (American Anthropologist, n.s., Vol. 3, pp. 532–41, New York).

1909 The Cruciform Structures of Mitla and Vicinity (Putnam Anniversary Volume, pp. 151–90, New York).

1916 Monolithic Axes and Their Distribution in Ancient America (Contributions, Museum of the American Indian, Heye Foundation, Vol. 2, no. 5, New York).

1917 *See* Anonymous Conqueror.

1920 The Goldsmith's Art in Ancient Mexico (Indian Notes and Monographs, Museum of the American Indian, Heye Foundation, New York).

1922 Turquois Mosaic Art in Ancient Mexico (Contributions, Museum of the American Indian, Heye Foundation, Vol. 6, New York).

1925 The Wood-Carver's Art in Ancient Mexico (Contributions, Museum of the American Indian, Heye Foundation, Vol. 9, New York).

1928 Ceremonial Axes from Western Mexico (Indian Notes, Museum of the American Indian, Heye Foundation, Vol. 5, pp. 280–93, New York).

1929a Votive Axes from Ancient Mexico (Indian Notes, Museum of the American Indian, Heye Foundation, Vol. 6, pp. 266–99, 335–42, New York).

1929b Tizoc, Great Lord of the Aztecs, 1481–86 (Contributions, Museum of the American Indian, Heye Foundation, Vol. 7, no. 4, New York).

SAYLES, E. B.

1935 An Archaeological Survey of Texas (Medallion Papers, Gila Pueblo, No. 17, Globe).

1936 An Archaeological Survey of Chihuahua, Mexico (Medallion Papers, Gila Pueblo, No. 22, Globe).

1937 *See* Gladwin, Gladwin, Haury and Sayles.

SELER, CAECILIE

1900 Auf Alten Wegen in Mexiko und Guatemala. Berlin.

1922 Alterthümer des Kanton Tuxtla im Staate Veracruz (Festschrift Eduard Seler, pp. 543–56, Stuttgart).

SELER, EDUARD

1901 The Tonalamatl of the Aubin Collection. Commentary. Translated by A. H. Keane. London.

1902 Codex Fejervary-Mayer. Commentary. Translated by A. H. Keane. London.

1902–23 Gesammelte Abhandlungen zur Amerikanischen Sprach- und Alterthumskunde (Vols. 1–5, Berlin).

1903 Codex Vaticanus 3773. Commentary. Translated by A. H. Keane. London.

1904a Ancient Mexican Feather Ornaments (Bureau of American Ethnology, Bulletin 28, pp. 57–74, Washington).

1904b The Temple Pyramid of Tepoztlan (Bureau of American Ethnology, Bulletin 28, pp. 339–52, Washington).

1904c The Venus Period in the Borgian Codex Group (Bureau of American Ethnology, Bulletin 28, pp. 353–92, Washington).

1904d Altmexikanischer Schmuck und Soziale und Militärische Rangabzeichen (Gesammelte Abhandlungen, Vol. 2, pp. 509–619, Berlin).

1904–09 Codex Borgia. Eine Altmexikanische Bilderschrift der Bibliothek der Congregatio de Propaganda Fide. 3 vols. Berlin.

1915 Die Teotiuacan-Kultur des Hochlands von Mexico (Gesammelte Abhandlungen zur Amerikanischen Sprach-und Alterthumskunde, Vol. 5, pp. 405–585, Berlin).

SOUSTELLE, JACQUES

1937 La Famille Otomi-Pame du Mexique Central (Institut d'Ethnologie, No. 26, Paris).

SPENCE, LEWIS

1923 The Gods of Mexico. London.

SPINDEN, E. S.

1933 The Place of Tajin in Totonac Archaeology (American Anthropologist, n.s., Vol. 35, pp. 271–87, Menasha).

SPINDEN, HERBERT J.

1913 A Study of Maya Art (Memoirs, Peabody Museum of American Archaeology and Ethnology, Harvard University, Vol. 6, Cambridge).

1916 See Wissler and Spinden.

1924 The Reduction of Mayan Dates (Papers, Peabody Museum of American Archaeology and Ethnology, Harvard University, Vol. 6, no. 4, Cambridge).

1928 Ancient Civilizations of Mexico and Central America (Handbook Series, American Museum of Natural History, No. 3, 3rd edition, New York).

1933 Indian Manuscripts of Southern Mexico (Annual Report of the Smithsonian Institution for 1933, pp. 429–51, Washington).

1940 Diffusion of Maya Astronomy (in The Maya and Their Neighbors, pp. 162–78, New York).

STARR, F.

1908 In Indian Mexico. Chicago.

STAUB, WALTER

1933 Zur Uebereinanderschichtung der Völker und Kulturen an der Ostküste von Mexiko (Mitteilungen der Geographisch-Ethnographischen Gesellschaft in Zürich, Vol. 33, pp. 3–26, Zürich).

STIRLING, M. W.

1939 Discovering the New World's Oldest Dated Work of Man (The National Geographical Magazine, Vol. 76, no. 2, Washington).

1940a Great Stone Faces of the Mexican Jungle (The National Geographic Magazine, Vol. 78, no. 3, pp. 309–34, Washington).

1940b An Initial Series from Tres Zapotes, Vera Cruz, Mexico (National Geographic Society, Contributed Technical Papers, Mexican Archaeology Series, Vol. 1, no. 1, Washington).

STREBEL, H.

1885–89 Alt Mexiko (2 vols., Hamburg und Leipzig).

STRONG, WILLIAM DUNCAN

1935a An Introduction to Nebraska Archaeology (Smithsonian Miscellaneous Collections, Vol. 93, no. 10, Washington).

STUDLEY, CORNELIA

1887 Notes upon Human Remains from Caves in Coahuila (Reports, Peabody Museum of American Archaeology and Ethnology, Vol. 3, 1880–86, pp. 233–59; cf. also pp. 10, 21, 32, Cambridge).

SWANTON, JOHN R.

1911 Indian Tribes of the Lower Mississippi and Adjacent Coasts of the Gulf of Mexico (Bureau of American Ethnology, Bulletin 43, Washington).

1911b See Thomas, Cyrus, and Swanton, John R.

SWANTON ESSAYS

1940 See Essays in Historical Anthropology of North America.

TEEPLE, JOHN E.

1931 Maya Astronomy (Carnegie Institution of Washington, pub. no. 403, Contributions to American Archaeology, Vol. 1, no. 2, pp. 29–115, Washington).

1935 Tenayuca (Departamento de Monumentos, México).

Tezozomoc, H.

1878 Cronica Mexicana (XVI Century) (in Biblioteca Mexicana, México).

Thomas, Cyrus, and Swanton, John R.

1911 Indian Languages of Mexico and Central America and Their Geographical Distribution (Bureau of American Ethnology, Bulletin 44, Washington).

Thompson, J. Eric

1927 A Correlation of the Mayan and European Calendars (Field Museum of Natural History, Anthropological Series, Vol. 17, no. 1, Chicago).

1932 Civilization of the Mayas (Anthropology Leaflet 25, 2nd edition, Field Museum of Natural History, Chicago).

1933 Mexico before Cortez. New York.

1934 Sky Bearers, Colors and Directions in Maya and Mexican Religion (Carnegie Institution of Washington, pub. no. 436, pp. 209–42, Washington).

1935 Maya Chronology: the Correlation Question (Carnegie Institution of Washington, pub. no. 456, contribution no. 14, Washington).

1935 See Gann, Thomas, and Thompson, J. Eric.

1939 Excavations at San José, British Honduras (Carnegie Institution of Washington, pub. no. 506, Washington).

Tonalamatl Aubin

1900 A Pre-Columbian Codex Preserved in the National Library, Paris. Published by le Duc de Loubat, Paris.

See Orozco y Berra, El Tonalamatl, 1887 (Anales del Museo Nacional, la Epoca, Vol. 4, pp. 30–44 and end of book, Mexico).

Torquemada, Juan de

1723 Los Veinte i un Libros Rituales i Monarchia Indiana (3 vols., Madrid).

Totten, George Oakley

1926 Maya Architecture. Washington.

Tozzer, Alfred M.

1912 The Value of Ancient Mexican Manuscripts in the Study of the General Development of Writing (The Smithsonian Institution, Annual Report for 1911, pp. 493–506, Washington).

1918 The Domain of the Aztecs and their Relation to the Prehistoric Cultures of Mexico (Holmes Anniversary Volume, pp. 464–68, Lancaster).

1921 Excavation of a Site at Santiago Ahuitzotla, D. F. Mexico (Bureau of American Ethnology, Bulletin 74, Washington).

1927 Time and American Archaeology (Natural History, Vol. 27, pp. 210–21, New York).

1930 Maya and Toltec Figures at Chichen Itza (Proceedings, XXIII International Congress of Americanists, New York, 1928, pp. 155–64, New York).

1937 Prehistory in Middle America (The Hispanic American Historical Review, Vol. 17, pp. 151–59, Durham).

——

1933 Tres Siglos de Arquitectura Colonial (Departamento de Monumentos, Secretaria de Educacion Publica, Mexico).

TRIBUTE ROLL OF MONTEZUMA (*See* CODEX MENDOZA)
A Pre-Columbian Codex Preserved in the Museo Nacional, Mexico.
See Peñafiel, Monumentos, 1890, Vol. 2, Pls. 228–59; Transactions of the American Philosophical Society, Philadelphia, 1892, n.s., Vol. 17, Pt. 2, Philadelphia.

VAILLANT, GEORGE C.
1929 On the Threshold of Native American Civilization (Natural History, Vol. 29, pp. 530–42, New York).

1930a Excavations at Zacatenco (Anthropological Papers, American Museum of Natural History, Vol. 32, Pt. 1, New York).

1930b Reconstructing the Beginning of a History (Natural History, Vol. 30, pp. 606–16, New York).

1931a A Bearded Mystery (Natural History, Vol. 31, pp. 243–52, New York).

1931b Excavations at Ticoman (Anthropological Papers, American Museum of Natural History, Vol. 32, Pt. 2, New York).

1932a A Pre-Columbian Jade (Natural History, Vol. 32, pp. 512–20, 557–58, New York).

1932b *See* Merwin and Vaillant.

1934 *See* Vaillant and Vaillant.

1935a Excavations at El Arbolillo (Anthropological Papers, American Museum of Natural History, Vol. 35, Pt. 2, New York).

1935b Early Cultures of the Valley of Mexico: Results of the Stratigraphical Project of the American Museum of Natural History in the Valley of Mexico, 1928–33 (Anthropological Papers, American Museum of Natural History, Vol. 35, Pt. 3, New York).

1935c Chronology and Stratigraphy in the Maya Area (Maya Research, Vol. 2, pp. 119–43, New York).

1935d Artists and Craftsmen in Ancient Central America (American Museum of Natural History, Guide Leaflet Series, No. 88, New York. Supplement: Chart in Vaillant, 1936, Guide Leaflet No. 103).

1936 The History of the Valley of Mexico (Natural History, Vol. 38, pp. 324-40, New York. Accompanying chart reprinted as Guide Leaflet No. 103, American Museum of Natural History).

1937a History and Stratigraphy in the Valley of Mexico (The Scientific Monthly, Vol. 44, pp. 307-24, New York).

1937b The Death Throes of the Aztec Nation (Natural History, Vol. 39, pp. 185-95, New York).

1938 A Correlation of Archaeological and Historical Sequences in the Valley of Mexico (American Anthropologist, n.s., Vol. 40, pp. 535-73, Menasha).

1939a The Twilight of Aztec Civilization (Natural History, Vol. 43, pp. 38-46, New York).

1939b Indian Arts in North America. New York.

1939c An Early Occurrence of Cotton in Mexico (American Anthropologist, n.s., Vol. 41, p. 170, Menasha).

1940 Patterns in Middle American Archaeology (in The Maya and Their Neighbors, pp. 295-305, New York).

VAILLANT, GEORGE C. (editor)

1940 A Sacred Almanac of the Aztecs (Tonalamatl of the Codex Borbonicus) (American Museum of Natural History, Limited Edition, New York).

VAILLANT, S. B. AND VAILLANT, G. C.

1934 Excavations at Gualupita (Anthropological Papers, American Museum of Natural History, Vol. 35, no. 1, New York).

VEYTIA, MARIANO

1836 Historia Antigua de México (3 vols., México).

VIOLLET-LE-DUC, E. E.

1863 *See* Charnay and Viollet-le-Duc.

WATERMAN, T. T.

1917 Bandelier's Contribution to the Study of Ancient Mexican Social Organization (University of California Publications in American Archaeology and Ethnology, Vol. 12, no. 7, pp. 249-82, Berkeley).

1924 On Certain Antiquities in Western Guatemala (Bulletin of the Pan-American Union, April, 1924, pp. 1-21, Washington).

WEIANT, C. W.

n.d. Manuscript on Ceramics of Tres Zapotes.

WEYERSTALL, A.

1932 Some Observations on Indian Mounds, Idols and Pottery in the Lower Papaloapam Basin, State of Vera Cruz, Mexico (Middle American Research Series, pub. no. 4, pp. 23-69, Tulane University, New Orleans).

WISSLER, CLARK
1938 The American Indian (3rd edition, New York).

WISSLER, CLARK, AND SPINDEN, HERBERT J.
1916 The Pawnee Human Sacrifice to the Morning Star (American Museum Journal, Vol. 16, no. 1, pp. 49–55, New York).

YANOVSKI, E.
1936 Food Plants of the North American Indians (U. S. Department of Agriculture, Miscellaneous Publications, No. 237, Washington).

ZINGG, R. M.
1935 *See* Bennett and Zingg.

ZURITA, A.
1891 Breve y Sumaria Relación de los Señores de la Nueva España (García Icazbalceta, Nueva Colección de Documentos para la Historia de México, Vol. 3, pp. 71–227, México).

INDEX

The rules for the pronunciation of Aztec names are simple despite the horrifying assemblage of consonants and vowels. *X* in general has a *Sh* sound; *Qu* has a *K* value; *Hu* and *Gu* have a *W* sound when preceding a vowel. All consonants and vowels are sounded as in Spanish. Rough English phonetic equivalents have been provided in the text and the index to guide the errant tongue.

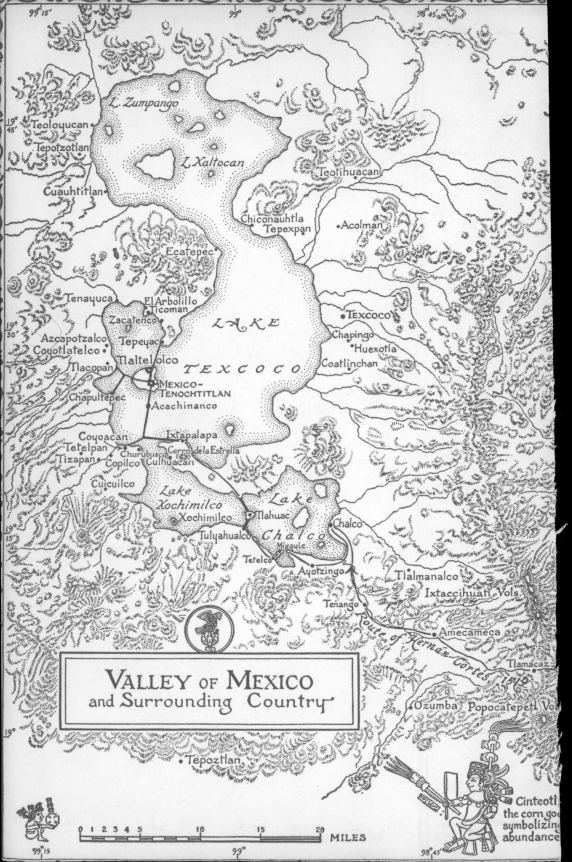

VALLEY OF MEXICO
and Surrounding Country

L. Zumpango

L. Xaltocan

Teoloyucan
Tepotzotlan

Cuauhtitlan

Teotihuacan

Chiconauhtla
Tepexpan

Acolman

Ecatepec

LAKE

Tenayuca
El Arbolillo
Ticoman
Zacatenco
Tepeyac
Tlaltelolco
Tlacopan
Chapultepec

Azcapotzalco
Coyotlatelco

MEXICO-
TENOCHTITLAN
Acachinanco

TEXCOCO

Texcoco
Chapingo
Huexotla
Coatlinchan

Coyoacan
Tetelpan
Tizapan
Churubusco
Copilco
Cuicuilco

Ixtapalapa
Cerro de la Estrella
Culhuacan

Lake
Xochimilco
Xochimilco
Tlahuac
Tulyahualco
Tetelco

Lake
Chalco
Chalco
Mixquic
Ayotzingo

Tlalmanalco
Ixtaccihuatl Vols.

Tenango

Amecameca

Tlamacaz

Ozumba   Popocatepetl Vol.

Route of Hernan Cortes 1519

Tepoztlan

Cinteotl
the corn god
symbolizing
abundance

0 1 2 3 4 5   10   15   20
MILES

99°15'

19°45'

19°30'

19°15'

19°

99°

99°15'

99°

98°45'

98°45'